The
DUTCH

The
DUTCH

A Portrait Study of the
People of Holland

By ADRIAAN J. BARNOUW

New York : Morningside Heights
COLUMBIA UNIVERSITY PRESS
1940

Copyright 1940

COLUMBIA UNIVERSITY PRESS, NEW YORK

First Printing, March, 1940

Second Printing, June, 1940

Third Printing, 1943

FOREIGN AGENTS: OXFORD UNIVERSITY PRESS, Humphrey
Milford, Amen House, London, E. C. 4, England, AND
B. I. Building, Nicol Road, Bombay, India

———

MANUFACTURED IN THE UNITED STATES OF AMERICA

To

HAROLD DE WOLF FULLER

PREFACE

THE TITLE of this book is a challenge to those Hollanders who are ashamed of the name Dutch. Why should they be? Because it is used, they say, in so many derisive and derogatory phrases that give the nation a bad name. I deny that they do. A nation's worth is appraised by its own actions, not by a foreigner's abuse. Besides, most of those idioms have ceased to be current. Dutch courage, Dutch concert, Dutch defence, Dutch widow, have passed from the speakers' lips to the pages of the dictionary. Many of my readers may have to look there to find out what some of them mean. We don't like to be called Dutchmen, these Hollanders tell their American friends, because your English ancestors poked fun at Dutchmen and everything Dutch. The best cure for that old sore is a little sense of humor. At the risk of getting in Dutch with my Dutch friends, I shall continue to call myself a native Dutchman.

Dutch is an ambiguous term. In America it also means German. That is, I admit, a more valid objection. But annoyance at the misuse of a good thing does not justify the cessation of its use. Would a housewife throw away a solid old breadknife, a family heirloom, because her little son used it to carve his name in the dining room table? She will always need a tool for cutting bread and she will use one that does cut. And Americans will always need a word to call us by, and they will use the one that is easiest and least cumbersome to use. That happens to be the name Dutch, the very one that we gave to ourselves and to our language when the nation was in its infancy. Its antiquity entitles it to the Hollander's love and respect, and instead of entreating the English-speaking world to desist from its use, he ought to be grateful to the English for having preserved in their language the original name of his own.

It may surprise American school teachers who have been trying valiantly to teach their students to speak of the Netherlands rather than Holland to find the latter term preferred by the author of this book. The Dutch themselves call their country Holland. They call it the Netherlands only when they write. There are Dutchmen, indeed, who resent the use of Holland as the name of the entire kingdom. Holland was, originally, the name of one province only, and inhabitants of other provinces protest against the use of a name which seems to imply that their own province is a part of the province of Holland.

Holland proper never forced its name upon the whole country. The whole country, and the outside world as well, adopted it at a period when, if it had not been for Holland, the Dutch Republic could not have survived. That the Netherlands exist at all as an independent nation is chiefly owing to Holland's leadership in the crucial days of the Dutch fight for freedom; Dutchman and foreigner alike expressed their recognition of that truth by identifying the entire country with the province of Holland.

I have heard it said that to call the Netherlands by the name of Holland is just as absurd as to call these United States Missouri. The absurdity is in the equation. It is a common feature in all languages that the name of a part is used for the whole. When the weather turns rough at sea, the captain orders "all hands on deck." He does not call his crew "feet," or "ears," or "mouths," for in such an emergency it is the sailors' hands that must do the work. It is the principal and most useful part that gives its name to the whole. If the inhabitants of the other provinces really feel themselves Netherlanders, they can not show the genuineness of that feeling more convincingly than by renouncing, as beneath their Netherlandish dignity, the petty provincialism that resents the use of the name Holland and Hollander.

ADRIAAN J. BARNOUW

COLUMBIA UNIVERSITY,

OCTOBER, 1939

CONTENTS

[xi]

CONTENTS

The
DUTCH

Chapter I

HOLLAND AMONG THE NATIONS

EARLY IN MARCH of the year 1937, the Netherland Social Democratic Labor Party made a momentous decision. The majority passed a resolution in favor of abandoning traditional opposition to all military expenditures. From the very beginning of Labor representation in Parliament, the Socialists had always voted as a man against the War Minister's annual budget. In the first decade of the twentieth century the Labor spokesmen firmly believed that measures of defense were a waste of precious money. They declared that the millions squandered on armaments could be used to better purpose—for the reclamation of the Zuiderzee, for the improvement of social conditions, for slum clearance and better housing for the poor, for government supervision of public health, for old age insurance and other social security measures. The possibility of war was remote. The ruler who should be so mad as to start a conflagration would find his army paralysed by the refusal of organized Labor to take up arms against their comrades of neighbor countries. The solidarity of the international proletariat was a firmer guarantee of national immunity from war than a costly defense machinery. The collapse

[3]

of that solidarity during the World War gave these Socialist dreamers a rude awakening. Nevertheless, they did not relinquish their opposition to any plans for military preparedness, for in the twenties they began to pin their hopes upon a new kind of shock absorber. Collective security as provided for by the Covenant of the League of Nations was sure to restrain the warmongers. No nation eager for conquest would dare to satisfy its land hunger in the face of international opposition under the aegis of the League. War was at last officially branded as a crime, and the threat of international punishment for a disturber of world peace was an effective deterrent.

Many Hollanders outside of the Social-Democratic Party shared this optimism of Labor. They were anxious to believe that the mirage of collective security was a substantial safeguard against war. There may have been doubts in their minds as to the reality of the pleasant vision, but to one hungry for peace and worn by the long and hazardous trek through the wilderness of international anarchy, it is difficult to resist the illusion that the Hôtel de la Paix is in sight, where hunger will be appeased and weariness assuaged. The experience of the past few years dispelled such daydreams. From the mountains of Abyssinia the smoke of battlefields and burning villages drifted across Europe and threw an ominous shadow over the Continent. The mirage vanished. The disillusioned found themselves back in the wilderness with not a glimmer of hope on the horizon. The Hollanders realized, then, that international action for the maintenance of peace was a forlorn hope: they must rely on themselves for the preservation of national safety. The Social Democratic Labor Party accepted the bitter truth, and did what it had never done before— approved the war budget.

Labor had come to its senses, was the comment of the Liberal press in Holland. That was a wrong diagnosis. Europe had gone out of her senses, and in a world gone mad and torn by dissension, Labor took the only course left open, reliance on national self-defense. Together with the so-called bourgeois parties, the Social Democrats now stand behind the Government in its determination to strengthen the military safeguards of the country's integrity.

If every other house in New York were an arsenal and its inhabitants, entrenched behind machine guns, recognized no moral obligation except to their self-interest, Police Commissioner Valentine would be absolutely powerless. Under such conditions law-abiding citizens would be forced to look after their own safety. If, after the World War, disarmament had been general instead of one-sided, an international police force might have saved the world from anarchy. Article 16 of the Covenant of the League of Nations calls it the duty of the Council of the League to recommend to the several Governments concerned what effective military or naval units each shall contribute to an armed force to be used against a Covenant-breaking State. In the light of our after-wisdom we can hardly suppress a smile at the naive optimism of the learned Versailles physicians who prescribed thus for world peace. The world has witnessed how punctiliously the Council lived up to its duty when the Negus appealed to the League for protection and justice.

Under that same article the Members of the League pledge mutual support in financial and economic measures invoked against an aggressor. We all know what became of the sanctions against Italy. The role Switzerland played in their enforcement is a case in point. The Swiss Republic, though recognizing its obligation under the Covenant to support its fellow Members in applying the sanctions, excused itself from subscribing to those whose enforcement by Switzerland might jeopardize Swiss neutrality. The League accepted the offer of conditioned coöperation without protest, admitting by its silence that the geographical position of Switzerland justified these reservations. But now that Italy has left the League and Switzerland finds herself wedged in between two military Powers openly hostile to international coöperation, she has all the more reason for caution in endorsing League action against disturbers of the peace.

The international position of the Netherlands is no less precarious. The Dutch do not delude themselves with the hope that the next European war will not involve their country. Holland is not a natural fortress. Its eastern frontier lies open to attack; only a small section can be inundated to impede the progress of an invading army. There is reason, then, for extreme caution in siding against the Covenant-breaking neighbor of League members in distant parts of the world. Fifteen years ago there were few people in Holland who were not enthusiastic supporters of the League. But the

League in action—or rather League inaction—belied their expectations. In a world rent by expansionist desires, and where disregard of treaties and international commitments had become a commonplace, they found no security save in their own determination to maintain a rigorous neutrality. The Dutch hate to make provision for military preparedness, but the hazards of the present situation have made them resigned to the sacrifice.

There was a time, not so very long ago, when military uniforms in Holland were an object of derision and scorn from the man in the street. That is changed. The realization of a national danger has taught the scoffers respect for the army. Three years ago a small group of prominent Hollanders formed a Society for National Safety. Its purpose is to acquaint the nation with the urgency of the defense problem—to bring home to the doubting Thomases the need of a strong army and navy, by pointing out the grave risk of involvement in war if the country cannot resist violation of its territory with a promptly mobilized defense force. Local committees of the Society in all the important towns of the country help to spread the propaganda for military preparedness. The army, once treated as a stepchild, is now the pampered young hopeful of the nation. It gets costly presents of fortifications along the eastern and southern frontiers; it has been given an increase in the annual contingent for compulsory military service; it is permitted to experiment with new aircraft, artillery material, caterpillar tanks, and armored cars. Its twin brother, the navy, is receiving an equal share of the popular favor. Holland is determined to maintain its neutrality also in the East

Indies: there naval bases are being fortified to accommodate a growing fleet. In short, the country, after a brief period of toying with collective security, has gone back to its soldiers and to the old policy of self-reliant neutrality.

Neutrality implies good will toward all nations and alliance with none. In temper and political outlook the Hollanders are akin to the Britons, but the nation fights shy of entanglements and would vigorously oppose a Government that would build the country's safety upon a treaty with England. The statesmen at The Hague will never make that mistake. They even refused to accept an undertaking proffered by the Third Reich not to violate Dutch territory. On January 30, 1937, the Reich Chancellor declared in the course of an address to the Reichstag that the German Government had assured Holland and Belgium of its willingness to recognize and guarantee these States as inviolable territories. That statement caused a flurry in the corridors of the States General at The Hague. Had Dr. Colijn's Cabinet actually received and accepted such a guarantee? Its reception was possible, its acceptance could not be credited. One member questioned the Minister of Foreign Affairs as to the nature of the alleged assurances. Jonkheer A. C. D. de Graeff replied that the Führer referred to a public announcement of March 7, 1936, which proclaimed the German Government's willingness to conclude, under guarantees from Great Britain and Italy, a nonaggression treaty with France and Belgium, and to admit the Netherlands as a party to the pact, if that country so desired and the other participants agreed to its inclusion. Jonk-

[8]

heer De Graeff added, however, that the Netherland Government, although fully appreciating the good intentions that the offer evinced, had notified Berlin that Holland declined to become a party to such a treaty. To the Netherlands the inviolability of her territory was a matter of course which did not lend itself to ratification.

This was the only reply that a self-respecting nation could give to a nation it respects. Acceptance of a non-aggression promise would imply a recognition on Holland's part of her neighbor's right to invade her. But Holland does not recognize such a right, nor is she willing to admit in writing that she holds any neighbor capable of claiming the right of invasion. A nation's inviolability is not a debatable question. It is an axiom, which even the brutal fact of conquest cannot invalidate. That was the import of Jonkheer De Graeff's dignified reply.

Holland has to reckon with the possibility of that brutal fact. The fate of Czechoslovakia and Poland serves as a warning. But that is all the more reason for remaining self-reliant and avoiding foreign entanglements. A protective alliance with one of the Powers called Great would not protect but would rather endanger the Dutch nation. What has the Franco-Russian alliance availed Czechoslovakia? In the summer of 1939 it transpired that Great Britain and France had secretly agreed to include Holland among the nations for whose independence, if attacked, the two Powers would go to war. The revelation caused no joy at The Hague. Holland does not want to be saved by a machinery which is automatically set in motion by an attack from the Third

[9]

Reich. If danger threatens, she claims the right to decide for herself whether her integrity is violated, and to invoke the aid that she considers needed. She cannot prevent other Powers from making secret plans for her safety, but she finds the best safeguard of that safety in refusing to become a partner to such an agreement. The best policy for a small nation is to go its own way and to find satisfaction in earning the name Great for achievements that do not depend on excessive wealth, numerical strength, or a powerful army.

The late Karel Capek, of Czechoslovakia, once visited Holland and published a record of his impressions in a slender volume called *Letters from Holland*. He had an axe to grind when he gave those letters to the press. For Holland, he thought, could teach his own country a wholesome lesson. Since Czechoslovakia became an independent state its people had been asking themselves questions. What does this small nation of ours amount to? Did we not count for more in the world's affairs when we formed part of the Hapsburg Empire? Some citizens of the new Czechoslovakia complained of their petty surroundings, while others daily warned them of the big, evil world which was preparing to swallow them up. So there was trouble among them, and Capek was interested in finding out "how they deal with this trouble in other places where the Lord of Hosts has assigned to the people the same sort of small scale national undertaking as He has to us. And that—next to Rembrandt—was the first thing I looked for when I went to Holland."

He did not get the impression that the Hollanders worried very much over the smallness of their country. But he did notice that they had developed a technique of living harmoniously adapted to the diminutive scale assigned to them. "There is a certain cosiness and frugality with regard to size which constitutes nothing short of an ingrained formal law." Nothing in Holland is overdone whether in architecture or in the way of living. Quality is stressed rather than quantity. "The national ideal does not aim at sizes but grades. You will discover this in everything: work, way of living, and even in nature itself. If you had to say on the spur of the moment what the Dutch are distinguished for, you would not think of anything huge, but of the fine, unusual and almost perfect quality of most things they produce." That was the lesson and the consolation that Capek wanted to convey through his Letters to those countrymen of his who were worried by the limited size of their country and the national insignificance that they feared would result therefrom. Stress quality, he told them, not only in material production, but also in the realm of ideals. "I cannot help feeling," he concluded, "that this small nation on the Rhine delta has acted like Mary in the Bible: it has chosen the better part."

What did Capek mean by the better part? To my mind the role of Martha suits the Dutch nation better. Like Martha, Holland is "careful and troubled about many things" and "cumbered about much serving": she must serve the interests of her people, their health and housing, their right to education, their will to work; she is troubled about the country's defense, about the growing menace of overpopulation and unemployment. She is working hard to wrest new polders from the sea and thereby add a twelfth province to the kingdom. She is administering an overseas realm much larger than her own home in Europe, and is building an air fleet to close the distance between those parts and the homeland. But she is attending to these troubles and cares with quiet, unostentatious thoroughness, and takes pride, as Capek says, in the quality of the work that is accomplished. Little is known in America of this Martha of the Low Countries going calmly but industriously about her tasks within her Dutch home, thinking her thoughts, and creating many things that carry, in their quality, a reflection of those thoughts.

The secret of that quality is in the Hollander's open-mindedness. He is willing to learn from foreigners and to adopt what is good wherever he finds it. And having to compete, in an envious world, with rivals economically much stronger than himself, he must improve on this composite selection by native skill and ingenuity, thereby putting the stamp of Dutch quality on the product. He is as hospitable to foreign ideas adopting such as may be made to suit the native character and way of life.

This eclecticism makes for moderation and tolerance. A nation to which all teachings and doctrines are freely accessible is least exposed to the danger of allowing one idea to run amuck. "Les idées marchent," to be sure, for a static idea would be a contradiction in terms. But the tempo of that march is regulated by the number of ideas. For ideas in the minds of men behave as do pedestrians in the crowded streets of New York. The individual walker's accustomed pace is retarded by the gregarious trend, the tempo of which is set by the slowest. To run himself out of breath is the lonely man's privilege; a streetful of individuals can only stroll. In totalitarian states, where the press is muzzled and all teachings adverse to the official ideology are decried as heretical and are promptly suppressed, the unchecked trend of the one triumphant doctrine will encourage autocracy to drive with ever increasing recklessness along the unimpeded track of political practice.

In Holland there is no danger of such madness. The public mind is safe from being rushed into error, because it is accessible to a diversity of political thought. The Hollanders do not worry over their smallness, as Capek observed; neither do they worry over the impact of the great world of ideas upon the life of the nation. For it has a shock-absorber in firmly rooted tradition, from which the nation draws its strength and those essential qualities that constitute its Dutchness. What those are is not easy to define. This little book is an attempt to suggest to the American reader a clearer conception than a definition could give of the characteristic traits that make the Dutch nation what it is—a nation closely related to the German and the English, and yet so clearly distinct from both that political independence is its natural and necessary habitat.

Chapter II

THE CHARACTER OF THE PEOPLE

COUNT KEYSERLING, the German philosopher who condescended, some ten years ago, to address American audiences, came to the conclusion—perhaps because crowds flocked like sheep to his lectures—that the American, as a species, has reverted to the status of an animal. This nation, he tells us in *America Set Free*, is still a wandering herd, a nomad tribe in the barbarian stage, incapable as yet of sharing a world civilization. Nomadism, to be sure, is not an exclusive feature of barbarity, for the wise Count himself has a tendency to wander, both in the body and in his thoughts. But in him it is an aristocratic indulgence; in the American it is an animalic urge.

The Count, in his wanderings, also visited Holland, but nothing worth praising did he find there. He found a native culture, it is true—for the Hollander has passed the animal stage—but only a culture based on ugliness. The Dutch, he tells us in *Das Spektrum Europas*, are physically an ugly people, and the psychic equivalent of their external ugliness is a kind of brutality which compares to Prussian brutality as a country fair by Teniers to a military drill in pre-war Potsdam. The language suffers from the same blight. A German hearing Dutch spoken cannot help thinking—at least the Count cannot, in spite of all his philosophy—that this speech must have been invented by a company of gentlemen at three o'clock in the morning. Is it possible that these profound speculations on Holland and the Dutch were made by Count Keyserling at four o'clock after midnight?

Another German author, Rudolf Mengelberg, shares this tendency to speculate and theorize, but owing to the mistake of making his home in Holland he has not been able to maintain that infallible accuracy of appraisal which Count Keyserling has kept intact by his judge-as-you-go method of studying mankind. Mr. Mengelberg naïvely believes that one has to surrender something of one's own self before one can fully comprehend a foreign culture. According to him all appreciation of what is alien demands a sacrifice from the appraiser. But this act of self-denial yields its reward in the discovery of new beauty and the enrichment of one's own spiritual life.

This is equally true of an expatriate returning to his native country. The Hollander who lives abroad is bound to surrender something of his old Dutch self in the process of acclimatization, and may be able, on a visit to the land of his birth, to appreciate traits of the national character that used to irritate him before he went to live abroad. The change is a measure of the distance that he has mentally traveled away from his own people. I found this to be true in my own case while traveling in the Netherlands one summer. A young woman carrying a baby and a heavy grip boarded the train at Antwerp. A commercial traveler, who occupied the seat by the window, immediately offered it to her, lifted her grip into the net, held the baby while she settled herself in the corner, and engaged her at once in conversation. He began with a self-evident question: "Traveling without your husband?" Yes, she had been on a visit to her parents. Was the husband going to meet her? Perhaps, if the boss would let him off an hour sooner than usual. What was his job? How long had they been married? How old was the baby? The baby was pinched in the cheek and given a watch to listen to. The little one's chuckling response to this entertainment weakened the mother's reluctance to submit to her inquisitor's persistence, and by the time we reached Rotterdam he knew her whole story, and they were chatting together as if they were lifelong friends.

I know what I would have thought of this if I were still living in Holland. I would have cursed the fellow for a vulgar, inquisitive, and meddlesome busybody, combining in his person some of the most objectionable character traits of the race. But my reaction to the scene was different this time. I could not help admitting that the man was punctilious in his attentions, that his manner of questioning her was never offensive, that he had an ingratiating way with the baby, and that he made the woman's train journey a pleasant experience in her probably dull and eventless life. His good-natured impertinence and her naïve response were somehow charming to the visitor fresh from New York and from daily travel in its dehumanized subway. The man's meddlesomeness seemed kindliness, and the whole scene enacted on the seat opposite the writer bore the aspect of a naïve idyll of kindly, simple-hearted people.

There is, indeed, one trait of the national character that in the eyes of the expatriate Dutchman will never assume the semblance of a pleasant virtue. That is the Hollander's finicky attention in trifling detail. He loves to stress the difference between things that to the casual observer are alike. Differentiation seems almost a national sport. The city of Rotterdam used to run a little steamer from Willemsplein, on the right bank, across the river to Feyenoord, where the ships of the Holland-America Line dock. The two shores are now connected by magnificent ferry boats that need not fear comparison with those on the Hudson. But ten years ago only a steam launch was plying between Feyenoord and the city. I had to cross one day on this tiny steamer and boarded the deck without more ado. But a sailor at the gangplank referred me to a little office on the quay, where I first had to buy a ticket at the rate of five cents for the first class or of three for the second. I went back and bought the ticket, handed it to the sailor at the gangplank, and stepped on board; but he called me back, tore the ticket in two, and handed me one half of it, retaining the other himself. As soon as we had left the quay, he went round among the passengers collecting the halves they had been allowed to retain. I asked him the purpose of this. Why could he not have collected the tickets untorn and spared himself the trouble of reassembling the parts? "I don't know," was his answer, "these are my orders." On the return trip I repeated the formalities in which I had been coached. I bought the pink-colored first-class ticket, handed it to the sailor at the gangplank, and waited obediently for the torn-off half. "Do you want anything, sir?" he asked. "I am waiting for one half of my ticket." "No, sir, that is not necessary here; that is done only on the Rotterdam side." "But what is the reason for this difference?" I enquired. "Don't ask me, sir; I simply follow instructions."

A passenger on a trolley car at The Hague finds himself confronted with various elaborate "don'ts" and warnings that make him self-conscious and embarrassed, there being apparently so many transgressions that one might commit without knowing it. It goes without saying that smoking is forbidden, but smokers have other ways of causing a nuisance, and the public must be protected against all eventualities; so besides being told that one may not smoke, he is warned not to carry a burning cigar, or pipe, or cigarette into the car. Fresh-air fiends should study the instructions before proceeding to lower a window pane, for they will find that this is a misdemeanor: they must ask the conductor; he alone has authority to open and close the car windows. Other notices tell the passengers to be quick in getting in and out, and not to put their feet upon the seat opposite. In short, all possible ways of misbehavior are foreseen and prohibited. Such irritating accuracy is an exaggerated form of a national virtue; conscientiousness in everything that the day's work calls for.

The neatness of Dutch homes and gardens, the tidiness of streets and parks, in such striking contrast with the litter that defiles public places in New York, are pleasing symptoms of the same painstaking attention to detail. If the Hollander insists on seeing his environment kept in scrupulous order, he must be satisfied to listen to paternal directions from the powers that be. New Yorkers, indeed, cannot help feeling ashamed of their own city at the sight of the impeccable condition in which the Dutch keep their streets and pavements and public parks. The town councils and the burgomasters take a justifiable pride in the communities for which they are responsible. They see to it that no street within the municipal precincts has its aspect spoiled by a garbage heap on a vacant lot or by the unsightly spectacle of an empty tenement falling into ruin. Even a haunted house must keep up a show of respectability.

South of Amsterdam, in a beautifully wooded section of the country, lies the rural town of Baarn, where many wealthy commuters have their homes. In 1926 the town council passed an ordinance declaring it unlawful for the owner of a house destroyed by fire to leave it in its disreputable condition and authorizing the town police to compel him either to demolish it or to rebuild it within a specified period. The Executive Committee of the Provincial States, to whom this ordinance had to be submitted for approval, objected to it on the ground that its enforcement would restrict the owner's right of property and would give too large a scope to the taste of the town police. Hence the Committee advised the Crown to veto the ordinance. But there is in Holland a State Commission for the Preservation of Monuments—the word monument to be taken in the sense of relic of the past that for its beauty or its historical value deserves to be saved—and this body, having been consulted by the Minister of Arts on behalf of the Crown, dug into the past and found that the Baarn ordinance was not a freakish innovation but in line with a well-established tradition, which could be traced back as far as the fifteenth century. In two ordinances of the seventeenth century the right of municipal magistrates to interfere was definitely based on aesthetic grounds; where negligence of a property owner was deemed to spoil the architectural beauty of the town, he could be compelled to remove the eyesore at his own cost. To judge from the aspect of the average American city, the Baarn ordinance would find little favor in this country, and it may well be that the property owner's liberty is a more precious principle than the aesthetic sensitiveness of the public at large. But since that liberty is already restricted in so many ways, the question might be asked whether a further limitation in the name of civic self-respect would entail a serious injustice.

Cleanliness is next to godliness. The Dutch have no equivalent of this proverb. But their language seems to imply that in their opinion cleanliness is next to beauty. For the word *schoon* in Dutch has the twofold meaning of clean and beautiful. With constant dusting and splashing and scrubbing and rubbing and polishing the housewife in Holland keeps her house clean and a pleasure to the eye. Saturday is a nation-wide *schoonmaakdag*, that is, "clean-making day." Then even the pavement in front of the house gets a good scrubbing. Foreigners who visited Holland in the seventeenth century were amazed and amused at this excessive zeal for cleanliness. An anonymous English writer of that period was annoyed at having to go outside to expectorate: "You must either go out to spit or blush when you see the mop brought."[1] The British envoy, Sir William Temple, tells an anecdote against himself that confirms the truth of this complaint. "Dining one day at Monsieur Hoeft's, and having a great cold, I observed, every time I spit, a tight handsome wench (that stood in the room with a clean cloth in her hand) was presently down to wipe it up, and rub the board clean: somebody at table speaking of my cold, I said, the most trouble it gave me was to see the poor wench take so much pain about it: Monsieur Hoeft told me, 'Twas well I escaped so, and that if his wife had been at home, though I were an ambassador, she would have turned me out of doors for fouling her house."

The Dutch adjective *klein*, meaning small or little, is the etymological equivalent of English clean. And indeed, there is a close connection between the Dutchman's love of cleanliness and his careful observance of detail. If the housewife wants her house to be in apple-pie order, she must needs watch out for the tiniest specks. Such finicky neatness is a form of thrift. If you take good care of your furniture, it will last the longer. When I was a youngster, the sun was carefully kept out of parlor and drawing room, the blinds being lowered to keep the upholstery from fading. The better educated among the present generation are wise enough to prefer the discoloring light to the thrifty darkness; still they form but a small minority, I am afraid.

A Dutch scholar, J. Huizinga, of the University of Leyden, while visiting in New York, was struck by the

---

[1] *The Dutch Drawn to the Life* (London: 1664), p. 68.

[21]

terrible waste which the unwieldy mechanism of city life makes unavoidable. "Goods that are the wonderful products of ingenious techniques and human labor are scarcely touched and remain unenjoyed. Precious woods are felled every day for the manufacture of paper that will presently litter the streets and the parks and the floors of the subway trains with dailies that have only been skimmed by indifferent readers. And passing on foot along the illuminated stores and theaters of Broadway, one might elegize upon all the light that burns without gladdening a soul, upon all the time that is wasted on aimless pleasures, on all the words that are never read, on all the shoes that are never worn, on all the silk that never drapes a shoulder, on all the flowers that fade behind the panes."

Careful husbandry is counted among the Christian virtues in Holland. After twenty years in New York I am not yet sufficiently Americanized to see good food wasted with indifference or resignation. I was brought up with the vulgar notion that it was bad manners to leave food on my plate. "Your eye should not be bigger than your tummy," my mother used to say. If I had taken too much, lack of appetite was no excuse. I had to finish it, willy-nilly. During the war Dutch eyes had little chance of overtaxing the stomach. Food of every kind was rationed, and, by force of its scarcity, good manners and emptied plates were the rule. When I came to America in 1919, I was amazed and pained to see my mother's lesson in thrift ignored by the best-mannered people. It was done so systematically that I could account for it only by assuming that dyspepsia was endemic in New

York. But the healthy look of the people who left half-empty plates on lunch counters and restaurant tables disproved that assumption. How was it, I asked one of my friends, that Americans' eyes were so much bigger than their stomachs? This waste, he explained, was not due to ocular hypertrophy; it was simply a demonstration of good breeding. You should not behave as if you were famished; show that you can control your appetite.

When Plutarch visited Rome, he asked the same question that puzzled me in New York. For the Romans also left part of the food on the table. In his *Quaestiones Romanae* he suggested various kinds of explanation: "Did they mean to signify that one should always remember to save part of the present store for the future, and today remember tomorrow? Or did they consider it becoming to restrain and keep in check one's appetite while it was still possible to indulge it? For they have less desire for what is out of reach who are accustomed to refrain from what they have at hand. Or did the custom arise also from kindliness to their slaves? Since they are better pleased at partaking than at taking, for so they seem to be in some sense the sharers of their masters' table. Or because no holy place should be left empty, and the table is holy."[2] Edward Clodd, the English folklorist, rejects all these explanations.[3] He sees in the Roman practice a case of sympathetic magic, the food that you leave untouched being a safeguard against starvation. Is it possible that the American custom has its

[2] Translation by H. J. Rose (Oxford, 1924).
[3] *Tom Tit Tot; an Essay on Savage Philosophy in Folktale* (London, 1898), p. 63.

[23]

root in that primitive belief? Could this thriftless demonstration of good manners be a magical device for exorcizing want by waste?

The Hollander draws the blinds not only upon his upholstery, but also upon his private life. In the early nineties of the past century an enterprising publishing firm brought out a Dutch *Who's Who*, but the book must have been a failure, as it never reached a second edition. The fault lay not with the publishers, but with the men and women who, through their autobiographies, must be the collective authors of the volume. Publicity is a state of exposure that the Hollander rather shuns than seeks, and he finds something indecent in the request of an inquisitive publisher that he write his own life story according to recipe. This dislike of self-advertisement accounts for the scarcity in Dutch literature of books of memoirs, confessions, and diaries. Autobiographies, if written at all, are kept in the desk for posthumous publication, and relatives who survive the author are seldom inclined to gratify his ambition to survive himself. A Hollander must leave his native country before he can publish the story of his life without qualms and misgivings. The most widely read autobiography ever written by a born Dutchman is the most convincing proof of the thoroughness of the Americanization of Edward Bok.

During the post-war period Holland's active participation in various international movements for peace and disarmament brought many Dutchmen of light and leading into European prominence, and this resulted in a growing demand from abroad for a Dutch *Who's Who*.

The well-known publishing house of Martinus Nijhoff yielded at last to this outside pressure and ventured to publish concise information concerning some twenty-five hundred Hollanders. The compiler was very discreet in drawing up his questionnaire. No one was asked to disclose any particulars about his family. The contributors to *Wie is dat* were listed as Government ministers, Members of Parliament, public officials, army officers, university professors, men of letters, clergymen, artists, doctors, merchants, industrialists, but never as bachelors, husbands, or fathers of families. Wives were ignored, as well as husbands. There was a way, though, to detect the existence of the latter, thanks to the custom for a married woman to add her maiden name, with a hyphen, to her married name. The heading *Boudier-Bakker, Ina* revealed that Miss Ina Bakker—a well-known novelist, by the way—was married to Mr. Boudier. The men did not commit such indiscretions. They were just plain Mr. So-and-so, without any clue as to the existence of a wife. In a few cases a female autobiographer was bold enough to volunteer the information that she was married to the man whose name she signed before her own. Only the women who had lost their partners by death made a regular practice of this boldness, for widows invariably confessed that the name before the hyphen was that of their departed husband. The book was equally reticent about political and church affiliations, club memberships, and personal hobbies. Not until one has perused the laconic entries in *Wie is dat*[4] does one realize to what

---

[4] *Wie is dat? Naamlijst van ongeveer 2500 bekende personen op elk gebied in het Koninkrijk der Nederlanden* (The Hague, 1931).

extent the contributions to *Who's Who in America* are loquacious, impertinent, and immodest. The modesty of some of these twenty-five hundred Hollanders went so far as to refuse, or fail, to permit them to fill out the publisher's questionnaire. This excess of virtue was to blame for many gaps and imperfections that diminished the usefulness of *Wie is dat*. The editor did his best in such cases to supply the desired information himself as well as he could, and in order to soothe the mental pain that his indiscretion might cause to these self-effacing persons, he gave due credit to their modesty by marking their names with an asterisk. Admirers of Willem Mengelberg will be interested to know that Holland's great conductor was starred among the unco modest.

When one sheep has crossed the dam, others will follow, says a Dutch proverb. In the preface to the second edition the publisher stated that the success which the book had scored both at home and abroad had persuaded many recalcitrants to supply the information they had withheld from the first edition. And the fourth, published in 1938, gave evidence in its bulk of a tendency among the Dutch to cast bashfulness and reticence to the winds. Still, Mr. Nijhoff found it necessary to appeal anew to the many who persisted in ignoring his questionnaire. His ambition is to extinguish all the stars.

To advertize oneself is vulgar, to fall for advertizing is foolish. Since the people in Holland are less gullible than those in the United States, one would think that, owing to the greater sales resistance, the art of salesmanship would have reached a high degree of development. But the contrary is true. The general distrust confronting publicity schemes and methods discourages attempts to introduce American ways of advertising. Since some one hit upon the slogan "Say it with flowers," the florists in the United States have done a flourishing business, I am told. It seems to make the readers rush in and buy before they have allowed themselves time to think of what it is they are going to say. A Hollander's reaction would be different. He is fond of flowers to say it with, whatever "it" may be, but he will not say it because he is urged thereto by a prompting phrase. The phrase will not make him buy; on the contrary, it will set him thinking, and the conclusion he arrives at will probably be that the next line of "Say it with flowers" is "Pay it with dollars." The frost of that afterthought will nip his floral eloquence in the bud.

The Hollander is, indeed, a cautious fellow. He has no spontaneity. There is something invigorating in the American climate that the humid, heavy atmosphere of Holland lacks. Edward Bok's hopeful outlook on life must have been an acquired characteristic due to his American upbringing. It is not typical of the Dutchman who stays at home. Bok's story of "The Man who saw the Sea," an eloquent sketch of Woodrow Wilson, concludes with a beautiful parable of an Indian boy who, in a race up a high mountain, was the only one to reach the summit. "My feet are torn," he panted, "and I am exhausted, and I have come late, but," and as a wonderful light came into his eyes, the young brave added, "I saw the sea!" That thrill of the distant vision suddenly revealed from the mountain top is not for the Hollander. The sea is always with him and impresses him more by its dangers than by its beauty. The sea's nearness and his own position below sea level are bound to make him a cautious and circumspect man. It is only for the inland dweller who has climbed the mountain top to rave over his first glimpse of the distant ocean. The Hollander does not easily fly into raptures. Exuberance in others makes him self-conscious. He possesses, indeed, a strong pride of country, but he is too shy, or too proud, to show it. Chauvinism is always arrogant, and the Hollander has an inveterate tendency toward self-criticism, which saves him from that indecorous lack of good taste. The habit of finding fault with their own country is common among the Dutch. But it is only a pose, serving as a convenient escape from the awkward confession that the Dutch *are* right after all. There are Dutch flagwavers who take this faultfinding habit in all seriousness and fear from it an enervating influence on the spirit of the people. They call it irreverent, profane, self-destructive. The humor and the instinctive wisdom of it escape them. The true Dutch patriot conceals his love of country not from profanity, but rather from a reverent fear lest his feelings be hurt. If a foreigner should repeat or join in with his critical remarks, he would bitterly resent it. For he feels that it is only the Hollander's prerogative to speak deprecatingly of the fatherland.

Erasmus often spoke contemptuously of his country, its climate, and its people, but that does not prove lack of love for his native land; on the contrary, he would not have been a true-born Hollander had he not availed himself sometimes of the privilege to vent his spleen on the stock from which he came. But when we find him going out of his way to give it praise, there is good ground for suspecting that he had a sincere love and admiration for his own people. In one of his *Colloquies* occurs a masterly description of a shipwreck. Adolph, who has escaped by a miracle from drowning, concludes his story with a tribute to "the incredible humanity of the people, who with great alacrity supplied us with lodging, fire, food, clothes, and means of transport." "What people was it?" asks Anthony. "The Dutch." "Ah," says Anthony, "no people are more humane, though they are surrounded with savage nations." Again, in his *Adagia*, he takes exception to the Latin phrase *Auris Batava*, which is used in one of Martial's epigrams to denote boorishness and denseness of mind. The Batavi, Erasmus explains, once inhabited that country which is now called Holland, "a land that I shall always honor and revere, as I owe it the origin of my life. If some one should maintain that this phrase of Martial still applies to the Hollanders of today, I would ask, what greater praise can one give them than to call them averse to the scurrilities of Martial? To judge from their home life, no other nation is more inclined towards humane and kindly manners and less capable of truculence or cruelty. They are straightforward, scorning trickery and all make-believe, and offend by no serious vices except a propensity to good living." And when he was dying and the death rattle upon him, two final words escaped his lips: *Lieve God!* Just as the drowning sailor or the soldier dying on the battlefield cries out for his mother, even so the Latinist, in the agony of death, turned for expression to his mother tongue.

[29]

Stefan Zweig, Erasmus' latest biographer, writing under the obsession of a new world war that threatens to destroy the culture of hate-torn Europe, sees in him the "supranationalist," the serene philosopher who, free from the narrow love of country, felt Europe to be his home. Since Herr Zweig intended his picture of the Age of the Reformation to be a mirror to our own, he had to confront his ideal of the European with the embodiment of sixteenth-century nationalism. "Erasmus, who was essentially the far-visioned man of intellect, the evolutionary, had as antagonist in the arena of destiny a man of action, a revolutionary, Luther, an emanation of the dark, daimonic forces of the Germanic peoples." As a Hollander I am near enough kin to Erasmus to feel distrustful of violent terms such as "daimonic forces of the Germanic peoples." What does it mean? Must we suppose that the Germanic peoples are blessed or cursed with a larger daimonic endowment than their neighbors? But Erasmus was also a son of those same peoples. How did he escape the hold of the racial daimons? If Luther was temperamentally so different from Erasmus, it was not because he was a daimonic Teuton, but primarily because he was Luther, and his antagonist, Erasmus.

Environment and breeding are also factors that account for the difference. The Hollanders, a nation of seafarers and traders, have freely mingled, since the early Middle Ages, with fellow men of other nationalities. Age-long rubbing of elbows with strangers has given them a polish and a tolerance that land-locked peoples have been slow in acquiring. The character traits that Luther the Saxon despised in Erasmus—his

moderation, caution, hate of violence, love of peace—
were part of his Dutch inheritance. With a Hollander's
dread of extremes, Erasmus deplored as signs of bad
breeding the stentorian voice and the fist on the table
with which Luther needlessly enforced the cogency of
his arguments. It was not the matter on which they dis-
agreed that caused the breach between the two, it was
the manner of disagreeing.

The heroic attitude did not suit Erasmus. In that he
was a true-born Hollander. His people do not love
danger for danger's sake, and the path to glory does not
lure them if it leads across the battlefield. They will
fight, if fight they must, for their freedom and their
homes, but never for the joy of fighting. Erasmus was
trained in the schools of the Modern Devotion, where
pacifism was taught as a Christian virtue. In that unheroic
milieu the example of Saint Cordula was revered. She
was one of the eleven thousand virgins who, according
to the medieval legend, suffered martyrdom in Cologne
at the hands of Attila's cruel Huns. The German mystic
Tauler devoted to Cordula one of his sermons, and this
homily was the first of all his writings to gain popularity in the Netherlands. Tauler singled her out from
among the host of St. Ursula's virgins because she was
the only one who feared martyrdom and concealed
herself from the barbarians. But she, who was the least
of them all, glorified her Saviour by her death as none of
her sisters did, for, said Tauler, "all that bloodshed and
death, those clubs and cudgels, and the hostile faces of
those wicked men, pierced her heart and imagination; so
that she died with each of her sisters a separate death in

[31]

her soul, whereas all the others died only once." The coward was the greatest saint of all, for she tasted death eleven thousand times through the vividness of her imagination.

The Dutch sense of realism evokes before the mind's eye all the horrors of which war is capable, and the mental picture teaches martial ardor deliberation. If that is cowardice the Dutch are a nation of cowards. But these same cowards will never brook suppression of the right to speak their minds. Freedom of thought and utterance has been theirs since the early days of the Dutch Republic. They possess a moral courage that transcends the physical bravery of the heedless, the courage to speak out for what they hold to be the truth, in open defiance of powerful authority.

Chapter III

PEACEFUL CONQUEST

"GOD MADE the country and man made the town," said William Cowper in *The Task*. An exception should have been made of the Hollander, for he made his own country. If you place side by side a map of the province of Holland as it was in the sixteenth century and one of the present day, you will see at a glance how much water has been converted into land. Large lakes, on which the Sea Beggars fought Spanish men-of-war, have disappeared, cows are grazing on what once was the bottom of the lake, and farmers live and labor where, more than three hundred years ago, lay the sunken wrecks of ships and the corpses of the drowned. But incessant watchfulness is the price that Holland pays for her safety. The water is her friend and ally as long as she keeps it subdued. If it once runs out of hand, it turns from an assistant to an enemy, destroying the homes that it protected, smashing the mills that it set to work, drowning the cattle that it gave to drink, spoiling the crops that it fertilized.

American children are told the story of the little hero of Haarlem who stopped a leak in the dike with his finger. I wish they would realize that little Jack Horner made better use of his thumb. That Haarlem boy is an impostor. I feel that Jenny Dobbs, who could not control her feelings in reciting the story, had much better choke in plums with Little Jack than in tears over that impossible hero. If thumbs could do the trick, then corks could serve the same purpose. But no Dutch farmer would rely on corks for protection against the water. He might use them to float upon after the disaster, but not in an attempt to prevent it. Unwieldy bags of sand, much heavier than the little Haarlem hero, are the only means of stemming the insistence of the oozing water. In idiomatic Dutch the teller of an incredible story is said to have "sucked it out of his thumb," and I have a suspicion that the little thumb which is supposed to have been the stopper of a leak, was itself the source from which this legend leaked into English and American schoolbooks. The schoolbooks of Holland do not know it.

There is no arbiter to whom the country can turn for justice in its age-long struggle against the water. If there were a World Court before which Holland could plead her cause she would not hesitate to join it, though Senator Borah should come over to The Hague to warn her against such a step. The country, in this instance, however, must judge its own case and be its own avenger, and with the aid of science must repeat the work that each preceding generation was forced to undertake in self-defense. Recent devastations caused by high water make the Hollanders realize what their ancestors, without the inventions of modern engineering, must have suffered from the inroads of the sea, and how much they accomplished with primitive means in spite of the

handicaps under which they labored. "Men's evil manners live in brass; their virtues We write in water," says
Griffith, in *King Henry the Eighth*, deploring the in-
gratitude of man. The Hollanders, a modest people by
nature, have written their own virtues in water, their
script being the curving lines of the dikes that shelter
what they have won from the waves by the virtues of
industry, persistence, and patience.

To keep the sea from coming in was an easier task
than to drive the inland water out. Windmills for drainage purposes were installed as far back as the early
fifteenth century. Marshland has been turned into pasture, lake after lake has been reclaimed, and the water
that remained within these reclaimed territories has been
tied in straight-jackets of canals and ditches from which
there is no escape except by permission of the jailers.
Holland proper is, indeed, a water prison. The cells of
the prison are called polders. A polder is an area of land
and water usually surrounded by dikes which serve both
as barriers to and as connecting links with the adjoining
area. The water cell or polder is not irretrievably cut off.
There are locks in the dikes which the jailers open from
time to time to let the captive out. This happens when
heavy rains have swelled the polder water above the
level that the jailers allow. A network of ditches running
crisscross through the polder serves as a provisional reservoir—called *bosom* in Dutch—for the overflow, which is
subsequently drained into outside *bosoms*. These may be
canals, or canalized rivers, or ancient lakes left unreclaimed for this very purpose of serving as receptacles of
discharged polder water. The outside *bosoms* are divided

into groups or units by an intricate system of dams and locks enabling the jailers to grade the water supply from *bosom* to *bosom* and to maintain that variety of gauge which is needed for the proper balancing of water levels. A polder, therefore, is not necessarily a reclaimed lake or pond. Its essential characteristic is the isolation of its water from the outside *bosoms*. Even the dikes are not an indispensable feature of the polder. For a polder may lie higher than the surrounding area, in which case no dikes are needed for protection against inundation. Hence not every polder is an erstwhile lake, but every reclaimed lake is a polder.

Considerable progress with the reclamation of flooded land has been made since the close of the sixteenth century. Between 1590 and 1615 some thirty thousand acres of polder land were added to the map of the province of Holland. The work was not undertaken by the Government, nor by the peasantry that reaped the chief benefits of the enterprise. Urban capitalists, enriched by commerce and navigation, invested their savings in these land-winning projects. They did not settle on the new land, but employed tenants to farm it for them. It became the fashion, though, for these city patricians to own a summer retreat by their farms, and thus they brought to the polder the amenities and the culture of city life. There is a fine picture by Thomas de Keyzer in the Rijksmuseum at Amsterdam showing one of these wealthy gentlemen and his family just descended, in front of his summer home, from the wagon in which they had arrived from Amsterdam. It is the best among many similar paintings that testify to the pride these burghers took in their new polder farms.

The largest lake of all, the one south of Haarlem, defied for a long time all attempts at reclamation. Hollanders do not like to "go over one night's ice." With this picturesque simile they describe their native caution in accomplishing the things they undertake. In the year 1641 the engineer Leeghwater draughted the first plan for the reclamation of the great Haarlem Lake, but not until 1852 was that inland sea laid dry and turned over to the cattle breeder and the tiller. This time, the Government took the initiative; private money poured in later, when the new land was offered for sale. J. P. Amersfoordt, a gentleman farmer, was among the first to buy a large tract in the polder, and at the very spot where in former days the people of Amsterdam had come to bathe, he began to drive the first steam plow ever seen in the Netherlands through the rich soil that was once the bottom of the lake. Badhoeve, Bath Farm, he called his place. Satisfaction with this new experiment made him an enthusiastic advocate of a still more ambitious scheme of reclamation. In 1849 B. P. F. van Diggelen proposed a plan for the drainage of the Zuiderzee, and Amersfoordt became one of its most ardent supporters. He designed, and made out of wood, a geological relief map to serve as an exhibit at the Centennial Exposition held at Philadelphia in 1876. The map bore this rhymed legend,

> Haarlem Lake is drained
> And drained is the Y.
> If peace be maintained,
> Zuiderzee will get dry.

As a matter of fact, it was just because peace was not maintained that the plans for the reclamation were carried into execution. The enormous expense at which the Dutch army was kept mobilized during the World War taught the Hollanders how little, comparatively speaking, the drainage of the Zuiderzee would cost them. The total expenditure, according to optimistic estimates of twenty years ago, would amount to no more than half the sum the country had to pay in one year for the maintenance of its neutrality in the war. If the taxpayers could bear the burden of those costly years of armed preparedness, they could certainly bear the smaller expense of an enterprise that would yield profits to the next generation. And so it happened that while the Great Powers were at war, the Netherland Parliament passed a bill for the reclamation of the Zuiderzee.

In 1933 the Zuiderzee ceased to be a sea. It became an inland lake cut off from the North Sea by a dike that was laid like a threshold across the only gate through which, in former days, it had free access to the ocean. It may still discharge water into the open sea beyond the dike, but man will henceforth control the outflow. In the past the little landbound sea was up to all the pranks that its big brother outside used to play. When the North Sea roared and lashed the beaches and dashed against the barrier of dunes, the Zuiderzee joined in the uproar and struck terror into the hearts of the womenfolk along its shores. But swells and spring-tides can no longer affect it. Its reservoir of water is now exclusively fed by the rivers that empty into it. These have turned the salt-water sea into a fresh-water lake, and this lake will, in the years to come, be forced into narrower confines by the reclamation of large areas that are to be annexed to the surrounding land.

One such polder has already been diked in and made available for settlement. Where part of the lake is thus laid dry and added to the mainland, the former sea dike becomes an inland highway, and erstwhile coast-dwellers involuntary landlubbers. Profound changes will, in consequence, alter the aspect of the landscape and the people's life. Much of the ancient charm will be lost forever. Quaint folklore, picturesque costumes, age-old customs, medieval architecture, will vanish wherever the farmer with modern methods and equipment replaces the conservative fisherman.

Seafaring people are arch-conservatives. The insecurity of life on the ocean seems to make them tenacious of all that they possess on land. They are willing to risk their lives on perilous voyages, but the things they leave behind must remain safely anchored in tradition. This aversion to change has maintained each fisher village as a separate community distinct from its neighbors in customs and costumes, in dialect and folklore, in the lines of its sailing craft and the weave of its nets. On the island of Terschelling two different languages are spoken, a dialectical variety of Hollandish in the west end, and Frisian in the east end. The linguistic border line runs, strange to say, across the village of Formerum. It seems almost incredible that one half the population of a small island village should speak a language different from that of the other half. Extreme conservatism has withstood the natural tendency to fusion, though the peculiar shape of the settlement may have aided in stiffening its power of resistance. The center of most Dutch villages is the parish church, but the kernel of Formerum is arable land. The settlers on the eastern edge of the rye fields moved up from the Frisian side, those on the western edge came from the Dutch-speaking part of the island. The two sections were never united into one parish, and that also may account for the tenacious bilingualism of the village.

Half a century ago the east and west ends of Terschelling were connected only by the Zuiderzee dike and a muddy footpath. In those days, no love was lost between the people of the two sections and rarely indeed were they united in marriage. Now the opposite ends of the island are connected by a motor road, and a member of the numerous Terschelling family bearing the curious name of Cupido has the monopoly of the insular autobus service. Cupido actually functions as a binder of hearts. The old antagonism is not proof against the locomotive power of Cupido, who, by his daily rides from one end of the island to the other, is promoting interchange of ideas and better understanding, and bringing together boys and girls whose grandparents were traditional enemies.

The isle of Marken and the village of Volendam on the mainland, with only a narrow strait between them, have never influenced each other. The island people are Calvinists, the Volendam folk are Catholics. The Marken women conceal and flatten their bosoms in tightly laced corsets, their Volendam sisters go corsetless revealing the forms that nature gave them. The Marken costume consists of several layers decked with a blaze of colors,

the Volendam attire is less complicated and more subdued in tone. Yet it takes only twenty minutes to cross
from one community to the other.

A stranger might not be able to see any difference between the various kinds of sailing craft in use, but a
Zuiderzee fisherman can distinguish at a good distance a
botter from a *blazer*, a *jol* from a *vlet*, and will tell you
from which port each vessel hails. The *jol* is a specialty
of Stavoren on the Friesland coast. It looks like a giant's
wooden shoe fitted out with a mast and a sail for his children to play with. With this clumsy-looking toy the
Stavoren people play the fishing game in dead earnest,
staking their lives on the catch that must yield them a
living. The largest *botter* bulks no larger than thirty tons,
the smallest *jol* not less than five. The skippers, as a rule,
are sole owners of their craft, and each has marked it
with a hieroglyphic sign of ownership that is handed
down from father to son. They bow to no master but
their God. This economic independence, which has been
theirs for ages, has bred into these Dutch fisherfolk a
spirit of rugged individualism. They earn a scanty living,
but are happier in their poverty than they would be with
ampler incomes received as wages in the employ of a shipping company. During the World War, when high
prices were paid for their fish, the average annual income
of a Zuiderzee skipper was $465, and that of his crew
$334 per man.

They are a race of optimists and console themselves
over mishaps and failures with the philosophy of ancient
proverbial lore. If a shoal of herring has eluded them,
they will say, "fish have fins," meaning they have swum

away, and resign themselves goodhumoredly to their disappointment with the mockery, "In the morning you will find out where you should have been at night." Sometimes they can account for their ill success. It may have been brought on by the presence of a stranger on board ship, or by their seeing a priest just before lowering the nets, or—I apologize to the clergy—by the sight of a pig, a dog, or a hare on the distant shore. Whistling on board is equally disastrous, for it challenges the winds to blow their worst. Pagan superstitions such as these are like ineradicable weeds in the garden of their religious concepts, which the churches have tended with assiduous care.

The fisherfolk have an unshakable trust in God. It makes them averse to insuring their craft and their own lives, as that would be tantamount to denying their faith in divine providence. If a man loses a ship, he can always find employment among the crew of another; if he loses his life and his body is washed ashore, the two gold buttons on his collar will secure him a Christian burial. That is their answer to any agent of an insurance company who would sell them a policy. But they seldom give a thought to the possibility of drowning. They feel so perfectly at home on the sea that the thought of danger does not occur to them. They do not even take the precaution of learning to swim. Only when the sea is frozen over do the fishermen fear it. Then they go fishing in sledges at a much greater risk of their lives. For the floor often cracks and sends them adrift on a floe of ice, to starve or freeze to death in a sea bare of ships that could come to the rescue. The islands of Marken and Urk lie isolated when the winter frost is persistent and severe. Formerly, it was necessary to organize expeditions to the mainland to fetch food supplies and meal and flour for the bakers. But the development of aviation has put a stop to these perilous adventures. The Royal Aircraft Company has concluded a contract with the Government for the maintenance of communications when ice drifts make the islands inaccessible otherwise.[1]

When the full reclamation program has been completed, both Marken and Urk will have lost their island status. Urk will be included in the Northeast Polder; it will lie close behind a dike shutting it off from a small lake—all that will remain of the Zuiderzee. Marken is to be incorporated with the Southwest Polder and will have no access to the new lake except by a long and winding channel following the old coast line from Amsterdam to Enkhuizen. A Dutch nursery rhyme pokes fun at the minister of Urk who, on the crossing to Schokland, another Zuiderzee island, forgot his sermon:

> The Dominie of Urk
> Went to preach in the Schokland kirk.
> Because of the roar of the sea
> He forgot his homily.

It is a silly little rhyme without the slightest literary merit, yet it has nation-wide currency, perhaps because it affords the opportunity for an irreverent chuckle. The

---

[1] In order to preserve for posterity a record of the quaintness and the beauty that are doomed, the publishing firm of Scheltema & Holkema, Amsterdam, brought out, in 1932, a richly illustrated volume containing contributions by experts on the history and various aspects of life along the shores of the Zuiderzee (*De Zuiderzee; een herinneringswerk door Dr. H. Colijn e. a.*).

ministers of the Dutch Reformed Church have always been a power in the land. Seafaring people, impressed by the minister's learning and conscious of their own inferiority, find a measure of relief in the discovery that as sailors they are his betters. It may be that these simple verses enable their ordinarily inarticulate souls to give expression to that sense of relief. However that may be, the Dutch nation has an affection for the rhyme out of all proportion to its wit or beauty. It is bound to survive the completion of the reclamation scheme, and when the children of later generations are taught to say these verses, they will wonder why the dominie who was such a poor sailor did not go to Schokland by car. For by that time both islands will be part of the mainland and autobuses will have replaced the sailing craft that used to ply between the two communities. The immortal preacher of Urk will then prove useful to the schoolmasters, who can employ his plight as a starting point for a lesson in the geography of Holland. In that way he may repay the nation for the undeserved fame it has bestowed upon him.

The four polders to be reclaimed will together have the size of a new province. They will add arable land and pasture to the territory of Queen Wilhelmina's realm, and open up opportunity for work to tens of thousands now unemployed and living on the dole. But there is also a dark side to the Zuiderzee picture. The Dutch have a saying, "Den een zijn dood is den ander zijn brood," that is, "One man's death is another man's bread." In this case the farmer's boon is the fisherman's doom. In June, 1925, the Netherland Parliament passed a Zuiderzee Relief Act which provides ways and means for indemnifying the victims of the reclamation. Some of the fisherfolk whom it will deprive of their livelihood may turn to agriculture, others may take up a handicraft, others again may want to enter the merchant marine, and those who are too fond of the independent life they have led thus far will want to move to a North Sea village, where they can carry on as of old. Such changes will involve considerable expense, part of which, under the provisions of the Act, will be borne by the State. If the fishery on the new inland lake should prove remunerative, the Zuiderzee fishermen who are willing to shift from the salt- to the fresh-water catch will be given their license gratuitously. The nation will see to it that none shall suffer or starve.

One dire foreboding of the fisherfolk has been pleasantly belied by a whim of nature. Since the Zuiderzee was shut off from the North Sea it has become a favorite haunt of *paling*,[2] for which the fishermen get much better prices than they used to be paid for their salt-water catch. *Paling* are a kind of eel that live in fresh-water lakes and pools; but when the spawning season

[2] Dutch *paling* has been a popular article in the London market ever since the Middle Ages. The Dutch fishermen who brought their catch to Billingsgate were known there by the name of *paling-men*. In an Act of Parliament of the year 1495 it was ruled that "Noe such marchante nor paling man shuld sell nor put to sale any Elys by barell." The word thus officially adopted into the King's English has puzzled the dictionary writers for centuries. Where did it come from? The etymologists came to the rescue. "*Palingman*," said Blount in his Law Dictionary, published in 1670, "seems to be a merchant Denizen; one born within the English pale." That settled the question. Blount's cautious "seems to be" became "is" in the definitions of his copyists, and as late as 1864 Webster's Dictionary stated that a *palingman* was "one born within that part of Ireland called the English Pale." So easy it is to make Irishmen out of true-born Hollanders and Frisians.

[45]

comes, which happens, it seems, only once in a *paling's* lifetime, they seek the Atlantic Ocean, where, at great depth and at great distance from the European coast, the new generation is born. According to the ichthyologists, the older generation never returns, but the young fry, by some mysterious intuition or guidance, find the way to the old haunts of their progenitors. "But how," I asked my informant, "do they get into the Zuiderzee, now that the Dutch engineers have bottled it up?" "That's quite simple," he said; "they crawl across the dike; they are used to traveling over dry ground." In former days they swam up the rivers that flow into the Zuiderzee and found their way through fields and meadows into the pools and lakes that dot the Dutch landscape. But now the Zuiderzee offers them a spacious fresh-water basin, and the fisherfolk no longer curse the reclamation scheme.

The first polder wrested by Holland from the Zuiderzee is called Wieringermeer Polder. It has three community centers, Slootdorp, Middenmeer, and Wieringerwerf. These villages have not grown up haphazardly, as villages did in the past. Little is left to chance in this new Netherland province. In former days a settlement just happened; a cluster of houses became somehow, in course of time, the nucleus of an expanding community. But the villages in the Wieringermeer Polder were opened as one opens a country fair, with a display of flags, a band playing, and speeches by representatives of the Government. The colonists did not come to a wilderness in which they had to build their own homes out of material found there; the homes were waiting for them, welcoming them to all the comforts that modern industries create. The kitchens were fitted out with electric stoves, a luxury of which the newcomers never dreamt in their former homes, the windows were screened to keep out the malaria mosquito, the drinking water supply was carefully supervised and guaranteed to be pure. Choosy settlers who preferred to have their houses built by an architect of their own selection could have their wish fulfilled on condition that the plans received the approval of the Wieringermeer Directorate, which sees to it that individual tastes do not clash with the general style of the settlement. Even the land was in a way prepared for the farmers. Experiments with various crops carried on by the Government experts spared the colonists costly disappointments and offered them guidance in the profitable use of the soil.

The settlers were not allowed to drift in, but were carefully selected with due regard to professional skill, physical stamina, moral fiber, and past record. No religion was granted special privilege, the Government's aim being to give Protestants, Roman Catholics, and agnostics the proportional strength that they hold in the country at large. And since political convictions are chiefly based on the confession, or the denial, of a creed, party divisions in the polder will fairly well tally with their strength in the nation. The Directorate also exercises control over the number of stores to be established. Only one baker, one butcher, and one grocer were admitted to the new village of Wieringerwerf, so as to preclude unnecessary competition and economic waste. As the village expands, the number of caterers to its physical wants will be increased to the limit which will insure to each supplier of meat and bread and groceries a decent livelihood. In short, adventure and romance, which are supposed to have glorified the risk of settling a new country in the past, were sternly barred from the Wieringermeer Polder. The Netherland Government frowns on dangerous living and favors for its substitute a planned economy.

This picture of the new Zuiderzee colony offers a striking contrast to the manner in which, fourscore years ago, new-won land was opened up for colonization. Haarlem Lake was reclaimed in the fifties of the past century and is now inhabited by a rich and thriving community. The farmers in this polder are among the most progressive and enterprising tillers of Dutch soil. Hendrik Colijn, Prime Minister, and Holland's strong man of the moment, was born among them. They were the first in the Netherlands to break with time-honored traditions, to experiment with modern machinery, and to change their methods in obedience to the lessons of science. They are a forward-looking race, not suspicious of innovations, not wedded to the routine of their ancestors, and acting as pacemakers to the rest of the farming population of Holland.

Their eminence is the crop of natural selection. The Government, eighty years ago, did little more than reclaim Haarlem Lake; it considered that its task was done when the water had been drained off. Colonists were invited in and left to shift for themselves. Anyone was welcome, no questions were asked, no proof of skill required, no record looked into. The settlers had to build their own homes, had to make their own experiments with the new soil, had to fight single-handed the rank growth of reed, weed, and willow that shot up all over the polder, had to fight the water that kept seeping in, turning the loam into a soggy marsh, and had to drink it at the risk of infection. The first year no grain could be sown on account of the high water. Penury was the result. Many wasted away through worry, undernourishment, and disease. The mortality rose to an alarming height, and the disheartened fled the scene of their misfortunes, impoverished and broken in health. The hardiest and the most skilled remained to fight it out with nature, and bred a race steeled by the struggle and made self-confident by the victory.

Nature did her work well in the Haarlem polder. Why then, seeing what excellent results she achieved, should the Netherland Government employ Science to improve on her planning? The believers in rugged individualism deny that Science can improve upon it. Governmental paternalism, they warn, will breed a race of weaklings, who, having been pampered from the start, will never develop those stern qualities of mind and body that thrive only on a fare of hardship, struggle, and want. Men who have worked their way up from the slums into a leading position in politics, industry, or finance are apt to talk that way in this country. No better discipline for a boy who has the makings of a man in him than the pangs of poverty and the blows of misfortune! This sounds fine and noble, but will the magnate, remembering his guttersnipe boyhood, send his own sons back to the slums for a training in that same school of hardship? He will hesitate to practice what he preaches, being well aware that the large majority of his former playmates never emerged from the slums.

Nature accomplishes great things, but harshly and at an appalling waste. The sacrifice and the suffering that she exacts as the price for her social planning are a cruel, because unnecessary, tax on human endurance. Science has proved them unnecessary by devising, as a substitute for Nature's relentless procedure, a rational method of selection that is less wasteful of life and is productive of immediate results. The product of natural selection may be superb in isolated instances, but Science insures a high average. Among the men who will till the soil in the Wieringermeer polder none may prove himself of the caliber of a Hendrik Colijn, but all will be good farmers, and their success in agriculture will not have been cruelly tested by their triumph over rivals who, weaker, or less skilled, or more shiftless, paid for their defeat with their illusions and their lives.

The nation's social conscience will not allow a return to the *laissez-faire* policy of former days. Even if the authorities could be convinced that Nature unaided is bound to turn out a hardier and more efficient type of men than is produced under the control of Science, they still would not give her free play. For that would mean taking chances with the lives of men and women and sacrificing them to the hope of great gain in a distant future. The stake is too precious to justify the gamble. And who can guarantee that the selective process which Nature achieves in her cruel way does not involve the irreparable loss of values other than those which distinguish the farmers in the Haarlem polder? These are hard-headed materialists; the fierce struggle for existence has stifled whatever yearnings may have stirred within the first settlers for the things of the spirit, love of music, literature, and art. The wildflower that thrives by the wayside is a hardier bloom than the hothouse orchid nurtured by Science, but the orchid's beauty is more precious than the wildflower's strength.

Besides, life in the Wieringermeer Polder, be it ever so scientifically planned, will never be a social hothouse. Enough struggle and strife will be left for the steeling of body and mind. Winter storms from the north, excessive rains, and the menace of high water in the spring will keep the men on the alert, and the need of social adjustments among settlers from all parts of the country, speaking various dialects, wedded to different traditions, and confessing several creeds, will prove a stern molder of character. There is no reason to expect that scientific planning will turn the polder people into a race of weaklings. The labor that the tilling of the soil involves cannot but harden them. And starting their new life under the most auspicious circumstances, they may develop into a rural community not impervious to the charm of pursuits that make for a fuller and a richer life.

Chapter IV

CITY PLANNING

THE CITY of Amsterdam is an inverted forest. Its pine trees do not rise from the ground, they bore into it, crown downward. The terrain is so soggy that each house must be built on a solid foundation of piles driven into the mud. The Hollander has a strange name for these subterranean trees; he calls them *juffers*, young ladies. I wonder why. A compliment to the erect build of Dutch girls may be implied. However that may be, the Hollander, in calling a pole a lady, is less offensive to the fair sex than the German who calls his women-folk female timber, *frauenzimmer*. That is inverting the comparison into a downright insult.

Since every house in Amsterdam rests on piles, it is clear that the entire underground city is a dense timber forest. But above ground it is a mass of brick and stone, with spare fringes of foliage along its canals and, here and there, dots of green parks. Where the city ends, the flat country begins, deep-lying polders with a criss-cross pattern of ditches lined with dwarfish pollard willows that do not obstruct the endless vista of pasture. There are no woods in the immediate neighborhood of Amsterdam to lure the poor away from the crowded city. The well-to-do have the means to spend their week-ends and vacations in Utrecht or Gelderland, or farther away in Switzerland or Germany. But those who can afford no more than a tram ride for an outing must find the pleasures and the benefits of rural life vicariously in the dusty city parks.

Since the larger part of the city's population cannot be brought to the distant woods, the municipal government has decided to bring the woods to the city. Amsterdam, built on a forest, will in the next few years be belted by a forest. A thousand men are employed in planting trees on the very outskirts of Amsterdam. Rather than have them come to the City Hall each week for their dole, the authorities will pay them for making the city a healthier and pleasanter place to live in for their fellow citizens and themselves.

The plans for this huge enterprise have been made by a committee of experts on forestry, landscape gardening, and botany. But the authorities count chiefly on the assistance of Nature, whose genius for landscape architecture will be given free rein after human adepts have done the planting. The pools and lakes near the city will not be drained but will be left intact for the recreation of anglers and lovers of aquatic sports, who will find there even greater beauty when these favorite haunts mirror sheltering girdles of foliage. The botanists and landscape architects are hunting all over the world for trees for the new Amsterdam forest. The Far East, Siberia, the Caucasus, and the North American continent will all contribute saplings to the polder landscape. A seventeenth-century poet pitied the worry-sick merchants on the Exchange, who with all their wealth lacked oak in Amsterdam. Twenty years from now the poorest slum dweller will be able to go picnicking of a summer Sunday in the shade of oak or beech or maple or whatever forest growth his fancy prefers.

A crowded city built, as Amsterdam is, among swamps and intersected by a network of stagnant canals that are the receptacles of garbage and sewage would seem to be a breeding place of contagion and disease. This has always presented grave problems to the authorities responsible for the city's sanitation. An Amsterdam physician of the early nineteenth century found the matter sufficiently interesting to devote to it a book in four volumes, to which he gave the curious title of *Medical Topography of Amsterdam*. The author, C. J. Nieuwenhuys, was a radical among his colleagues, a forward-looking practitioner with advanced ideas about hygiene, physical culture, nursing, medical legislation, and many other related subjects. His book dealt with the Amsterdam climate and its effects upon the people's physique, with the city's water supply, the municipal inspection of foodstuffs, the control of infectious diseases, the training of physicians and surgeons, of dentists and midwives, with infant mortality, population statistics, hospital care, prison conditions—in a word, it might well be called a sociological survey of early nineteenth-century Amsterdam. But the word Sociology had not yet been invented in the good doctor's lifetime, and Medical Topography was the best he could think of. And it must be admitted that his best is very good.

When he began to compile the data for his survey,

Amsterdam and the rest of Holland were passing through a depression that was much more serious, probably, than the one from which the city is slowly recovering at present. The Napoleonic wars, in which the country had become involved, had left in their wake a general stagnation of trade. Amsterdam's commerce was at its lowest ebb, unemployment caused much suffering among the lower classes, and emergency relief drained the resources of the well-to-do. Yet no one seemed to care, says Dr. Nieuwenhuys. He noticed with pained surprise that public places of amusement were always crowded, that the collapse of business and loss of capital were borne with indifference, and that petitions in bankruptcy were filed by the insolvent with brazen disregard for personal reputation. People seemed to spend more since they possessed less. Divorces increased and marriages decreased in number. The young people, unable to marry on account of the critical economic conditions, disregarded legal conventions, and the number of illegitimate births rose, consequently, to an alarming height. According to the doctor's statistics, one-fifth of all the children born in the period from 1812 to 1815 were born out of wedlock. Daughters of good families visited dance halls of ill repute, where they mingled with the better class of hetaerae frequenting those places. In a population of about 220,000, more than 800 of these women were known to the police. Soliciting by streetwalkers was an open scandal. Venereal diseases were common, and the author's professional experience had led him to believe that there were few men in Amsterdam who, once at least, had not been infected by gonorrhea. In short, our

[55]

outspoken doctor paints a picture of the city's public morals such as the literature of the period does not reveal. It is instructive to read such a matter-of-fact account of actual conditions of a past age. It makes one suspect that the general breakdown of self-restraint which the moralists of our day deplore is not a sign of our depraved modernism but the recurrence of a phenomenon that comes and goes with wave-like periodicity.

When James Howell, the author of *Epistolae Hoelianae*, visited Amsterdam in 1619, he gave in a letter to his father the following description of the city's water supply: "They have neither Well or Fountain or any spring of fresh Water, in or about all this city, but their fresh Water is brought to them by boats; besides, they have Cisterns to receive the Rain-water, which they much use." Two hundred years later that description was still applicable. The rain water which was collected in cisterns was, according to Nieuwenhuys, the cause of many intestinal complaints, and the water that was imported in lighters from the Vecht, a small river that flows into the Zuiderzee south of Amsterdam, was even less reliable. It was transferred from these lighters into stationary barges that were moored to the quays of the city canals. The owners of these barges were not organized in a guild and were exempt from official inspection. Their boats were often in a decrepit condition and let the polluted canal water ooze into their liquid cargo. Domestic garbage, refuse from vegetables and butchers' shops were thrown into the canals in defiance of city ordinances against pollution. Besides, the majority of the privies discharged into the public canals, in spite of an early ordinance of 1663 forbidding such disposal. We of the twentieth century, who have learned to guard ourselves against an invisible host of germs and microbes, cannot but wonder how anyone in those unsanitary days could defy the curses that flesh is heir to and survive to a lusty old age.

The fourth and final volume of Nieuwenhuys' masterpiece was published in 1820. In the century that followed, the city, aided by Science, transformed itself into a healthier place than the medical topographer could have believed possible. The dunes along the North Sea are now being used as filters for the purification of the water that is supplied to every home in Amsterdam. An excellent sewerage system keeps the canals from pollution, and hydraulic engineers, by varying the levels of the water within and outside of the city, keep the water from stagnating and compel it to steer its impurities seaward. Slums have been cleared away and the city's death rate has been greatly reduced. And during the past two decades Amsterdam has built modern quarters for its growing population that attract the attention of architects from all over the world.

The man who was the moving force behind this latest expansion was Dr. F. M. Wibaut. He was *Wethouder* of Amsterdam, and in that capacity did excellent work in the clearing of slums and the building of decent dwellings for the laboring class. The *Wethouders*, of whom there are six in Amsterdam, form with the Burgomaster an executive committee of the City Council, from which they are elected. The Burgomaster alone holds his office as an appointee of the Crown. He presides at the meetings of both the *Wethouders* and the Council. The literal translation of *Wethouder* is "Law Keeper." The name seems better applicable to the Burgomaster, who is, as such, head of the city police, than to the administrators of the various departments of the municipal government. Dr. Wibaut, when elected *Wethouder* in 1914, was put in charge of Housing and Labor. He was then the only Socialist on the Board, but later on two, and finally three of the six, were members of the Social Democratic Labor Party.

Wibaut did not spring from the proletariat. He was a son of middle-class parents of the Roman Catholic faith. His father destined him for a business career, and he became a prominent executive of a lumber business at Middelburg, in which capacity he traveled widely in Russia and southeast Europe. But the acquisition of money for money's sake was not to his taste. Having lost his faith in the tenets of the Catholic Church, he became an ardent advocate of Socialism. He moved to Amsterdam, entered politics as a candidate of the Labor Party, and was elected a member of the City Council. From that time on he devoted to the welfare of the city all his energy and his love for his fellowman. He had no ambition to play a role in national politics. He felt that he could do better work in the municipal field, where his Party had fewer spokesmen, than in Parliament. First as a member of the City Board of Health, and later as *Wethouder*, he led the movement for slum clearance.

The census of 1899 had startled the public conscience by the appalling revelation that eighty percent of the lower income groups of the nation were living in one or two room dwellings. In Amsterdam large families were living in single rooms, dozens of families were cooped together in small houses, where they shared one steep, narrow staircase and one evil-smelling latrine; parents slept in closet beds with shelves above their heads for the larger children and with the smallest one tucked in at their feet. A subterranean population huddled in cellars, damp and moldy, where never a ray of sunshine penetrated.

The indignation aroused by these disclosures prodded the legislature into passing the Housing Act of 1901. This provided for State subsidies to municipalities, but left the initiative and the responsibility for the building program to local administrations. These, however, were allowed, and even encouraged, to enlist the enterprise of the citizens. Form your own building societies, the inhabitants were told, and we shall help you to finance your schemes. In 1906, the first coöperative housing society, formed by low-wage employees of the city of Amsterdam, applied to the central Government for a certificate. Only a properly certified housing society can obtain public funds for its building program.

The conservatives shook their heads over this dangerous innovation. It was downright socialism, they warned, for the Government to delegate so much responsibility to a group of small-wage earners, whose business capacity was, no doubt, to be rated in proportion to their incomes. In spite of all warnings the grant of the certificate was made, the building project of the architect employed by the applicants was approved by the city government, and this in turn applied to the central Government for a loan. In the ensuing years the demand for certificates grew apace, coöperative building projects were launched in cities, towns, and even rural districts, and the success of all these enterprises soon shamed the calamity howlers into silence. It was abundantly proved that low-wage earners were perfectly capable of running their homes coöperatively. Members of the society elect from their midst an executive board whose decisions are subject to approval by the municipal government. When a society is responsible for several blocks of houses, the tenants of each block appoint from their number a tenants' committee, which advises the board, settles disputes between neighbors, and organizes courses of instruction and entertainment for the children.

Members of these coöperative societies are, in general, workers who earn an average weekly wage of thirty guilders. They can afford to pay the rentals in these new houses, which are less than six guilders a week. But what about the poor slum dwellers whose homes were condemned by the Board as unfit for habitation? They could not be forced to pay rents exceeding one-fifth of their scant earnings. Adjust the rents to their meager incomes, was Wibaut's advice. That, however, was a socialist scheme which even the humanest members on the Board of Health could not swallow. They were willing to consent to much that Wibaut advocated: they agreed that the city should supply building capital at low interest, and should offer building space at cheap rates; they approved of municipal administration, free of charge, of apartment blocks. But they balked at a policy which would allow families of the laboring class, with regular incomes above the maximum entitling them to relief, to pay a rent in proportion to their earnings. Nevertheless, the experience that Wibaut had gained during his seven years' service on the Board of Health had convinced him that no solution of the housing situation was possible unless the city were willing to lease dwellings at less than cost price to families unable to pay the full rent. As *Wethouder* he succeeded in realizing even this part of his program. Thanks to State subsidies for the construction and upkeep of new homes to replace slum dwellings declared unfit for habitation, the city adopted the policy of leasing them to low-wage earners at reduced rentals. *Wie bouwt?* (who builds?) was a burning question in those days, which was answered by its echo. For the name Wibaut and that question are homonyms. He was, indeed, the chief builder of modern Amsterdam, and the workmen's quarters that he erected are admirable not only from the point of view of the sanitarian, but equally so from that of the artist and the architect. Wibaut deserves no small part of the credit for Amsterdam deslummed and beautified as it looks today, one of the most modern and spacious cities of Europe.

Wibaut was fortunate in finding the greatest among Dutch architects supporting his plans and willing to execute them. Hendrik Petrus Berlage was the acknowledged leader of modern Dutch architecture. I remember the sensation which he caused in the late nineties of the past century by his design for the Amsterdam exchange. Its severe simplicity and the rejection of all ornament that did not organically evolve from the construction itself were decried as the symptoms of a vitiated taste. People were so accustomed to look upon a profusion of ginger-bread decoration as the test of beauty in architecture that they could not recognize beauty in a building devoid of all fortuitous finery. It was fit for a prison or a madhouse, but to offer that solid block of brick to the Amsterdam merchants for a meeting place was an insult to the city and its commerce. Such were the comments that one heard even as late as 1903, the year in which the new Exchange was inaugurated. But gradually the popular taste and temper were won over first to acceptance and finally to admiration of Berlage's art. A new generation grew up that heartily detested the meaningless frills in which late nineteenth-century architecture had found such pleasure, and few Hollanders now would dare to ridicule Berlage's creed that the function of a building should dictate its form and that beauty evolves from the architect's obedience to that truth. Our grandparents built Protestant churches that were copies of Greek temples, laboratories that pretended to be Gothic monasteries, and villas that looked like huge canary cages. It is hard for us to understand what beauty they saw in those misshapen hideosities.

But Berlage did more than create a new style based on sound, aesthetic principles. The rapid expansion of Amsterdam during the past two decades called for artistic leadership in city planning, and Berlage was entrusted with the task of laying out the new quarters on the outskirts of the city that I knew in my young days. This commission gave him the opportunity to create the ideal setting for the type of town house that he had taught a younger generation of architects to build. And that applies not only to the rich man's home, but also to the workman's simpler quarters. Artistic colonies have arisen on the outskirts of Amsterdam and many other Dutch cities, where the worker can live in a comfortable home that is well-aired, well-lighted, and an aesthetic pleasure to the eye. There is no better way to teach people to understand and to love art and beauty. Given a home that is a daily demonstration of those two, they will learn to feel that life without them is a mental discomfort. Berlage and his school have made the Hollanders aware of what is beautiful in architecture, and that, perhaps, is his greatest contribution to the life of the nation. He has changed not only the aspect of town and country, he has changed the attitude of town and country dwellers toward their environment.

Hence at every fresh visit to my native land I find new beauty in it. This may be partly due to a change in myself which makes me look at old, familiar scenes with new and unaccustomed eyes. The scenery of both town and country seems richer in color and variety of form to one who comes from the greystone canyons of New York. But a change has come over Holland, too, thanks to a new generation of architects who see in Berlage their master. Beauty of architecture, in the minds of sight-seeing travelers, is a monopoly of the dead past. The sights of The Hague displayed to tourists by professional guides are the old buildings in the heart of the city whose age can be counted in centuries. Visitors are wisely kept from the more recent purlieus where, from about 1880 to 1920, speculators in real estate erected interminable rows of common-looking houses, each a faithful copy of its neighbors to right and left. The eternal sameness of those dwellings, it would seem, must affect the spirit of their tenants and merge them into a dull, impersonal crowd of standardized automatons. But the builders of these atrocities have had their day apparently. North of The Hague, in the direction of Leyden, a new garden city has sprung up which is a sight worth visiting. A too obvious striving after originality, it is true, has resulted here and there in something ludicrous and absurd, but the general impression is one of charm and exquisite taste. The intrusion of the city, for once, has not despoiled the country of its loveliness; on the contrary, it has turned the landscape of field and wood and dune into a garden of delight.

An even more interesting departure from the style of the recent past may be seen in Amsterdam West. Here each block represents the homogeneous work of one architect; it is not a dull square of exactly similar houses, but each house in it forms an integral part of the whole, the entire block, not the house, being the unit. No gingerbread decorations spoil the severe simplicity of these façades. The sense of beauty which they evoke is created by the contrast of straight lines and curves, by the right proportion of window space to wall space, by the color of the brick, and by the consistent use of that material in every detail. Thirty years ago the class of people inhabiting this modern section of the city was forced to live in sinister streets where there was nothing beautiful to cheer their existence. May we not believe that the new generation growing up in these bright, artistic dwellings will show the wholesome effect of that environment in greater vitality and love of life than their parents possessed?

Chapter V

LOVE OF GARDENS

THE DUTCH are a race of painters. Even the Hollander who has no gift for the painting craft possesses the love of color. He turns his garden into a canvas and, using flowers for paints, enlists the aid of nature in composing a picture. The nursery is his palette; no artist ever found a richer selection of colors in his paint-box. The Dutch garden painter adheres to the style known as stippling or dotting; he does not mix his colors, but achieves brilliance by their juxtaposition. His flower picture is not a still-life scene; it is a kaleidoscopic picture, exhibiting a succession of imperceptibly changing phases, a fading of fierce canary yellow into pale lemon, a bursting of green buds into fiery-red blooms, a dimming of bright blue into faint lilac, a shifting of the high spots in the color scheme from one side of the picture to the other. Hence it never bores by monotony, as does the stereotyped painting of fruit and flowers in the dining room. The family, indeed, have long since ceased to notice the still-life over the sideboard. For the picture that draws their eyes is a living one, framed by the wide-open garden doors, and constantly painted afresh by the successive seasons of the year.

[65]

The florist round the corner sells hyacinth bulbs in fancy jars of colored glass. The jar bears a faint resemblance to a lady of the Directoire, whose bell-like skirt gathered up below the breasts is suggested by the cone-shaped base that holds the water, the bust by the curving rim and the head by the bulb that crowns the whole. In the warmth of the living room or of the sunshine on the window ledge the bulb will shoot its roots into the water and lift its chandelier above the jar. I do not care for the hyacinth in such a setting. It does not belong indoors. A single flower cuts a stiff and awkward figure, and a bunch of hyacinths makes a sullen, choked-up group, as if their own fragrance were too much for them. They look self-conscious in the presence of a vase of tulips, who are born aristocrats and know instinctively how to carry themselves in a drawing room. These bend their supple stems into graceful attitudes and tilt their heads intelligently, as if to catch each other's fragrance, or in response to the vibrations astir in the room.

The hyacinth is made of coarser fiber. He is a soldier born, at home in the field, and at his best when merged in the mass, one of an army on parade. There are various regiments that can be distinguished by their uniforms. There are the whites, and the yellows, the pinks, and the blues, the lilacs, and the purples. They hold maneuvers once a year, towards the end of April or early in May. Those among my readers who can take the time off for a trip to Holland at that season will see a pageantry of military colors such as no other army can display. Take your stand at the foot of the dunes west of the battle array. The wind in Holland is nearly always from

the west, and if you let the army charge in your direction
with the wind behind it, the overpowering scent of
hyacinth might fell you to the ground. At the foot of
the dunes you are safe. See how they are arrayed in
serried ranks, each regiment a solid block of color and
ready, it would seem, to charge that peaceful village in
the distance. Its cottages seek shelter behind hedges and
under the shade of spreading trees; and above that cower-
ing scene a windmill lifts its cross against the eastern sky
as if in prayer for peace and safety. The sun breaks
through the clouds and sets the colors of the regiments
ablaze. The west wind rises and blows a trumpet call, the
army bends under its lash into position for the attack.
The spring maneuvers are on.

Once in ten years there are special maneuvers. They
take place in May and usually cover an area of sixteen
thousand acres. The hyacinths are not the only com-
batants. Daffodils and dahlias and tulips are good soldiers
too and make a brilliant showing in their bright yellow,
blazing red, and dark purple uniforms. The parade
grounds are established at Groenendael, once a private
estate and now a public park belonging to the village of
Heemstede. These special maneuvers were last held in
1935. An army of tulips, five hundred thousand strong,
lined up, on that occasion, in front of the General Staff's
Main Hall and played a symphony of colors against a
background of foliage and fountains. Experts from abroad
were invited to come and review the floral parade. A
delegation from the Horticultural Society of America
sailed on the Holland-America liner *Statendam* to attend
the military show. They nearly arrived too late, for

there never was an army more impatient to show off. The daffodils in the fields around the village of Hillegom were reported to be marshaling for the parade by the time the party embarked at Hoboken. The oldest inhabitants of the region could not remember such an early turnout. The mild winter was to blame for this impatience. The troops in their subterranean barracks were scenting the spring breeze and the sunshine, and rose from their beds with flying colors ahead of time.

Within easy motoring distance from Heemstede is the village of Aalsmeer. On a visit to Holland, a few years ago, I revisited its flower gardens. I retained but vague recollections of earlier visits. The place itself stood out less clearly in my mind than did the steam launch that used to take us there, and the treat of strawberries and cream which for children was the chief attraction of the trip. For in those days, half a century ago, Aalsmeer strawberries were famous, and when they were in season an excursion from Amsterdam to Aalsmeer was a delight for young and old. We used to stop at the sign of *De Drie Kolommen* (The Three Columns), where we could sit by the water's edge in a garden at the back of the house and watch the little boats with fruit and vegetables for the Amsterdam market glide past while we relished our strawberries and cream.

The Three Columns still stood in the same place, but Aalsmeer looked different. It had risen high above its former station. I should insult it now, I felt, if I went there for the sole purpose of eating strawberries and cream. Aalsmeer has outgrown strawberries and grows roses instead. One goes there now to feast

[68]

the eye, not the tongue, though I must admit that I
ate an excellent luncheon at my old haunt *De Drie
Kolommen*. The meal was only an incident in the adventure of the day, which was a quest for color and
fragrant beauty. It was the season of roses, begonias,
and dahlias; the chrysanthemums were just opening into
bloom. About four million rose bushes are grown under
glass at Aalsmeer, and about half that number in the open.
There were the dark-red *Hadley*, one of the most fragrant varieties, the *Golden Ophelia*, the pink *Columbia*,
the salmon-tinted *Aspirant Marcel Rouyer*, the creamy-
white *Kaiserin Augusta Victoria*, the yellow *Souvenir de
Claudius Pernet*, the copper-colored *Wilhelm Cordes*,
and several other varieties without other blight or blem-
ish than their names. "Give a rose a bad name and cut
her," seems to be the slogan of these nurserymen. They
cut roses by the millions in Aalsmeer and ship them by
airplane to Bremen, Hamburg, Copenhagen, Malmö,
Hannover, Berlin, Frankfurt, Basle, Brussels, Paris, and
London. Schiphol, the Amsterdam airdrome, is only a few
miles' distance from Aalsmeer. The flowers are taken
there by trucks, transferred into the planes with little
delay, and reach their various destinations within four or
five hours almost as fresh as when they left the nursery.

The rapid growth of aviation in Holland has made
Aalsmeer the cut-flower market of all Europe. The rose
especially has benefited by this winged transport. Lilacs
used to be the chief product of Aalsmeer some years
ago, but they are too heavy for transport by air. Hence,
in 1928, the rose, for the first time in the history of
Aalsmeer, yielded a bigger profit than the lilac. In that

year the number of cut roses sold in the Aalsmeer market surpassed that of the previous year by more than seven million.

Lilacs too heavy for transport by air? It does sound incredible. But if you could see them in bloom in the Aalsmeer hothouses, you would believe it. They are the chief pride of the nurserymen. For nowhere else will lilacs flourish as they do in Aalsmeer. They thrive on the mud—*bagger* they call it in Dutch—which is dredged from the bottom of the *Groote Poel*, the Big Lake, whose edges are fringed by the nurseries. When you look down upon Aalsmeer from an airplane, the flower gardens look like square little islands dotting the mirror of the *Groote Poel* along its frame. As each nursery is surrounded by water, the flowers are carried to the auction house by boat. The barges with their fragrant cargoes slip noiselessly into the very center of the spacious building, where the flowers, in great sheafs, are transferred to movable counters, which one by one are wheeled into the auction room. You cannot hear yourself bid here, not on account of the noise, but because the bids are not made by word of mouth. No sound is heard in this model salesroom except the voice of the auctioneer. He holds up a bunch and appraises it. As long as there is no bid, he keeps lowering the price, until a buyer strikes the bargain. This is done by pressing a button in front of the buyer. Facing the audience is a huge dial, studded with little electric bulbs, as many as there are seats in the amphitheater opposite. The bidder, by pressing the button, lights one of these bulbs and thus reveals upon the dial a number corresponding with the number of his seat. At the same time the hand of the dial indicates the price at which the item has been sold. The first bid is a purchase, no outbidding being allowed. Thus with the least noise and the least loss of time, tens of thousands of flowers are sold in a couple of hours.

There are two of these auction houses in Aalsmeer, each the property of a coöperative society of nurserymen. These societies accommodate their members with money loans for the purchase of tools and supplies, repayment being made by deductions from the proceeds of the sales; they organize collective exhibits of Aalsmeer nursery products at international flower shows; they subsidize horticultural experiments, and award scholarships to students in the Government College of Horticulture at Aalsmeer. The daily auctions which are held under their auspices attract hundreds of buyers to the village, causing a continuous stir and traffic strangely in contrast with its usual rural quiet. Coöperation is the very lifeblood of Aalsmeer's garden industry: the nurserymen have their own employers' union, they have a common garden for experimentation purposes, they run their own coöperative bank, and have formed a society for the collective purchasing of horticultural supplies; the exporters of cut flowers are coöperatively organized; the graduates of the Horticultural College have their Alumni Association. All these coöperative organizations are held together by one inclusive organization, the Aalsmeer Horticultural League (*Aalsmeersche Tuinbouwbond*), whose secretary is the busiest man among the seven thousand people that make up the village population.

The high quality of Holland's horticultural products is not due solely to the excellence of the soil. It is true that the narrow strip of land behind the North Sea dunes yields an ideal soil for the cultivation of tulips and hyacinths, and that the *bagger* from the *Groote Poel* deserves credit for the richness of Aalsmeer lilacs. But the aid of Science should not be discounted. The Dutch nurserymen are not satisfied with the lore that tradition has handed down to them. Inherited practice must be reinforced with the theory that science teaches, so they send their sons to agricultural colleges to learn botany and plant pathology. The services of the laboratories are always available when problems baffle their experience or disease threatens to destroy their crops.

Dutch nurserymen and plant pathologists resent the inference, drawn from the name, that "Dutch elm disease" originated in Holland. Its first symptoms were observed along the west coast of northern France, Belgium, and Holland, and from that center it spread in the next ten years into England, Germany, southeastern Europe, and Italy. Holland, it is true, was among the first to be visited by the plague, but she was also in the forefront of the battle waged against it. The beauty of her canals was at stake. All over the country, these are lined with elms, I suppose because the *iep*, as the elm is called in Dutch, is a tidy sort of tree such as housewives favor. In the fall it does not clutter up doorsteps and the pavement in front of the house with sticky fruit and slippery leaves. Other qualities that recommend it, especially to municipal park commissioners, are its rapid growth and its deep-digging roots. I remember a terrific hurricane which struck The Hague on September 30, 1911, and uprooted some four thousand trees, many elms among them. They fell across canals, impeding the barge traffic, and struck their crowns against façades, smashing windows and roof tiles. But that was an exceptional disaster. Hurricanes are rare phenomena in the Low Countries. The atmosphere's worst fits of temper are gales that seldom gather strength enough to uproot an *iep*.

Since the summer of 1919 the elm has been the victim of attacks much more dangerous than those of blustering winds. An insidious enemy began to sap its strength in a mysterious way that baffled gardeners and botanists. Early in June the leaves would begin to shrivel, the twigs to curl at the top, and after a few days the withered leaves would fall off, except the one at the end of the curled twig, which kept fluttering in the breeze like a tiny vane. A cross section of a diseased branch showed under the microscope that the wood vessels of the outer rings were filled with a brown, resin-like substance. The youngest, tenderest twigs were affected first; from them the infection spread to the older branches, until it finally reached the trunk. There was no means of saving the patient. It might survive into the next year and make a brave show of lingering vitality, but the new leaves remained undersized and underhued, they shriveled and dropped, and soon only the diminutive vanes were left as ominous signals of death. The plant pathologists were divided in two camps, one calling the treacherous enemy a fungus, the other a bacterium. The chief bacterium baiter was a Russian artist, who after the World War exchanged the brush for the microscope. He must have peered into it with an artist's eye, which sees things no one else can see. He came to the conclusion that the soil of Western Europe was infested by a bacterium especially prone to poison elms, and he called the vile creature *Micrococcus Ulmi.* It was confronted by a rival called *Graphium Ulmi*, a fungus whose claim to the distinction of being the real elm fiend was supported by the other camp. The controversy was settled in the late twenties in favor of the murderous fungus. A German scholar proved the nonexistence of *Micrococcus Ulmi*, and a Dutch scientist, Christine Buisman, succeeded in producing the disease in healthy trees by infecting them with *Graphium Ulmi.*

That was a Pyrrhic victory for the fungus. For after the exposure of *Micrococcus* as a fake and impostor, *Graphium Ulmi* became the sole butt of the elm-saving campaign. Mycologists and entomologists joined forces in testing the fungus in their laboratories. They found that its spores grow in the wood vessels of the outer rings, whereupon the tree retaliates by closing up these vessels. But since the elm employs the vessels of the outer rings especially for the circulation of the needed moisture, it wages a suicidal struggle. While fighting the fungus, it starves itself to death.

But how did the murderous fungus migrate from tree to tree and from the west coast of Europe to the east and south of the Continent? That mystery was solved by three entomologists of the Wageningen laboratory. These G-men of the insect underworld tracked *Graphium's* accomplice and proved him guilty. The secret agent is a tiny beetle, which lays its eggs in the bark of sick or dead trees. The corridors which they dig for this purpose offer the spores of the fungus space to develop. The beetle's larvae winter in the bark and when, in May and June, they emerge as beetles they carry with them spores of the fungus with which they infect untainted trees. For the baby beetles need the juicy wood of tender elm twigs to make them sexually mature. This maturation period lasts but a week, but in that time the harm is done. The elm must die that the beetle may breed.

To convict the beetle of complicity was one thing, to counteract its damage was another. The spraying of trees with chemicals has proved useless; they do not kill either the fungus or the beetle. An effective way of fighting the latter is to deprive it of its hatcheries by cutting down all infected elms and burning the bark. Another is to develop a species of elm that is immune to the disease. Miss Buisman, who played a prominent part in discovering the cause, undertook the task of testing various kinds of elm as to their susceptibility to the blight. A Siberian variety, *Ulmus Pumila*, was found to suffer no harm from the fungus. But it does not thrive in the moist Dutch climate. Better results were obtained with a cross between the Dutch elm and a species of the European field elm imported from Spain. The attempts to grow a blight-resisting variety have developed so many new kinds that the botanists have apparently run out of names. This promising cross at any rate is prosaically labeled No. 24. The gardeners and municipal park commissioners in Holland are pinning their hopes on No. 24 as the elm that will restore shade to the denuded city canals and parkways.

If Holland must figure in the name of the disease,

let it be in recognition of the part taken by her scientists in tracing its cause and finding a remedy. First among these was Christine Buisman. She was taken away from her research by her sudden death three years ago. But she had the satisfaction of knowing, before she passed away, that she was near the goal. Richard Bright was the first to describe the true nature of the kidney disease that bears his name. In like manner, Dutch elm disease should be understood to mean a disease first diagnosed by Dutch scientists.

Chapter VI

THE DUTCH IN SCHOOL

THE GREAT SCHOLARS of the age of Erasmus held a position not dissimilar to that now occupied by popular radio speakers. When they mounted the rostrum to broadcast their learning, students flocked to the lecture halls in larger numbers than ever crowd the classrooms of a modern university. When Hieronymus Aleander announced a course of lectures at the *Collège de la Marche* in Paris, two thousand gathered to hear him, and he had to move with his audience to a larger hall in the Portico of Cambray. He spoke for two and a half hours, and although it was in midsummer, neither the heat nor his long-windedness proved too much for the endurance of his listeners. On the contrary, they were avid for more; on the third day all seats were taken by eleven, though the lecture did not begin until one o'clock. And the teacher did not discuss current events, or preach social justice, or counsel the weary and the downhearted with the voice of experience; his subject was the fourth-century poet Ausonius! Aleander, you must remember, lived in the semidarkness of the late Middle Ages, when only a faint glimmer heralded the advent of our wiser modern age.

To our times, Erasmus is as distant and awe-inspiring as Ausonius was to Aleander's. But this enlightened generation, which has forsworn folly, does not flock in thousands to the lecture room where scholars discourse upon Erasmus. Nevertheless, there were some eight hundred still foolish enough to fill the seating capacity of Low Memorial Library at Columbia University, when three scholars of international repute paid homage to the memory of the Dutch humanist four hundred years after his death. And if we may add to those eight hundred the thousands who listened in on the radio that late afternoon of November 18, 1936, Aleander—praised be folly—found his peers in Dr. Rufus M. Jones, Sir Robert A. Falconer, and President Butler.

It was fitting that Erasmus was remembered, four hundred years after his death, at Columbia and other American universities. For the entire western world is indebted to him for the wholesome reform he effected in the medieval system of education. He trained a new type of schoolmaster by his precept and example. Try to make the study attractive to your students, he told his fellow pedagogues. A dull man cannot be a good teacher. Do not inculcate too many rules; simplify grammatical instruction, and start at once with the reading of texts; exceptions to the rules should be illustrated in the reading material. Reward industry and good behavior, and refrain from bodily chastisement. The teacher who canes his boys is more fit to be a hangman. And do not train children to be parrots. Let them read the lesson over from beginning to end so that they grasp its general tenor. Let them then study it, first for its

[78]

grammar, next for its style, making notes of striking passages, trying to make clear to themselves why the author expressed his ideas in just that way, and committing proverbs and fables to memory.

One recognizes in those instructions the author of the *Colloquies*. I know no schoolbook so rich in wit and wisdom and entertainment. If its Latin is too hard a nut to crack, read it then in the racy rendering that Nathan Bailey made of it in the early eighteenth century. These amusing dialogues will teach a student Latin without tears, unless they be the tears of laughter. Here are no rules of grammar, but only reading matter replete with idiomatic phrases, metaphors, proverbs, and stories. The clash of opinions strikes sparks of wit from the argument, and profound thoughts that carry the seeds of revolution are casually dropped in a simple exchange of compliments. In one of his early *Colloquies* Erasmus teaches a polite way of interviewing a traveler upon his return from abroad. Our youthful press reporters might read it with profit. The wanderer has been in France and found the people there all talking about war.

The interviewer: "Whence come all these tumultuous wars?"

The traveler: "Whence should they come but from the ambition of monarchs?"

"But it would be more their prudence to appease these storms of human affairs."

"Appease 'em! Ay, so they do, as the south wind does the sea. They fancy themselves to be gods, and that the world was made for their sakes."

"Nay, rather a Prince was made for the good of the commonwealth, and not the commonwealth for the sake of the Prince."

That was a fruitful maxim dropped incidentally. It fell into fertile minds and bore seed again and again in successive generations of Dutch schoolboys, until the word was turned into stern practice by the grandsons of the youth for whom Erasmus wrote. When in 1581 the States General abjured allegiance to their sovereign, Philip II, King of Spain and Lord of the Netherlands, they justified their revolt by reminding the tyrant that "a Prince is appointed by God to be the shepherd of his people, and that the subjects were not created by God for the benefit of the Prince."

Holland gave birth to Erasmus, she gave a home to Comenius. The Dutchman preferred the cosmopolitan life of a wandering scholar to an anchorage in native soil; the Czech, Johan Amos Comenius, a wanderer not from choice but by compulsion, settled in Holland and lived there the fourteen last years of his life. He belonged to that European élite of seventeenth-century thinkers and reformers who, exiled from their native lands, found a refuge in the Dutch Republic. He was a member of the *Unitas Fratrum*, better known by the name of Moravian Brotherhood, a sect of radical Presbyterians, who laid stress not on doctrine but on conduct. They were a powerful organization in the early seventeenth century, and, through the schools they had founded, exercised great influence upon the young who were entrusted to their care. But they fell upon evil days at the outbreak of the Thirty Years' War. After the battle of the White Hill, in 1620, the Catholic Counter Reformation invaded Bohemia, and the Brethren were driven from their homes. Spanish soldiers, in the service of the Emperor Ferdinand II, pillaged Fulnek, where Comenius was pastor of the Brotherhood, and robbed him of all that he possessed. He became a wandering scholar, visiting the scattered communities of the *Unitas*, preaching and teaching in foreign countries, in Poland, Hungary, England, Sweden, Germany, and finally in Holland. And while he labored for the maintenance of unity between the Brethren in their dispersion, he wrote books on pedagogy that made him famous all over Europe as a reformer and the leading educator of his age.

The task of the school, he taught, was not merely to give instruction, but to mold and develop life. But life cannot unfold unless it grow up in an atmosphere of joy. The school should be an attractive place, pleasing to both the eye and the heart. He shook his head over those foolish parents who pictured to their children the master as a bugaboo and the schoolroom as a place of torture. When the time approaches for a child to go to school for the first time, the parents should talk about it as of a festival just as joyful and alluring as the annual fair or the harvest of the wine. For schools should be the pleasure-gardens of mankind; but alas, they have been turned into treadmills. I have seen teachers, he wrote, who threw assignments at their pupils as one throws bones to the dogs, and these same men would fly into a rage when the work the children handed in was badly done. You cannot be a teacher if you cannot act as a father.

[81]

Six hours in school was the maximum Comenius would allow. The children might be employed at home for two additional hours in various domestic tasks, but there should be no homework. The school was to be the only workshop. And he insisted on games and athletics as a necessary relaxation, ball games and bowls, and running and jumping and wrestling. Swimming was excluded from that list; the naked body was the devil's bait, and should be hidden from the children's eyes, for the little ones learn most through the eyes, both good things and bad. That is why he insisted on the value of visual education. Show your pupils the things you tell them about. Do not make them think and talk of what they do not comprehend; do not raise parrots but men. Schoolbooks ought to be picture books.

To set his contemporaries an example of a good schoolbook, he published in 1658 his *Orbis Sensualium Pictus.* This was an illustrated edition of an earlier work of his, the *Janua Linguarum Reserata* or "The Door of Languages Reopened"; in it he worked out a new method of teaching language by combining instruction in expression with information about the things expressed. Words without things, he said, were shells without kernels. In the *Janua* he taught his pupils eight thousand words in one thousand sentences, which, divided into a hundred chapters, discussed all phases of human knowledge and experience, from religion, science, and politics, down to the material need of clothes and food. He intended his *Janua* as a model for the instruction of each nation in its own mother tongue; for to teach a child a foreign language before it had mastered its own was like

[82]

teaching a boy to ride before he could walk. As a model handbook it gained recognition all over Europe, and outside the continent.

When Comenius visited Leyden in 1642, he was told that the book had been translated into Arabic, and that a Turkish and a Persian edition were in preparation. Even Indians in New England were given the *Janua* to study. There were two Indian students at Harvard in the class of 1665, one called Joel Jacoomis, the other Caleb Cheeschaumuk. The former's signature has been preserved in two places of the copy that he owned of the 1649 edition of the *Janua*. The two made such progress in their studies that John Winthrop, Governor of Connecticut, sent samples of their Latin papers across the ocean to the Honorable Robert Boyle, Governor of the Corporation for Propagating the Gospel in New England. If we are to believe Cotton Mather, Comenius himself was invited by John Winthrop to come to America to assume the presidency of Harvard. "That brave old man Johannes Amos Comenius," he wrote, "the fame of whose worth has been trumpeted so far as more than three languages (whereof every one is endebted unto his *Janua*) should carry it, was indeed agreed withall by our Mr. Winthrop in his travels through the Low Countries, to come over into New England, and illuminate the College and country in the quality of a President, but the solicitations of the Swedish Ambassador diverting him another way, that incomparable Moravian became not an American."

The pedagogic theories of Erasmus and Comenius were counsels of perfection. Although the average Dutch schoolmaster's actual performance fell far short of the ideal, the high example set by them stimulated the better type of teacher to conscientious effort. Especially the Latin schools of the Dutch Republic were staffed with masters who earnestly tried to follow in the footsteps of the leaders, and each Dutch town was ambitious for its Latin school to excel the Latin schools of other cities. Local pride kept education up to the mark. "In Holland," says the English historian G. N. Clark, "where urban conditions were commoner, the general level of education was probably higher than in most parts of France and the British Isles."[1]

Awareness of his own worth gave the Dutch schoolmaster a certain standing in the community. A curious incident in the history of New Netherland testifies to his self-assertive sense of importance. The town of Bergen, N. J., was laid out in 1660 by Jacques Cortelyou, a teacher by profession, and one Engelbert Steenhuysen was appointed precentor and schoolmaster at an annual salary of 250 guilders in wampum. One day some soldiers were quartered on the town. Each family was to take in one. But Steenhuysen refused to receive his boarder, asserting that "a schoolmaster should be exempt from all village taxes and burdens, as is customary everywhere in Christendom." His fellow citizens did not agree with him. They reasoned that since Steenhuysen was "the owner of a house and lot and a double bouwerie in the jurisdiction of the village," he ought to bear his part of the common burden. This aggrieved the schoolmaster so much that he resigned his office, whereupon the *schout*

[1] *The Seventeenth Century* (Oxford, 1929), p. 297.

and *schepens* appealed to the Council, arguing that he could not resign without giving six months' notice.

I do not pretend to know what the present-day schoolmaster's problems are everywhere in Christendom, but I can safely say that his controversies with the parents do not bear upon his duty as a taxpayer. He is less fortunate than the worthy schoolmaster of Bergen in New Netherland, for though his work is undoubtedly better it is much more severely criticized. Complaints about the school have increased in number and asperity in proportion to its improvement. Since Comenius' days, the school has amply demonstrated its capacity for development; each change, however, has been accompanied by warnings from the conservatives and by cries for more change from the progressives. Before the nineteenth century, the school changed its program and curriculum hardly at all. It taught the same things in the same way to one generation after another. But the school that understands its duty must say one thing to one generation and another to another. And it has to say the other thing in a different way. It has to present a new aspect of life in a new manner. In a time of great social upheaval, when people learn to look at life with different eyes, the school cannot escape the general drift towards readjustment.

In Holland, as in all the countries of Europe, education, as a result of the war, passed through a severe crisis. The war was felt to have demonstrated the bankruptcy of the prevailing educational system. This time it was not a case of the schoolmaster versus the people for taxing him unduly, it was the people versus the master for taxing the children's brains in the wrong way. The war, of course, had not created this discontent with the school, it had only accentuated a long-felt grievance. And, strange to say, the grievance was not that the teaching was inefficient, but on the contrary that it was too good. It was excellent in its way, but the way was felt not to be the right way. It led the child not into the life he was destined for, but away from it.

The school, during the nineteenth century, had labored industriously and incessantly to perfect itself, and it had done this to an extent that makes one marvel at the progress achieved in so short a period. But while engaged in improving itself, it lost sight of the life beyond the walls of the school house. The school became a law and an end unto itself, forgetting that its reason for existence was to function as a part of the larger organism of society. In the school everything was school-ish; reading matter, mathematical problems, geography and history were taught very thoroughly, but never with an eye to the world round about. Madame Montessori has well illustrated this aimless excellence by her attacks on the classroom seats, which, from the scholastic viewpoint, approach perfection inasmuch as they make it easier for the child to sit still, but to sit still is the very thing the child does not need. The needs of the child were not considered; the demands of the school were the law. The school did not serve the child, it served itself.

The parents themselves were to blame for this development. Parental indifference as to what was being done for their children forced the school to become self-reliant, and once self-reliant, to become self-sufficient. The parents judged the school by the children's report cards and by their success in passing examinations. If they failed it was not the subject matter of the exams that was called in question, but the efficiency of the preparation for them. This misdirected criticism urged the school authorities to proceed still further on the way to scholastic efficiency: more drilling, more memorizing, more parsing, more home work. It was a common saying in Holland before the war that during the summer holidays one half of the nation was engaged in examining the other half. This examination of the candidates was according to the teachings of the school, to find out what rank they would take in the classroom, not for what place in life they might be fit. Still, without school ratings the graduate cannot hope to enter a profession, for such is the respect commanded by the school among the laity that its stamp of approval is held to declare one fit for the business of life.

In the summer of 1931, a Dutch schoolboy, Henri R. M. Hoof, of Overveen, Holland, won the world's championship in high school oratory over six other contestants. That was a phenomenal victory, for the Dutch have never been known to excel in eloquence. Their national hero is William the Silent, and they honor his memory more by practicing the virtue that gave him his name than by making speeches, as young Hoof did at Washington, on William's greatness as a statesman. I know from my own experience how difficult it is to teach Dutch children the art of public speaking. They hate to get up on a platform and address a crowd, be it only an audience of their own classmates.

Educational methods are to blame, I believe, for the self-consciousness that seals their lips on such occasions. The average Dutch schoolmaster may be an expert in instilling facts into young brains but he has little notion of how to mold his pupils into self-reliant men and women. A retentive memory and intelligence is all he cares for; the child's character is none of his concern. In papers and quizzes he finds the clue to a pupil's worth. Strict obedience he expects as a matter of course, contradiction is put down as impertinence, and no allowances are made for individual peculiarities, moods, and tempers. The parents, from a sense of duty, impress upon their offspring the terrible shame of flunking at the end of the year; failure to be promoted to a higher grade or form casts disgrace not only upon the unfortunate derelict, but on the child's whole family.

"That boy knows a lot," is higher praise than "that boy is a manly little fellow." A system that aims at making children "know a lot" is apt to neglect training in the art of living. The many who know less than a lot are apt to be self-conscious, awkward, and suppressed. The art of speech can be developed only when the individual is free from diffidence and the obsession of his own inferiority. During the past two decades the know-a-lot fetish has suffered a decline of worship. Dutch educators have begun to realize that German pedagogy is not the infallible science that, before the war, it was believed to be. English and American methods are being studied with increasing interest, and the application of Anglo-

Saxon ideas begins to have a beneficial effect upon Dutch schools and Dutch children.

The emphasis laid upon the acquisition of facts made for a spirit of emulation, for a desire to outdo others in knowing much. The best pupil was the child that came nearest in knowledge to the teacher. It was not realized that the child who is in closest sympathy with the greatest number of his little fellows is a better pupil than the promising prig. The boy who, from a kindly fellow feeling, would assist a less clever comrade at his task must go about it clandestinely, because to help one's neighbor, which is a Christian duty in society, is an offense in the school. There was nothing the children could do or create together; they had only their knowledge which could not be possessed in common, but must be acquired and measured individually. A Dutch poet, Petrus Augustus de Genestet, addressed a century ago a hymn to Holland's youth, who held the promise of a better future for the nation; but he pictured her young people not at their desks in the classroom, but at play in the open. Without any intention of criticizing the school, he instinctively felt that the future generation might be preparing itself to better purpose in the communal ardor of the game than by individual effort in the school.

Games, since the time of that poet, have become an essential part of the Dutch child's education, thanks to the growing tendency, after the war, to imitate England rather than Germany. But it was difficult to convince the parents of the generation to which this writer belongs that games should be part of the school curriculum.

They were approved of as a healthy exercise outside of school hours, but were not accepted as of equal importance with the subjects taught in the classroom. In this negative way parents of that day showed their interest in the school. To win positive assistance in bringing the school into closer relation to society was a different matter. Some private schools, under progressive management, followed the American example and instituted parents' meetings; progressive educators made the ideas of John Dewey and other American writers known in the Netherlands. But innovations entailing an entirely new departure from the beaten track are difficult to bring about in Holland. Tradition, custom, prejudice, have a stronger hold on people over there than in this new country of ours, where nothing has been settled very long. Parents' meetings were ridiculed as a new fad of troublesome busybodies, harmful for the education which they pretended to serve. Nothing good could come of inviting the parents' active interest, the schoolmen and public objected, for they would not stop at showing interest, but would proceed to interfere. It was clear that only by artificial means, by legislative enactments, could parents and teachers be made co-workers in the interest of the child.

The churches were, before the war, the chief critics of the public schools. Nineteenth-century Liberalism saw in the public, nonsectarian school the best promoter of social unity, because it brought together under one roof the children of Protestants, Catholics, and Jews. But this very aspect of the school was most bitterly assailed by Calvinists and Roman Catholics alike. They did not want a neutral, purely rationalistic education for their children. They finally succeeded, after the war, in writing into the Constitution the principle of absolute equality of sectarian and public education, which meant that the costs of both must be defrayed from the public revenue. Hence all primary education, whether it be given in private or in public schools, is now charged to the Dutch taxpayer. The Elementary Education Act provides that, if in a community of less than five thousand inhabitants a denominational school is demanded by the parents of at least forty pupils, the government must comply with the request. The communes are divided, on the basis of their population, into five groups, and the minimum number of pupils required for each school is made progressive in accordance with this scale.

Thus the Liberal ideal of public education transcending disparity of religion came to naught. But the change was a gain insofar as it stimulated parental interest in the school. Parents were encouraged to take the initiative in the founding of schools, as it was believed that, having been instrumental in establishing one, they would be more inclined to retain an interest in their own creation. It was on the strength of that assumption that the legislature wrote into the Elementary Education Act an article providing for the establishment of parents' councils.

Too short a time has passed as yet to judge of the value of these councils. The teachers will probably find it more difficult to accept a coöperation forced upon them from above than if it had come about by mutual initiative. The good that is accomplished voluntarily has always greater value than the good done under compulsion. And will the parents, now that the law compels them to take an interest in the school, know how to use their influence to good account? C. P. Gunning, a modernist among Dutch headmasters, feels sceptical on that point. After a few years' experience with parents' councils he has come to the conclusion that parents, as a rule, have plenty of beautiful pedagogical theories, but that, in practice, the majority seem to value no other appraisal of ability than the purely intellectual one expressed in class ratings, and no other hope or ambition than that their children may pass their exams. If parental interest is to improve the school, it must be through bringing the atmosphere of the wider life of adult activity and interest into the isolation of the classroom. The parents must be the agents who shall keep the teaching in constant touch with the actual, so that the knowledge of the school may make the child receptive for the wisdom of life. For wisdom is not of the schools. "Wisdom," says the Book of Proverbs, "crieth aloud in the streets, she uttereth her voice in the broad places; she crieth in the chief place of concourse; at the entering in of the gates, in the city, she uttereth her words."

It is for the school to impart such knowledge to the child as will enable it to understand the message that wisdom utters in the street and the broad places. And it is for the parents to keep open the windows of the schoolroom that wisdom's voice may enter and remind the teacher that wisdom, not his own knowledge, is the end he has to serve.

Chapter VII

CONSERVATIVE YOUTH

THE UNIVERSITIES of Holland are old institutions if compared with even their most ancient sisters in America. But among the venerable universities of Europe which trace their history back to some medieval founder they are but modern upstarts, upon whom the moss of old age is yet to grow. They have no recollection of the Middle Ages. They came into existence when monasticism, in the northern Netherlands, had become a thing of the past, and owe their origin not to the private devotion of a pious founder but to the collective initiative of a young democracy. That gives them their peculiar character, so different from Oxford and Cambridge. The college with its quadrangle and its cloister, its chapel and its dining-hall, and with a name that perpetuates the memory of the donor, is here unknown. The Calvinist rulers of the Dutch Republic would not admit such monkish relics into their modern schools of learning. They were to be schools exclusively, not hostels for a monastic brotherhood. It was learning alone, at first theological learning especially, which constituted the brotherhood of students, not the community of roof and board. Hence the care for his physical welfare is the

[93]

student's private concern. He must find himself a lodging, he must cater for himself. The university will supply him with the knowledge which he seeks and, incidentally, watch over his morals.

In the days of the Republic there were as many of these universities as there were provinces in the Union. For provincial pride did not allow the province of Holland to remain in sole possession of a school for higher learning. Three of those old provincial institutions were taken over, in 1815, by the new Kingdom of the Netherlands, those of Leyden, the oldest of them all, of Utrecht, and of Groningen. Amsterdam possessed within her walls an *Athenaeum Illustre*, which in 1876 was raised to the rank of a university. But it still differs from its three sisters in that it remains a municipal institution, whereas the others are State universities.

The attendance at these four universities is comparatively small. The largest of them can not compete in numbers with an American college of modest size. But the two should not be compared, as their aims and methods are entirely different. Holland has no equivalent of the American college. The curriculum at her four universities provides exclusively for what in America is called post-graduate work. The Dutch boy and girl leave the high school at eighteen sufficiently prepared to specialize from the outset in one of the five university faculties, be it law, or theology, or philosophy, or medicine, or science. What the American undergraduate learns in his four years at college is condensed in the curriculum of the two last years at the Dutch *gymnasium* and high school.

Having successfully passed the final examination at one or the other of these schools, the student holds in his certificate the key to the gate of the university. An entirely new life is awaiting him, attractive for its freedom from the dull routine of the school, but more so for its remoteness from parental control. He will be his own master, unless he becomes his own slave. The hardest test of his character is at hand.

The university in Holland does not distinguish between winter and spring terms, the academic year from about the twentieth of September until about the tenth of July being reckoned as one term interrupted only by a month's vacation at Christmas and an Easter vacation of three weeks. The Freshman whose parents do not live in the university town or within commuting distance from it must secure rooms there in the early summer. Unnecessary to advertise for addresses. Householders who make an industry of letting rooms to students put a Latin notice up over their front door informing the prospective Freshmen that here are *Cubicula Locanda*, "Rooms for Rent." He spends a pleasant day, full of novel experience, in climbing up dark, winding staircases, inspecting luxurious and simple quarters, interviewing landladies of various physiognomies and tempers, from the forbidding virago to the ingratiating gossip, praising to each the rooms just visited before hers in the ever disappointed hope of beating down the rent, finding it more difficult to make up his mind after each fresh inspection, and returning home in the evening with an anxious misgiving that the rooms he finally took were about the worst of the lot. But he will think differently when he is properly installed in September, the proud monarch of all he surveys.

Beyond the narrow compass of that monarchy, however, he will have nothing to say for the first three weeks of his student life. For he and all the fellows of his class are on probation, and, being greenhorns just released from mother's apron strings, must go through the process of *ontgroening* or "de-greening." They are made to live under a depressing conviction of their total insignificance to the entire scheme of life. They may not sport an artistic shock of hair, a close-cropped pate being the regulation *coiffure*; hats, high collars, and fancy scarfs are considered contraband, the unimportance of the Freshman deserving no better than a cap, a low collar, and a skimpy black bow. Thus accoutred they descend upon the town on the first day of the *groentijd*, the hazing time. There is no way of escape from the trial. Their uniform marks them the lawful prey of the older classmen, who can order them about, command their services, summon and dismiss them at will. Their own will counts for nothing. What their seniors and—for the time being—their betters wish them to do is law to them; they carry a compendium of that law in their breast pocket in the form of a three weeks' diary for the masters and tyrants to write their orders and engagements in.

The Leyden Freshman gets one day of respite in those three weeks of serfdom. That is on the third of October, the day on which, in the year 1574, the city was relieved from its Spanish besiegers. That event is annually commemorated by both citizens and students, and the greenhorns, being deemed unworthy of sharing in the festivities, leave Leyden in a herd to find in the gaieties of Amsterdam as welcome a relief from their oppressors as Leyden did from hers in the sixteenth century. It is on that visit to Amsterdam that the class elects its president. Headed by him they return to the place of their captivity for another week of probation. But those final days hold a foretaste of the freedom and the pleasures to come. They give a theatrical performance for the entertainment of the other classes; they compete among themselves in boat races and athletic games; they spend a day in the dunes for military drilling; and on the night of their inauguration into the sacred bond of the students' Corps they perform a snake dance across the town in the fantastic glare of torches.

Not every Freshman is thus initiated into the mysteries of student life. No one who goes to the university to study is compelled to join the students' Corps. The Corps is the social bond between the students, as the university constitutes their scholastic unity. But the latter includes the entire student body, the Corps only those who believe that knowledge alone does not make men. Friendship, conviviality, games, the luxury of laziness, the romance of nightly escapades, these also add an indispensable element to the stuff a real man is made of. In former days, three generations ago, it was still a matter of course that entrance into the student body meant initiation into the Corps. But the students in those days were few in number and chiefly sons of well-to-do families. A university education, at that time, was the gentleman's prerogative; it is now a privilege obtainable by any boy with brains. It was formerly a shame for a student not to be in the

Corps, and pigs was the nickname for those unfortunates; now the number of those who stay out of it exceeds its membership list. Some would join if they could afford to, others who might join, do not care to. Many students commute and have, therefore, no inducements to enter the Corps, as they are only in town for lectures and leave it when the pleasures begin. While these "rail-students," as they are called, may do honor to the university, they contribute nothing to the community life of the students.[1]

The Corps has, in consequence, lost its representative character. It could speak, in former days, on behalf of the entire student body. It elected, and still elects, each year a Senate or, as they say in Leyden, a *Collegium*, a government of five to represent the Corps at all the ceremonies and official functions occurring in the university. They do so still, but only as the spokesmen of a privileged minority. Nonmembers have now their own organization, whose officers act as their spokesmen on these same occasions. But the real student life remains centered in the Corps and those who want, and can afford, not only to study but to be students as well will enter it when they enter the university.

Each annual class splits up into smaller groups of seldom more than fifteen, which are called clubs. The club is the student's substitute for the home he has left. Among fellow club-members he finds the daily companions of his leisure hours, and in the intimacy of the small circle

[1] Women students have their own organizations, but these are of very recent date and have accordingly not developed characteristic customs and traditions. What there is of these is mostly copied from the men's Corps.

friendships are formed that will last a lifetime. In Amsterdam the club is not a group of class fellows; the freshmen there are invited to join permanent clubs consisting of students who belong to different classes. In that way the classes are intermixed and the younger students brought into closer contact with their more experienced seniors. Still, the club that consists of contemporaries does not lead an isolated life. The entire Corps has a club house officially called the *Societeit* and in students' slang the *Kroeg* (the pub). This is the common meeting ground for all classes, and the permanent home of the entire Corps family. The family itself changes from year to year, but the *Kroeg* is the symbol of perpetuity. The alumnus who revisits his university town after a twenty years' absence will find there a welcome and, perhaps, an old friend in one of the faithful attendants.

Between the lecture hall, where he gathers with his fellow students, the digs, where he keeps vigils with his club friends, and the *Kroeg*, where he mixes with his Corps fellows, the student spends most of his happy, care-free life. His only worries are the exams. When he feels confident, or when his coach assures him that he is sufficiently primed he calls on the Secretary of his Faculty to have a day and hour fixed for the ordeal. The date is officially announced to the public at large by means of a notice posted *ad valvas academicas*, on the doors of the academy. The trial is open to the public, but it is not considered good etiquette to attend it without the victim's permission. The victim is taken to the trial by his club. In Leyden he waits for the summoning ring of the bell in a little room whose white-plastered walls

[99]

are covered with the signatures and literary effusions of many predecessors who spent an anxious quarter of an hour in that same place. It is known by the name of *Zweetkamertje*, the "Sweating room," and over the door on the outside it bears the inscription from Dante's, *Inferno*: "Lasciate ogni speranza voi chi entrate."

The bell rings, the usher, called *pedél*, conducts the candidate before the judges, and his friends go for a walk while he is under fire. He is released after three-quarters of an hour, and the door that lets him out is shut again upon the deliberations of the court. His friends are there again to cheer him up during those moments of suspense. Another ring. If the usher throws the door wide open, it is a sure sign that all is well: his friends may come in to hear the good opinion of his judges. But when the candidate is admitted alone, they know that he has flunked. There are, however, various degrees of failure. The extent of the deficiency is expressed in the number of months which must elapse before he may come up for re-examination. Three is the minimum, twelve the most ever assigned to a candidate. He who gets a year's postponement may consider himself doomed. He knows that it means a *consilium abeundi*, a hint to quit the university.

It is not customary for a student to leave for another university after the first exam. The ties that bind him to the one first entered hold him until the completion of his studies. He may go abroad for a year, to England, Germany, France, or Italy, in order to collect material for his doctor's dissertation, but he will return to his own university to take that degree. By his first exam he obtains the title of *Candidatus*, a successful second exam makes him *Doctorandus*. After that he must prepare his dissertation, which will win him the degree of *Doctor*. The ceremony which accompanies this final act of his university career, the *Promotion* so-called, is an impressive survival of olden times.

The student's life is very conservative of ancient traditions; to uphold the *Mos*, honored customs handed down from father to son, is considered a debt of honor that one owes to the past. And at no moment of his life in the university does the student show himself more attached to tradition than when he prepares to leave it for good. Innovations would seem to profane the solemnity of a last farewell. The doctor *in spe* drives up in state to the university building, the horses in front of his carriage waving plumes in the colors of the candidate's faculty. He is accompanied by two intimates, his *Paranymphi*, who will stand by him throughout the trial. They are the masters of ceremonies in the day's proceedings. They have made the arrangements for the dinner which the young doctor will give to his friends on the eve of his departure. They have on his behalf sent out the invitations and received the responses. They have taken every burden from their friend's shoulders so that he may give his mind entirely to the difficult task of defending his thesis against the attacks of the Faculty.

That trial over, the *Paranymphi*, as a faithful bodyguard, stand to the right and left of him while he listens to the speech with which the *Rector Magnificus*, on behalf of the university, confers upon the candidate the degree of *Doctor*. Then follow cheers and congratulations from a crowd of friends and relatives; whereupon the three, in the carriage with the plumed horses, drive to the *Kroeg* where the Doctor is the hero of the day. At seven he sits down to dinner with his club and with what other friends he may have made among the members of the Corps. His father, or his guardian, and his *promotor*, i.e., the professor under whose guidance he wrote his thesis, are also present. The *Paranymphus Primus* is toastmaster, and will be kept busy later in the evening, for on those occasions academic eloquence flows freely, with the wine. The *Paranymphus Secundus* is in charge of the nougat cake, a marvel of the confectioner's architecture copied from some edifice which figures largely in the Doctor's life. It occupies the center of the table and will be raised to still greater prominence at a late hour in the evening, when the *Paranymphus Secundus* will carry it, at the head of a torch-lit snake dance from the house where they dined to the home of the Corps. The snake dance does not end there. It winds itself through the *Kroeg*, over chairs, over tables, it jumps across the bar, and dives into the cellar; out at one door and in again at the other, while all the time the leader, who carries the nougat cake, exerts his utmost to keep it in balance and deliver it whole for the hero of the feast to cut up and divide.

In the same way, the club is broken up and the friends are scattered. But those whom he holds dearest will not be lost to him. They will meet once a year, at least, for a chat, as of old, over their wine. And once in five years the entire class and the classes of other years will meet at a great reunion, when the university celebrates the passage of another *lustrum*. Then all the alumni who can spare the time flock to their old university, and for a week festivities keep the town in feverish excitement. The chief item on the program is a historical pageant, which attracts not only the alumni but crowds of spectators from places far and wide. For the students are known to enlist all the talent and ingenuity and wealth among them for the perfection of these spectacles.

Each student, on that day, throws his rooms open to the friends and relatives who have come to see the pageant. Especially popular students are those whose windows look out upon the procession. They are not there themselves to act as hosts, their place being in the pageant, which winds its splendor of shining armor, waving crest, caparisoned courser, and floating banner along streets and canals, across arched bridges and through dark, narrow alleys, under the red, white, and blue of the national flag which flies from every housetop. In the evening, after supper, the procession again meanders through the town in the red flare of torches, and offers in that illumination and against the picturesque background of old façades a fantastic, unforgettable scene. On the following day, the masqueraders usually perform some play or other—a knightly tournament, an episode from medieval romance or national history— using some public park or building of ancient architecture in the town as a setting for the show.

It was my privilege, in the summer of 1936, to represent Columbia University at the celebration of the tercentenary of the University of Utrecht, Harvard's coeval among Holland's seats of higher learning. I found it difficult to believe that the two were of an age. In Utrecht

the university's three-hundredth birthday was commemorated in solemn retrospect; at Harvard the celebration took the form of a learned symposium, at which
not the past of the university, but the present and future
of mankind claimed the attention of the assembled
scholars. Harvard, in spite of three centuries of teaching,
retains the forward look and the disregard of past
achievement which are the essential traits of youth,
whereas Utrecht, in the reminiscent mood of ripe old
age, celebrated her three-hundredth anniversary as a goal
attained, without giving expression to the thought
whither the road might lead beyond.

Both universities owe their origin to the need of a
training school for learned ministers of the church. In
the Harvard symposium, however, theology was given a
back seat and no voice; in Utrecht, on the other hand,
the Dutch Reformed Church supplied the setting and
the substance of the ceremonies. These were opened with
a solemn convocation in the Church of St. Peter, and in
the afternoon the *Rector Magnificus* addressed a
crowded audience of Faculty members, official delegates,
and guests of the university from the pulpit of the
ancient cathedral. This imposing monument of medieval
architecture was, in the days of the Reformation, taken
away from the Church of Rome and handed over to the
Protestants, and it has remained a Dutch Reformed house
of worship ever since. There is a close connection between that transfer and the founding of the university,
for the same creed that claimed the building for its worship created the school for the church's need. Theology,
therefore, was not forgotten in the commemoration; it

justly played a major part at the three-hundredth birthday of its foster child.

The students of Utrecht celebrated their Alma Mater's tercentenary in their own way, not by paying tribute to the creed that gave her life, but nevertheless in the same retrospective mood that presided over the university's official proceedings. The Dutch student's traditional attitude is to look back, not forward. The class to which he belongs calls itself after the year in which it entered, not, as in America, after the year in which it will graduate. This year's Freshmen form the class of 1939, and the class of 1943 will not come into existence until the enrollment of that year's Freshmen has been completed. The newly made doctor who prepares to leave his Alma Mater talks of entering "the cold, workaday world," as if the best part of his life were over and the presentation of the doctor's bull were not the symbol of a promising Commencement, but the regretful marking of an End. Maintaining that retrospective attitude, Utrecht's student body turned their backs upon the future to pay tribute to the early days in which their university was born. They masqueraded through the city in costumes of three centuries ago, one of them acting the part of William, Prince of Orange; and they staged around midnight an open-air play which symbolized the Dutch revolt against the tyranny of Spain and the cruelties of the Spanish Inquisition. While Dr. Willem Mengelberg was conducting a concert on the final evening of the celebrations, the student who impersonated Prince William entered the hall with his retinue, and took the seat of honor reserved for him. After listening to Peter van Anrooy's *Piet*

Hein Rhapsody, His Highness sent one of his attendants to the platform to summon the conductor into his presence, and Dr. Mengelberg, entering into the spirit of the masquerade, came down from the podium and made his bow before the Prince in humble response to the latter's praise of his performance. The professors, the students, and the citizens of Utrecht lived during that week with their minds in the past, and even the famous conductor, who may well consider himself one of the great of his own age, was willing to pay homage to a greater one of a greater age.

The four universities mentioned so far are not the only institutes of higher education in Holland. A private corporation, the Society for Higher Education on a Dutch Calvinist Basis, founded in 1880 the "Free University" at Amsterdam. A similar university for Roman Catholic students was recently established at Nijmegen. Until 1905 only the three State universities and the municipal university of Amsterdam possessed the right to give degrees *cum effectu civili*, but in that year a law was passed which placed privately endowed institutions on an equal footing with the others.

The State Institute of Technology at Delft was founded in 1842. Reorganized in 1905, it received the official name of "Technical University." Its student life has been modeled on that of Leyden and Utrecht, which it resembles in nearly all particulars. As in the older universities, one finds here the Corps with its home and the *Kroeg*; the classes are similarly divided into clubs; the Freshmen must be "de-greened" before their initiation; and once in five years there is a general reunion of all the alumni and a week of festivities including some kind of pageantry or masquerade. The Delft Corps, though younger than those of the three State universities and Amsterdam, is treated as the equal of these four older sisters. Its Senate represents the Corps at the lustrum celebrations in Leyden, Utrecht, Groningen, and Amsterdam, and these, in their turn, honor Delft in its reunion week, in the same official fashion. In the varsity boat races the competing crews are usually from Leyden, Amsterdam, and Delft. And though the four other universities derive some superior distinction from their comparative antiquity, that of Delft may pride itself on being numerically the most important.

There is a Veterinary College in Utrecht, an Agricultural College in Wageningen, both maintained by the State, and a Commercial College, founded in 1913 by a private corporation, in the city of Rotterdam. These are young institutions lacking the stamp of dignity which the four older ones derive from age and an inherited devotion, now unfortunately on the wane, to the study of Latin and Greek, a knowledge of which is still required from Freshmen wishing to enter the faculties of Law, Theology, and Letters. Student life in these younger institutions is still in the making. It has not had time to mature and develop a sacred tradition whose very essence is its age. And it is this tradition which really constitutes the student life. Without it, there would be no tie between the classes, nor any devotion to the Corps. Tradition saves the Corps from being a continuous experiment in democracy. If tradition did not rule, each new class would bring its innovations with it and break

[107]

the continuity of the Corps. The alumnus in Reunion Week would not care for the Corps which he found so changed. He likes to know that the son whom he sends to the university will live there in the home that his father knew. Only tradition can keep that home intact, and the student body upholds the tradition from an instinctive recognition of its value. If the student community is a microcosm of the State, politicians may learn a lesson from unconscious youth who, while preparing for the future, remain devoted to the inheritance of the past.

Chapter VIII

FLYING DUTCHMEN

THE STORK is called *ooievaar* in Dutch, an ancient word of obscure origin, but probably meaning "bringer of luck." Little children who are acknowledged blessings to their parents know that the *ooievaar* brought them. But in these days of depression, children are dubious blessings, and the luck-bringing bird's popularity has consequently suffered a decline. On the campus of Columbia University they tell a story of an instructor in the English Department who, having explained to her Oriental students the meaning of the phrase "penny-wise pound-foolish" inquired whether there was an equivalent idiom in any of the languages spoken by her students. "In my country," said a stolid Chinese, "we say, You go to bed to save a candle, and you beget twins." If in China the arrival of twins is deplored as the costly effect of penny-wisdom, one need not wonder that in Holland, with its high standard of living, the birth of even one child is not always a case of single blessedness.

Formerly, Dutch farmers invited a pair of storks to spend their summer honeymoon on the place by laying a cart wheel on the roof or on the top of a high pole for the *ooievaars* to build their nest on. These perches are becoming very rare, and a stork's nest on a housetop is a thing of the unhygienic past. The bird still graces, in effigy, the coat-of-arms of The Hague. Until recently, its living counterpart stalked among the slithery offal of the fish market opposite the City Hall. I wonder why he was removed. Perhaps the city magistrates thought it too sad a degradation for an erstwhile accoucheur to be employed as a scavenger. Indeed, the *ooievaar*, who in the past was held to be the national bird of Holland, has fallen upon evil days. And what little prestige he had retained was taken from him, a few years ago, by the sudden ascent of a rival to national fame and to first place in the affection of the people.

The usurper was the pelican. There is some comfort for the stork in knowing that he was not supplanted by a worthless upstart. The pelican has an honorable record. She is that noble bird who fed her starving young with her own heart's blood and thus became the symbol of Christ shedding His blood on the Cross to atone for the sins of mankind. In December, 1933, a "pelican" flew from its nest at Schiphol, the airport of Amsterdam, to the Netherland East Indies, carrying Christmas greetings from the motherland. Before the year was out she was back at Schiphol with New Year messages from Java. From Amsterdam to Batavia in one hundred hours and thirty minutes, from Batavia to Amsterdam in one hundred hours and forty minutes, or twice over a distance of about 9,800 miles in less than a week's time! In the days of the Dutch East India Company a ship that made the voyage from Amsterdam round the Cape of Good

Hope to Batavia in one hundred days had an auspicious passage; voyages that took from four to six months were nothing out of the common. The *Pelican*, with a crew of four, reduced the one hundred days to as many hours.

The first of these flights, in the twenties, took from twelve to more than fifteen days. The men who blazed the trail were Thomassen à Thuessink van der Hoop and Van Weerden Poelman, names which, said a reporter of the London *Times*, "have just the swing of the opening couplet in a Bab Ballad." They flew from Amsterdam to Batavia in a Fokker monoplane. Within three days of the start engine and radio trouble brought them down in a forced landing at Phillipolis, between Belgrade and Constantinople, where they had to wait a month for a new engine. As soon as this arrived they continued the voyage by way of Constantinople, Baghdad, Karachi, Calcutta, Rangoon, Bangkok, and Sumatra. "The net time of the whole flight," said the London *Times*, "allowing for the enforced delay at Phillipolis, was less than three weeks, and as the result of its success the establishment of a regular air service between Europe and the East Indies will, in all probability, be only a matter of time."

The *Pelican*, nine years later, flew to Batavia and back in less than half the time it took those two pioneers to reach Batavia. Better engines, improved landing facilities at the intermediate ports, and the accumulated experience of the intervening decade made the four days' voyage to Java possible. The four men of the *Pelican's* crew would not deny their indebtedness to the precursors who showed the way; but all honor was due them for the courage and the skill with which they beat all previous records.

The Dutch nation paid a tribute to these heroes such as few Dutchmen ever received from their countrymen. They were welcomed with an impressive outburst of national enthusiasm, and the *Pelican*, sharing in the honors of her masters, was proclaimed the symbol of Holland's conquest of the air. In the early evening of December 30, 1933, when the four Flying Dutchmen were reported to be heading for Schiphol, along the narrow highway from Amsterdam to the airport thousands poured into the aerodrome. Automobiles, bicycles, pedestrians passed for hours by the quaint old farmhouses that line the winding road. The waiting crowd on the landing field clustered round huge open fire pots, and those who could not come close enough to the warming glow tried to keep circulation active by stamping a tattoo on the frozen ground. Suddenly, at twenty minutes of ten, the ground lights flooded the field. A surge of excitement, then silence and breathless suspense, all ears on the alert to catch the first purr of the plane. There she was, not visible yet, for a fog enveloped the airport. The roar overhead dwindled down again to a distant hum. The flyers were evidently circling round to get their bearings. The purr grew again to a roar, the *Pelican* suddenly pierced the fog, and settled gracefully down upon her nest. Hats flew up in the air, hands waved frantically, shouts of joy greeted the flyers, the national anthem rose above the tumult, but many, overcome with emotion, could not sing. There were speeches by Cabinet Ministers and Generals and aviation officials, and messages from all parts of the country, including one from Her Majesty Queen Wilhelmina, who conferred upon the four national heroes the cross of Chevalier in the Order of Orange-Nassau.

In days gone by Java was a place of exile to which despairing parents sent their wayward sons. If the boy made good in the service of the Dutch East India Company, so much the better; if he did not, there was hardly any chance of his ever turning up again from the other end of the world to pester his father for further support. Having seen the scapegrace off on an East Indiaman, papa washed his hands of him for good. But see what would happen nowadays. A week after the boy's arrival at Batavia, his employer might call the old man on the telephone to tell him that he had found the young scapegrace useless, and would send him back by the next plane; and a week later the prodigal might literally drop from the sky on the doorstep of his parents' home. Java is no longer at the end of the world. It is, through the radio-telephone, within hearing distance of The Hague and can be reached by air in a dozen hops. A German writer of the seventeenth century called the island the dumping ground for Holland's human garbage. That time is past. From a land of exile, Java bids fair to become a pleasure ground for holiday makers, in which to pass a delightful year-end.

Greater safety is the only condition that must be fulfilled before that pleasant prospect can be realized. The development of radio, by which the pilot remains in constant communication with the solid ground, has made flying less hazardous. But the skies have not been charted yet in the meticulous fashion by which the oceanographers have marked all the dangers and pitfalls of the seas. Two years after the epoch-making flight of the *Pelican*, the Douglas air liner *Uiver*, of the Royal Dutch Airways, came to grief in the Arabian desert. She was a good ship and had proved her mettle that same year in the race from London to Melbourne, in which she finished second. The New York *Times* said editorially of the *Uiver's* achievement, "The American contribution demonstrated with a commercial load that London is now but four days distant from Australia." That sounded as if the wonderful Douglas air liner, like a robot of the skies, had itself piloted its commercial load across three continents. I yield to no one in respect for the engineers of the Douglas Aircraft Corporation, and subscribe wholeheartedly to the *Times* editor's eulogy. But to represent their achievement as the decisive factor of that successful flight was going a bit too far in provincial self-applause. The Dutch pilots who finished second in the race deserved better from America's leading newspaper. It was the skill and endurance of K. D. Parmentier and J. J. Moll that brought demonstration of the Douglas liner's superiority, and no praise of the shipbuilders should go forth without due mention of the crew that manned the ship. Was it confidence solely in the craft and its Wright cyclone motors that gave the three passengers courage to undertake the hazardous voyage? Or was it their trust in the two men and in their skill to ride the cyclone? "Some English editors," said a dispatch from London, "considered the methodical flight of this plane, until almost within an hour of Melbourne,

as the most sensational achievement of the whole race."
And I would ask the *Times* editor, Was the method the
engine's or the men's?

Before the end of that same year the *Uiver* perished.
The conquered element, as if whipped into fury by defeat, hurled its lightning upon the craft and left it a
wreck amid a sea of sand. The story of Holland's navigation to the Indies is a record of many such wrecks. The
sea was a more treacherous enemy to sailing craft than
the air is to modern aviation. But the Dutch merchant
marine could not be daunted by the terrors that lay in
wait along the sea route to Java, nor will the Dutch flyers
give in to the terrors of the sky. The heroes who found
an untimely grave in Baghdad died not in vain. Any
worthwhile victory demands its sacrifice. They paid
with their lives for the triumph which by their death
was brought nearer. For it spurred their comrades on to
greater exertion. Each new flight across the spot where
the *Uiver* came to grief is a salute to their memory and
a vindication of their fate. The roar of the engine calls
to them from above, "Rest ye in peace; we carry on."

There is in Java a small group of educated natives—
small in comparison to the sixty millions whose spokesmen they claim to be—who, fired with nationalistic fervor, are agitating for autonomy and the right of self-
determination. They are trying to steer their people away
from the contact with the Dutch and to sever the ties
that bind the islands to Holland. Aviation, on the other
hand, is counteracting that nationalistic movement.
Three-day flights twice a week will bring the Indies so
much closer to Holland that Dutchmen at home who

seldom gave a thought to what was happening in Java will have East Indian affairs thrust upon their attention from day to day; and the islanders will be impressed with increasing cogency by the fact of their proximity to the motherland when newly arrived visitors can tell them that five days earlier they were walking through the snow in Amsterdam.

In the dawn of Greek civilization the people of Ephesus laid down a rope, seven furlongs in length, from their city to the temple of Ephesus, in order to place the city under the protection of the temple. It was a symbolic act which was none the less believed to be efficacious. The Ephesians mistook an imaginary for a real connection. The transatlantic cable of today seems a modern realization of that make-believe of primitive magic. But our age has found means to dispense with the tangible link without severing the connection once established. The Government at The Hague maintains by radiotelephone a daily contact with Batavia, and birdmen fly at its command along the invisible airways of the sky. Modern science has made fact of the magic by which Prospero ruled on his enchanted island.

The word wonderful is no longer adequate to express our amazement at happenings that are full of wonder. It has been used so often in praising what is merely nice, or beautiful, or interesting, that, when a wonder does happen, we must avoid the Anglo-Saxon term and resort to miraculous. Our age has need of the Latin word, for miracles do happen nowadays.

Although he knows that no supernatural agency controls them, aviation and radio are miracles to the layman, and radio is the greater miracle of the two. I base my conclusion on the imaginings of our ancient ancestors. To imitate the birds and explore the sky seemed to the early Greeks a possible achievement for man; even to imitate the fish and explore the submarine world did not seem an impossibility two thousand years ago. Alexander the Great, says the Greek legend, made a large framework of iron, like a cage, wherein he placed a thick glass vessel, and in the bottom of the vessel was a hole large enough for the hand to pass through. This opening was closed from inside, so that when the whole apparatus was submerged, the traveler might open it quickly and, putting his hand through, draw in whatever struck his fancy. To the cage he attached a chain, two hundred cubits in length, by which this submarine chamber could be lowered from the deck of Alexander's ship. But no fable or myth of the ancients ever imagined that man could speak to man across the seas. Only the voice of a God could accomplish that miracle. Daedalus and Icarus are the mythical precursors of Lindbergh; Alexander of legendary lore anticipated the exploits of William Beebe. But human imagination in the remote past never fancied that wonder to be humanly possible which Marconi actually accomplished in our day. His discovery enables even the humblest layman who has no notion of how it is done to avail himself of the miracle. Man will never learn to fly with a bird's native ease; it will remain to him a difficult art to be practiced at the danger of his life. But he can speak, as the Gods spoke of yore, from coast to distant coast across the ocean, without the need of acquiring a God-like utterance.

[117]

Chapter IX

THE NATION'S PATRON SAINT

MORE THAN SIXTY percent of the country's inhabitants are Protestants. The majority of the nation does not worship any saints. But there is one among the saints of the Roman Catholic church who is honored by all Hollanders regardless of the creed they confess. However much the people be divided religiously, politically, and socially, Protestants, Catholics, and Jews, Conservatives, Radicals, and Socialists, aristocrats, bourgeois, and proletarians are united in their common affection for St. Nicholas. The popularity he enjoys finds expression in the name by which they prefer to call him. Every Dutch boy who was christened Nicholas is simply Klaas to his relatives and friends. That is the familiar and affectionate form of the name. And St. Nicholas is so close to the hearts of the people, that they never call him anything but Sinterklaas. Sinterklaas he was to the early Dutch settlers in this country. Pronounce Santa Claus, and you will come pretty close to the Dutch pronunciation. For Santa Claus is Sinterklaas pronounced in the American way.

Once in a while some wise educator denounces Santa Claus as a public menace. I preserve among my clippings a news item from the New York *Times* of December, 1931, bearing the startling headlines, "Santa called dangerous. Jersey Professor warns of effects of parents' deceit." The disillusionment which must follow the discovery that Santa Claus does not exist is bound to lessen the children's faith in their parents, an authority on child psychology was quoted as having told the students at the New Jersey College for Women. "Sooner or later," he said, "the Santa Claus myth must be exploded and frequently this is done with unfortunate circumstances. I believe that parents lose a certain amount of standing in the eyes of their children because of this small deceit."

It must be a very shaky standing that is so easily thrown out of balance. And what terrible little prigs these children must be who, remembering all the fun this small deceit has given them in the past, blame their parents for the deceit rather than thank them for the fun. I am afraid that psychology, if it teaches this kind of learned veracity to women students, will lose more than a small amount of standing in their eyes by the time they have children of their own to deceive about Santa Claus for the fun that he brings.

The professor was, indeed, aware that his craving for super-honesty would rob the little ones of a lot of pleasure, but he suggested, by way of substitute, that children be permitted to dress up as the North Pole toy-maker and distribute gifts on Christmas morning. Would not that be tantamount to training the innocents in practicing the very fraud condemned by the professor in their parents? My experimental, and wholly amateurish, psychology has taught me that the fun of acting is

[119]

in the belief that your audience believes in your impersonation. The actor's best reward is the illusion he is creating; would it, therefore, be good psychology for a parent to let Johnnie play the role of Santa Claus and spoil his pleasure in advance by telling him that everyone in the audience knows that Santa Claus is Johnnie?

It would be a dull and dreary world for the little ones if all make-believe were banned from the nursery. Fortunately, Santa Claus, who does not exist if we must believe the New Jersey authority on child psychology, will easily survive such attacks on his entity. For he has lived so persistently in the imagination of our race that no philosophy of the schools can teach him out of existence.

Santa Claus has been used to these tilts at what the attackers call his myth for more than a thousand years. They occur periodically, for the good of the children, it is claimed. The truth is that they are made for the sake of some doctrine which happens to be in vogue at the time. In seventeenth-century Holland Sinterklaas was bitterly opposed by the good ministers of the Dutch Reformed Church. They warned their flocks against celebrating his feast on the fifth of December, and petitioned the secular authorities for a ban upon all Sinterklaas booths in the market place. They wisely attacked at the source the evil they wanted to suppress. By prohibiting the sale of toys they hoped to put Sinterklaas out of business. They fought him not in the name of child psychology, but in the name, more impressive and powerful, of the Reformed religion. How could believers in the Calvinist creed honor a saint of the Church of Rome?

That was an argument of greater weight than modern psychology can put forward. The Hollanders had suffered persecution under the Spanish Inquisition, the Sea Beggars had fought the Spaniards under the slogan "rather Turkish than Popish." The very thought of popery was a bugbear to frighten women and children out of their wits. How then could St. Nicholas maintain his esteem among a people so hostile to the saints and the Church of Rome? Yet he did. By a strange perversion of logic the Reformed people of Holland managed somehow to make fun, once a year, in honor of St. Nicholas, while they made fun of all the other saints all the other days of the year. They hated Rome much, but they seem to have loved St. Nicholas more. And can it be said of a power so strong as to overcome hatred that it is no more than an empty myth?

Calvinism fought St. Nicholas in vain. The Roman Church, centuries before Calvin, had been confronted with the very same problem, when the feast was celebrated by our pagan ancestors and St. Nicholas did not yet preside over the fun. In those early days it was Wodan who, on his horse Sleipnir, rode through the wintry sky scattering gifts among the people down below. The Roman missionaries succeeded in unseating the heathen god, but since the good horse Sleipnir continued to haunt the sky and the people's imagination, the preachers lifted St. Nicholas into the vacant saddle. The fancy of a superhuman being in the clouds dropping gifts through the chimneys upon the hearths has an ineradicable charm. No matter what you call him, whether Wodan, or St. Nicholas, or Santa Claus, no matter how you picture him, as a one-eyed god, as a bishop of the Church, or as a jolly old gentleman from the North Pole, the thing that counts with the people is that they have an embodiment of the spirit of giving.

One would think that missionaries and priests and divines would be only too glad to foster that spirit. In their zeal for veracity, be it the true faith or scientific truth, they take offense at the fiction that lends charm to the giving. I do not remember losing a particle of the love and respect that I felt for my parents when I saw Sinterklaas unmasked and found myself a wiser child. But I would now respect them less, I believe, if they had been as wise and veracious as the New Jersey expert in child psychology.

On St. Nicholas Eve, which falls on the fifth of December, the little children of Holland sing songs to St. Nicholas.

> Santa Claus, good holy man,
> Put your finest tabard on,
> Ride in it to Amsterdam,
> From Amsterdam to Spain.

Incantation is needed to speed the good bishop's arrival. For in spite of his holiness and episcopal dignity, he still retains some of the attributes that belong to the supernatural beings in whom our pagan ancestors believed. These entered the house through the chimney flue, the traditional passageway of spirits, and St. Nicholas, true to his supernatural origin, still comes in through the chimney. Before they go to bed, the children place their shoes under the dark, mysterious hole, after filling them with hay and black bread for the horse, a survival, no doubt, of a pagan offering to Wodan's horse Sleipnir. When the children wake in the morning, they will find bread and hay replaced by presents from the saint.

In Jan Steen's picture of this scene in the Rijksmuseum, the boy on the left has found a rod instead of the hoped-for presents. He stands crying his eyes out while his sister holds shoe and rod up for derisive inspection by the others. An older boy stands under the chimney and shows the baby on his arm the big black hole through which St. Nicholas has come and gone, while his little brother gapes up open-mouthed in wonder and awe. A tiny girl in the foreground has her arms full of toys and seems afraid that her mother, who reaches out for her with open arms, will take her new-found treasures from her. St. Nicholas, as the phrase goes, has ridden well for her. In the background, an old woman, a grandmother or nurse, lifts up the curtain of a bed and, with a sly smile on her face, beckons to the girl to come and look. I am sure a big cake in the shape of a young man lies hidden between the sheets. For Sinterklaas is not only a patron saint of children, he is also an expert in match-making.

The historical St. Nicholas was Bishop of Myra, a town in Asia Minor. The story goes that the good prelate once saved three daughters of a poor man from a life of prostitution by providing each with a handsome wedding gift. On three successive nights he threw a bag of gold in at the window. In medieval iconography he is usually represented in bishop's attire, with staff and mitre and on his left arm a heavy book, on which he carries three solid balls—the sculptural representation of the three bags of gold. The Lombard merchants, who in the Middle Ages were the professional money-lenders all over Europe, turned St. Nicholas' three golden balls into a business sign over their front door. Thus the bags that were given to the three poor maidens by an anonymous, unselfish donor, became the emblem of the usurious pawnbroker.

Three is the usual number of the recipients of the saint's blessings. He brought back to life three little scholars whom a wicked butcher, under whose roof they spent the night on their way to Myra, had slaughtered and chopped up into meat balls. He rescued from the hangman three innocent youths whom the consul had condemned to death. Three generals of the Emperor Constantine, imprisoned on a charge of treason, owed their release to the saint, whom the Emperor, in the dead of night, beheld in a vision.

Three times is ship's right, says a Dutch proverb. The saint who liked to triple his miracles was also a patron of seafaring folk. On a voyage to the Holy Land he prophesied to his fellow pilgrims an oncoming storm, and when it struck the ship he calmed it with his prayer. His patronage of sailors made him popular along the seacoasts. That is why Amsterdam, which grew from a humble village of fisher-folk into a prosperous seaport, chose St. Nicholas for its patron saint and dedicated to him its oldest church.

There is good reason, then, for the summons in the children's song to ride to Amsterdam. They call St.

Nicholas to the city which is his very own. He will surely answer and will make his entry on a white horse. From the steamer which has brought rider and steed from Spain, he will disembark in front of the new St. Nicholas church. At that moment the bell in the tower of the Exchange will play the melodies of various popular St. Nicholas ditties. He will be attended by his faithful henchman Black Peter and a small band of colored servants carrying in large bowls the golden oranges from Spain that figure in one St. Nicholas song among the saint's traditional gifts. Students of the university of Amsterdam accoutered as Spanish noblemen will escort the bishop on horseback. They will head a procession of wagons loaded with all sorts of good things which the holy man will distribute among the school children of the city.

A hundred years from now the good people of Amsterdam may be telling one another that this festive entry of St. Nicholas is a tradition as old as the city itself. But the historic truth is that it happened for the first time in 1934. It was done so well and met with such general applause that its originators were encouraged to repeat it the following year, and a third and a fourth time, until it seems to have become an established custom. The actor who took the bishop's part in 1934 made it a condition of his participation that on his progress through the streets of Amsterdam he should not encounter any rival Santa Claus. The wholesale extinction, for one day at least, of this cheap breed of impostors must have added to the popularity of the "real" St. Nicholas. I wish some one would hit upon a device for driving the department store Santa Clauses up the chimney and out of sight.

Popular gratitude has repaid the good bishop's generosity by enriching his legend with an abundance of miraculous stories. He gave evidence of his sanctity, says the *Breviarium Romanum*, before he could stammer, for on Wednesdays and Fridays he took the breast only once, whereas on other days he showed a healthy appetite for his mother's milk. Chaucer's prioress, on that account, was always reminded of St. Nicholas at the sight of a devout little schoolboy saying his prayers to Christ and the Virgin:

> Saint Nicholas stant evere in my presence
> For he so yong to Christ dide reverence.

He was beloved among the people of Myra before he became their bishop. For the legend tells the story of a young mother among his parishioners who, at the news of his election, ran to the church to give thanks to God, forgetting that she had left her baby in a tub full of water on the hearth fire all set for his bath. But no harm was done. Though the water was boiling when she came home, the baby, thanks to the good bishop's power, sat happily splashing in his steaming bath. Even Jews, says the legend, believed in his power to work miracles. One regarded his image as a protection against thieves, and made it the guardian of all his treasures. He was robbed, none the less, and in his anger he struck at the statue. St. Nicholas, meekly returning good for evil, appeared in a vision to the frightened burglars, and made them return the stolen treasures. The Jew, overcome by re-

morse, prayed the saint to forgive him, and was converted to the Christian faith.

That is, of course, a legend that has come down to us
from the "dark" Middle Ages, when people were taught
to hate Jews for being non-Christians. The Nordic
supermen, whose apostle is Herr Julius Streicher in
Nürnberg, would have us hate Jews, converted and
unconverted, for being non-Aryans. The all-inclusive
generosity of St. Nicholas is dead in present-day Germany. The story of the holy bishop and the Jew is illustrated in a stained-glass window in the south aisle of the
cathedral at Freiburg. It was, at least, a year ago. But it
may well be that storm troopers, after the murder of
Herr Vom Rath, in righteous indignation smashed it to
smithereens, the damage to be charged to the Jewish
community of Freiburg.

Chapter X

THE DUTCH LANGUAGE

IN AMERICAN USAGE the name *Dutch* is somewhat confusing, because it may refer to the language and the people either of Holland or of Germany. Pennsylvania Dutch is a dialectal variety of German, Dutch toys come from Nürnberg, a Dutch treat is a form of entertainment that is totally unknown in Holland, and most of the Dutch butchers on American Main Streets never spoke a syllable of Holland Dutch. One has to dig deep into the past to find the cause of this vagueness in connotation. The Netherlands did not always form a distinct political entity. In the Middle Ages they were a part of the German Empire, and the people then inhabiting the eastern provinces of present-day Holland were not conscious of being nationally different from their German neighbors on the east. The political frontier between Holland and Germany separates people whose medieval ancestors did not look upon each other as foreigners. They all belonged to the Dutch race and spoke varieties of the Dutch language.

The name *Dutch* has a curious history. It is derived from an ancient Teuton noun meaning "people," but its first use to denote the language of the Germanic tribes

of northwestern Europe occurred, not in the speech of
these tribes, but in the written Latin reports of Anglo-
Saxon missionaries who brought Christianity to those
unreclaimed regions. They were the first to call the language of their prospective converts *lingua theodisca*, de-
riving the Latin adjective from the Old English *theod*,
that is "people." The plural of this noun was used in
Old English in the sense of "the heathen," just as the
Latin plural *gentes* was used to denote the pagan races.
Lingua theodisca, in the reports of the missionaries, doubtless meant the language of the heathen. The new coinage
soon found its way from the correspondence of the
missions into the chancelleries of Charlemagne's empire,
but it took more than a century for the word to be
adopted by the people themselves. At the end of the
eleventh century *Duutsch* was a common term in the
vernacular. Since by that time Christianity had ousted
paganism, officially at any rate, from all German lands,
it is not likely that the new converts would have called
their own speech "the language of the heathen." Being
aware of its derivation from the native word for "people," they accepted the name, not in the sense that St.
Boniface and his fellow missionaries had given it, but in
that of "the popular, the people's own, language," as
distinct from Latin, the language of the Church. Pre-
viously, the Franks, the Saxons, the Bavarians, the Ale-
mans, had called the vernacular after their own tribal
names, but after the eleventh century it was possible to
express by the name *Dutch* the relationship of Fran-
conian, Saxon, Bavarian, and Alemanic. The term thus

became a symbol of the linguistic unity among the various West Germanic tribes of the Continent.

Within the limited area of the Low Countries the name served a similar useful purpose. There was, and still is, a rich variety of dialects, but *Dutch* was the family name that proclaimed them all sisters. At the same time it proclaimed them sisters of all the dialects that were spoken in Germany. In the Middle Ages this was not felt to be misleading, as the Netherlands had not yet developed into a closely knit political unit distinct from the rest of the Dutch-speaking Continent. When Chaucer in *The House of Fame* mentions "pypers of the Duche tonge," one cannot tell whether he refers to pipers from the Netherlands or from Germany. His English contemporaries could not tell either; nor did they care, for to them there was slight difference between the inhabitants of Germany and the Low Countries. The more discriminating among them possessed the means in their language to express that difference, Germany being known as Almaine and the speech of the Netherlands as Flemish, but the average Englishman of Chaucer's time did not trouble about such fine distinctions. Neither did the poet of a folksong of much later date, to whom all people from Continental cities whose names ended in *dam*, whether these were situated near Berlin or by the North Sea, were damned Dutchmen:

> When you hear the beat of the big bass drum,
> Then you will know that the Dutchmen have come,
> The Amsterdam Dutch, the Rotterdam Dutch,
> The Potsdam Dutch and all the damned Dutch.

Dutch must mean "German" there, for Hollanders never felt the urge nor the need to follow the drum as hirelings of a foreign monarch. The song may be a reminiscence of the Hessians who took the King's shilling to fight the American rebels. By that time the Hollanders had ceased to call themselves Dutchmen.

When the Dutch Republic won its independence from Spanish rule, it also obtained, by the peace of Westphalia, the severance of all ties that still bound it officially to the German Empire. The treaty put its seal on the estrangement by which the Netherlands had gradually divorced themselves from Germany. From that time on the citizens of the young Republic and the inhabitants of the Reich were foreigners to each other. The Germans, impoverished by the devastations of the Thirty Years' War, scowled with envy at the prosperous Republicans in the Rhine delta, and these repaid envy with mockery and disdain. The Hollanders made fun, on the Amsterdam stage, of the penniless German *junkers* and the ragged Westphalian farmhands who sought rich Holland brides and wages in Dutch guilders. The nickname *Mof*, by which the German is known in Holland, dates from that period of incipient estrangement and antagonism. "To be silent as a Mof" is still a current phrase in Dutch, expressive of inarticulate stupidity, and the Germans still echo their ancestors' envy of the merchant princes of seventeenth-century Amsterdam when they refer to their Dutch neighbors as *steinreiche Holländer*. Nations that are neighbors are seldom good friends, and the closer the contact between them, the more inclined they are to stress their differences and to caricature the traits they dislike in each other.

In that same period the Hollanders began to discard the name *Duitsch* for their language: *Duitsch* meant German; the language of the Hollanders was the independent speech of a free nation and deserved a name of its own. Nor did *Nederduitsch* satisfy them; it stamped their tongue as a low form of high German. So its place was taken by *Hollandisch*. As a result, in present-day Dutch the word *Duitsch* means exclusively "German," and *Dutch* as a name for the Hollander's speech is now exclusively English. But to the Dutchman's annoyance Americans use it also in the sense of Hollandish *Duitsch*, thus obliterating the distinction between Hollander and German and denying the Dutch nation the independent existence which it has won and maintained against heavy odds.

No Scot likes to be called an Englishman, and yet Scot and Englishman owe allegiance to the same monarch. How then can one blame the Hollander, who has never been subject to Berlin, for objecting to being called a German? For the indefinite use of the name *Dutch* amounts to that. This is not a childish quarrel over a trifle. The Dutchman's national distinctness is no trifle to him, and he resents the American's carelessness of phrase which ignores both the political frontier and the divergence in temper by which German and Hollander are divided.

The ambiguous use of *Dutch* in American English is especially resented among Dutch merchants, for it is felt to be harmful to the trade relations of the Netherlands with the United States. When the persecution of Jews in Nazi Germany provoked in the United States a Jewish boycott of German goods, Dutch products became suspect among the many who are ignorant of the difference between *Dutch* and *Deutsch*. No wonder manufacturers and exporters in Holland object to being called Dutchmen if that name discredits them and their wares in the eyes of prospective buyers. It was for this reason that the Netherland Government, in the fall of 1934, issued orders to all civil servants to avoid the word *Dutch* in official correspondence written in English and to replace it, in "Dutch East Indies" and similar names, by *Netherland* or *Netherlands*. This was in conformity with the usage in the Netherland language, in which the term *Hollandsch* has the same colloquial connotation as *Dutch* has in English. Hollanders never refer to their Asiatic territories as *Hollandsch Indië*, but call them *Nederlandsch Indië*; and it is only consistent with that usage that civil servants, in English communications, shall use the name "Netherland Indies." The form without the final *s* seems to me more correct than the use of the plural as an adjective, for the English speak of the Scottish Highlands, but of a Highland chief, a Highland lass. The use of *Netherlands* as an adjective, however, could be defended on the analogy of *Hollands* in the phrase "Hollands gin," which form is, of course, not a plural but the Dutch adjective *Hollandsch*, or *Hollands*, the *ch* in the former spelling being mute. The phrase "Netherlands Indies" might, accordingly, be explained as the phonetic equivalent of *Nederlands(ch) Indië*.

The Government also issued a circular letter to all

school authorities requesting them to have the children taught the avoidance of the term *Dutch*. This document elicited from J. F. Bense, a Dutch authority on English, a bitter diatribe against the authorities who "presumed to improve the English language." I cannot believe that it was the intention of the Minister of Education at The Hague to teach Britons and Americans how to write English. Teach the children, he evidently meant to say, to be careful in the use of the term *Dutch*; teach them to avoid it wherever it might be mistaken for "German." If American children were properly taught to translate *Deutsch* by "German" and to use *Dutch* exclusively for the language of the Netherlands, the authorities at The Hague would not feel called upon "to improve the English language." I do not believe, however, that anything the Hollanders can do will be able to remedy their grievance. The official attack on the term *Dutch* will never oust it from the English language. It would be unwise, even if it were possible, to discard it because of its misapplication. It is terser and therefore more useful than the trisyllabic "Netherland" and its clumsy derivative "Netherlandish." I, for one, have no intention of using these in preference to the firmly established term *Dutch*. The best we Dutch-Americans can do is to protest, not against the use of *Dutch*, but against its misuse as a synonym of "German."

The Dutch language might be called a halfway house between German and English. It is less conservative than its neighbor on the east, and less radical than its neighbor across the North Sea. Its treatment of the ancient grammatical genders exemplifies that middle position. German

[134]

has preserved the three genders intact, English has effaced the distinction altogether, and Dutch has retained only two. How does one know the gender of a noun? The speaker born to the language can tell by the form of the definite article that goes with it. Dutch nouns are either neuter, that is to say they take the definite article *het*, or they are not, which means that they take the article *de*. But there is no way of telling whether these *de* words are masculine or feminine; we can only state that they are not neuter. The definite article in Dutch has become an uninflected prefix to the noun; in the written language, and especially in the language of poetry, it is still used in various case forms, but these have been dropped from the speech of every day. As the sole clue to the gender of any noun lies in the form of its article, the unchangeable *de* form—the rubber stamp of all non-neuter words— compels us to the conclusion that the Dutch language has effaced the distinction between masculine and feminine nouns.

The English language has done the same, but in a more thorough and consistent fashion. For it has turned the names of all things into neuters. In English the pronouns *he* and *she* cannot refer to inanimate objects. But in Dutch there are numberless things that are *he's* and *she's*. What answer shall a Dutch housewife give to the question, "Where is the butter?" (*Waar is de boter?*). Since *boter* is a *de* word, that is, a non-neuter, she cannot reply, "It is in the cellar; I'll go and get it." Since the dictionary says that *boter* is feminine, the correct answer would be, "She is in the cellar; I'll go and get her" (*Zij is in de kelder; ik zal ze gaan halen*).

But many speakers will substitute *he* and *him* for *she* and *her*, and not even the grammarian will take offense. According to the word lists a table is a *she* and a chair a *he*, but most speakers disregard the distinction and will say, referring to the table, "Put him by the window."

In writing there is a tendency to keep *he*-things and *she*-things apart, but it is never done consistently except in official documents. Language teachers will no longer waste time on cramming lists of feminine and masculine words into children's brains, as the spelling reformers have succeeded in obtaining official recognition for the uninflected article. This was perhaps the most radical of the changes proposed by the reformers. But they found other faults to be remedied. The sound which in English is spelt *sh*, is in Dutch spelt *sch* as in German. The Hollander, however, pronounces it differently from his neighbors. When he says *schip*, the Dutch equivalent of *ship*, the initial *s* is followed by a velar spirant sounding very much like the *ch* in the Scottish *loch*. But *sch* sounds that way only at the beginning of a stressed syllable. At the end of a word and at the beginning of weak syllables, *ch* is mute. Hence the Dutch equivalent of the English *fish* is pronounced *vis* and its plural is *vissen*, although the official orthography of 1864 prescribed the spellings *visch* and *visschen*. "Away with this superfluous *ch* where it is not heard in the spoken language," say the reformers. "And why spell *e* and *o* in open syllables in two ways, single in some, double in others? The variants sound exactly alike—why then this discrimination? They were different once, it is true; *ee* and *oo* developed from diphthongs, while *e* and *o* were always single vowel sounds. But the two coalesced long ago, and why should our modern spelling have to reflect ancient history? Precious time is wasted in our schools on teaching an intricate and antiquated orthography. Simplify the system, and devote the hours thus gained to the study of literature and the technique of writing. Instruction in these subjects, rather than in dull spelling rules, will arouse in them a love of their native tongue."

Social conventions have a tenacious life, and the philologist does not, as a rule, command much prestige in the community. In the estimate of the public at large a philologist is a superior kind of schoolmaster, a helpless fool in the practical affairs of the world, and wise only in the knowledge of forgotten lore that is of no value to anyone. But the foolish language professors who advocated spelling reform did so purely on practical grounds; the lay public that prides itself on its common sense defended, without knowing it, the preservation of fossilized lore embedded in the traditional spelling. The bitterest opposition to any change in the established practice has come, in the past decades, from the professional men of letters, the poets, critics, and writers of fiction. To their artistic sensibilities there is an element of beauty in the old spelling tradition. "Nonsense," say the reformers, "orthography has nothing to do with aesthetics. An audience listening to a public address cannot tell whether the speaker's manuscript is written in the official or the simplified spelling, and a sonnet by Shakespeare, respelled in phonetic script, will sound the same in the recitation as it would if read from the original edition." That is true. It is also true that, for the most part, we read, not aloud, to an audience, but silently, to ourselves. Thus, while conveying to the mind the meaning of the printed words, the reader's eyes may be affected, either pleasantly or painfully, by the visible form of those words. The reformers call that self-deception; but imaginary pain is pain, all the same, to the deluded sufferer.

The conservatives object, and, rightly, in my opinion, to the demand of the reformers that present-day speech shall determine the norm of Dutch orthography. The spoken language is only one form of Dutch. There is also the archaic diction of poetry, which uses the definite article in four different forms, *de, des, den,* and *der,* and thus preserves the distinction between masculine and feminine nouns. This literary idiom may seem a dead idiom to the practical-minded average Hollander, but to the man of letters and the cultured reader it has not lost its freshness and vitality. There is, indeed, a wide rift between the spoken language and this written record of literature: is it desirable, the conservatives ask, to widen the rift still further by rejecting the inaudible flectional endings from the visible record of the language?

This war between sentimental conservatives and utilitarian reformers has been waged for the past forty years. Its effect upon Dutch orthography has been disastrous. Attempts at a compromise foundered on the intransigence of both the sticklers for old-fashioned correctness and the zealots for radical simplification. The result was chaos. The schools, of course, had to teach the official rules, but many a master sided in his heart with the reformers and taught the traditional spelling with little conviction and less effect. Hence children grew up without a fixed standard and learned to spell as they saw fit. It was a *reductio ad absurdum* of the individualistic spirit on which the Hollander prides himself.

In the year 1933, the Minister of Education, although himself not in favor of simplified spelling, appointed a committee of five philologists to draft a spelling reform that would be a compromise between the opposing factions. They submitted their plan to the Minister in April, 1934. He gave it his sanction, and September the first was fixed upon as the date on which the new system would officially begin to operate. It was a euphemism to call the plan a compromise. It was a complete triumph for the reformers. The definite article was officially shorn of its inflectional final *n*; *sch* was to shed its redundant *ch*; *e* and *o* in open syllables were always to be spelled with a single letter; and the children in primary schools were allowed to make bonfires of their obsolete spelling books. The publishers protested against the immediate introduction of the revision: valuable stocks of unsellable schoolbooks would be left on their hands. They foresaw financial ruin unless the final *n* and the superfluous *ch* and the double *e* and *o* were given a few years of grace. Holland's New Deal in orthography created just as much confusion with the letters of the alphabet as did Mr. Roosevelt's New Deal in this country.

The problem of spelling reform is aggravated by the lack of uniformity in spoken Dutch. Within the borders of Queen Wilhelmina's kingdom there is a recognized standard language which, thanks to the schools, is more or less known and accepted by all her subjects. But the

Dutch language covers a larger territory than Her Majesty's realm. The northern half of Belgium is also a Dutch-speaking area. Belgian Dutch, called Flemish, is a patchwork quilt of local idioms, many of which have preserved the inflected article and other archaic traits such as have not survived in Holland Dutch except, in a fossilized state, in the now discarded spelling. The educated Flemings are doing their best to adopt standard Dutch as their model, but they find it hard to reconcile themselves to the new orthography, as it bears less resemblance to their local speech than did the old. They are anxious to promote a cultural *rapprochement* of Flemish Belgium to Holland, and they regret the official adoption of an orthography that tends to emphasize the difference between Belgian and Holland Dutch. The Dutch race in South Africa, on the other hand, has no cause for sharing the Flemings' objections. Their language is a radically simplified form of Dutch, and its speakers find it easier to read Hollandish, which to them is almost a foreign language, in the reformed than in the archaic, spelling.

The rift between spoken and written Dutch is not only a matter of inflection and spelling. When a Hollander sits down to write, he does not feel at ease. The pen in his hand and the blank paper in front of him make him self-conscious. The words that he commits to paper will be scrutinized by others. He must prove to them that he is an educated man. School education has made him afraid of trusting to impulse. He must choose his words carefully and in conformity with polite usage. In everyday speech he may show spontaneity of utter-

ance by creating words and similes from personal vision
and feeling, but as soon as he sits down at his desk his
style becomes cramped. Then words crop up that he
would never use in conversation, and which, if he did use
them in speech, would sound ridiculous. The word for
today, in the spoken language, is *vandaag*, but in writing
it is *heden*. *Mooi* is the common term for beautiful, but
when the Dutchman writes about something *mooi* he
calls it *schoon*. The spoken language uses *schoon* too,
but only in the sense of clean. A lover will send *kussen*
(kisses) to his girl by letter, but if he should ask her for
a *kus* when he meets her face to face, she would think
he was a pedantic ass. She would grant him only a *zoen*.

In every tongue, of course, the written language is
richer than everyday speech, but few, I am sure, are
cursed with so many pairs of synonyms, one for use in
speech, the other for use on paper. Even the equivalent
for the English *you* has a split personality in Dutch.
Good friends say *je* to each other, but many hesitate to
use this pronoun in writing. They have a feeling that
something common or vulgar attaches to it when it takes
visible form on paper, and prefer as a substitute *gij*. But
gij does not exist in the spoken language. It is absolutely
impossible for a Hollander to use it in conversation. How
shall we account for this strange aversion to a harmless
little word, which in speech is not only inoffensive but
absolutely indispensable? Its vulgarity cannot be in the
sound. It is as light and toneless a syllable as the definite
article *de*. Yet *de* is never banned from the written page.
Je is vulgar only in comparison to *gij*. For *gij* is an

aristocrat leading a secluded life on noiseless paper aloof from common everyday speech.

The written standard is largely based on the speech of Brabant and Flanders, the two leading Dutch-speaking provinces of present-day Belgium. The southern Netherlands, being nearer to France, attained prosperity and culture much earlier than the northern Low Countries. Dutch as it was written in the south served as model for the north. In the early seventeenth century Amsterdam became the cultural center of the Low Countries, but the literary tradition of the south was by that time so firmly entrenched that the writers of Holland, rather than use their own idiom for literary purposes, molded their style after southern models. Hence the written language still bears the imprint of its Flemish origin, whereas everyday speech derives from the vernacular of Holland proper. In other words, when a Hollander writes, he employs words and phrases that belong to the speech of the Dutch in Belgium; when he speaks, his vocabulary is pure Hollandish. The pronoun *gij* is still a living word in Belgian Dutch. If you ever meet a Dutchman who addresses you with *gij*, you may be sure he is a Fleming.

The Dutch, whether they live in Holland, Belgium, or South Africa, are extremely fond of the use of diminutives. A great Danish philologist, Otto Jespersen, has called the Dutch people, on account of that fondness, "innocent, genial beings with no great business capacities or seriousness in life." No business capacities in the Dutch? By what miracle, then, did they become rulers of a colonial island realm forty times the size of their own country? Jespersen is mistaken not only in his conclusion—the premise from which it is inferred is also wrong. "In Dutch," he writes, "every child is a *kindje*, and every girl a *meisje*; every tree may be called a *boompje*, every cup of coffee or tea a *kopje*, every rabbit a *konijntje*, every foot a *voetje*, every key a *sleuteltje*, etc., etc." Hearing the Dutch converse among themselves, a casual observer might easily be led to believe that every noun may be a diminutive. But from a philologist a more accurate statement might be expected than the assertion that the frequent recurrence of these endings happens "without any apparent necessity."

Every Dutch mother could tell Jespersen that, on trying occasions, her little *kindje* denies that fond appellation by becoming a naughty *kind*. Every Dutch girl, it is true, is a *meisje*, but for this very good reason that, without the diminutive ending, the word would mean "maidservant," or would be a term of abuse. The little *meisje* who has incurred her daddy's anger will at once become a *stoute meid* in his vocabulary. Every little tree may be called a *boompje*, but a big tree cannot be called otherwise than a *boom*. In Holland the Danish professor would be offered a *kopje* of tea, and would actually have to be satisfied with a diminutive cup, a quarter the size of a good English breakfast cup. Tom Thumb trips on *voetjes* in the Dutch version of the fairy tale, but his parents, not to mention the giant and his wife, walk on *voet*. The key that by its blood stain betrayed poor Mrs. Bluebeard's disobedience was never called a *sleuteltje*, and the Dutch boy who goes poaching in the dunes will let the *konijntje* escape, if for the same trouble he can have a fat *konijn*. It is true that the Dutch language has an unlimited capacity for the formation of diminutives, but their employment depends on definite conditions which, though not apparent to foreign listeners, are very clear to the speakers themselves.

The diminutive ending does not always indicate smallness of dimension. It may also serve the purpose of changing the meaning of the word to which it is affixed. The word *man* acquires the meaning of "male animal" when used in the diminutive form, irrespective of the animal's size. The male mastodon and the male rabbit are both *mannetjes* in Dutch, and their mates are called *vrouwtjes* or *wijfjes*. In the same way, a man's personal name in the diminutive becomes a woman's name. *Jan* and *Jannetje*, *Piet* and *Pietje*, *Klaas* and *Klaasje* belong to opposite sexes, and *Jannetje* may exceed her male namesake in bulk. The adverb *toe*, meaning "in addition," when turned into a noun by the suffix *tje*, acquires the meaning of "dessert," but the guest who praises the *toetje* to his hostess does not imply an ironic allusion to the smallness of the helping on his plate.

Who does not admire in the genre painters of the early Dutch school the artists' attention to picturesque detail? The Hollander's speech reflects a similar tendency to stress the distinction between the little and the big; but this close scrutiny of the world he lives in does not unfit him for business, nor make him incapable of any seriousness in life. His very seriousness may find expression by means of this diminutive speech. For the use of the suffix may also serve to reflect the mood of the speaker. Scorn, irony, contentment, compassion may be effectively voiced in this way, and when this is the case

[144]

the speaker will form diminutives of words that otherwise would be incapable of diminution. *Lekker weertje*, "nice little weather," is a commonplace expression of well-being or an ironical sneer at a wet or a stormy day. I have heard an old woman console herself with the thought, *Ons Lieve Heertje zal daarvoor wel zorgen*, "Our dear little Lord will take care of that," and God's name in the diminutive form did not sound irreverent to me, but told me of her naïve trust in His love and power. Even adverbs are capable of taking the diminutive ending, and in that form help to soften the sternness of a command or to express the speaker's pity. *Kom es eventjes hier* ("Come here just a moment") is spoken more kindly than *kom hier*. *Hij ziet er povertjes uit* ("he looks poorly") is said with a commiserating shake of the head. *Hij lachte witjes* (literally, "he laughed whitely") retains something of the brightness and kindness of that smile. If the Hollanders, hurt in their pride by Jespersen's description of them as "innocent, genial beings with no great business capacities or seriousness in life," should self-consciously make an effort to abstain from the use of diminutives, they would sadly impoverish their language. But they never will. They could not. For this race of painters needs the diminutives to indicate all the subtle shades and half tones that social intercourse requires: to speak without them would be just as impossible as to speak always in the same tone of voice. The intonation of the sentence is the audible record of the speaker's feelings, and the diminutives are helpful illustrations to that record. You would make a Hollander tongue-tied if you persuaded him to speak without the telling "little" words.

Some poets of the seventeenth century have stretched the possibilities of diminutive speech to the utmost. Joost van den Vondel wrote an exquisite song in which the *je* endings clatter down like raindrops on a window pane:

> Eetje slaatje met een eitje?
> Drinckje niet dan schapeweitje?
> Pluckje moesjen uit den tuin?
> Backje struifjes van de kruitjes?
> Treckje heen, na zomerbuitjes,
> Om lamprey en knijn in duin?

Another, Dirck Raphaelsz Camphuizen, exulting in the glory of a May morning, gave thanks to God for its beauty in tender little words such as *dauwtje* (dew), *veetje* (cattle), *veldjen* (field). These helped him to say, more eloquently than he could otherwise have expressed it, that all was well with the world. I know one English poet who would have relished the charm of this diminutive word coinage. Robert Herrick equalled his Dutch contemporaries in love for little words. He coined forms such as quarrelet, pipkinet, shepherdling. But the virile language he was born to was not equal to the creation of all the diminutives that he needed for the seven three-line stanzas of his Ternary of Littles:

> A little saint best fits a little shrine,
> A little prop best fits a little vine,
> As my small cruse best fits my little wine.

Chapter XI

THE PRINTED WORD

"BOOKS are sepulchres of thought," said Longfellow. I am afraid that in many a case the corpse will be found missing when the tomb is opened. I have before me a statistical survey of such burials that took place in Holland during the year 1936. The thoughts of 6,118 authors were interred in that period, an average of seventeen funerals per day. And this figure does not take into account the ephemeral thoughts that are covered up by periodical sepultures. The Dutch presses turn out weeklies and monthlies and quarterlies to the number of 1,910. The total number of publications has more than tripled in the past thirty-five years. Does that indicate an increasing tendency towards meditation, or a greater willingness on the part of the thinkers to bury their thoughts?

To judge from the fact that fiction has the lion's part in this increase of literary output, I feel inclined to believe that many of these funerals were fake ceremonies that covered up but empty graves. In the year 1900 the number of novels published in Holland was 231, and the publishers turned out 261 books for juvenile readers. In 1936 the children were supplied with 377 new books and

[147]

the grown-ups were given a choice from no fewer than 849 novels. Have Dutch parents, in this age of the child, become more voracious readers of fiction than their children in the past thirty-five years? Or must we account for the comparatively slight increase in the output of juvenile literature by the assumption that the modern child precociously reads his elders' literature?

A surprising fact revealed by these statistics is the high percentage of translations among this output of fiction. Almost half of it is foreign literature. One would think that, thanks to the excellent language teaching in the Dutch high schools, adult readers of fiction would need no interpreters to relish English, French, and German novels in the original. The Dutch publishers seem to rate the reading public's knowledge of these languages rather low. They brought out, in 1936, 643 translated books, 395 of which were novels. These figures seem to discredit the Hollander's reputation as a linguist. The Dutch Association of Modern Language Teachers ought to protest against the scepticism of the publishers.

Dutch book translators are often the butt of public ridicule and scorn. The tortures to which foreign authors are subjected in Holland ought, indeed, to be investigated and exposed. The real culprits, though, are not the translators but the publishers, who pay such paltry wages for translation that no writer worth his literary salt can be induced to act as interpreter. Hence the task is handed over to people who neither understand what they read in the foreign language from which they translate, nor know how to write well in their own. There is a League of Netherland publishers which should consider it a point of honor to devise ways and means of fighting this evil, but since the League remains inactive, a group of writers, publishers, and lovers of literature came together some years ago to start a campaign for the prevention of cruelty to books. "Treat animals kindly, spare the birds," is a slogan that is advertised all over Holland. A fitting counterpart would be, "Treat authors kindly, spare their books."

The daily press of Holland is a very dull, straight-laced, and respectable old lady. Her conduct is hemmed in by inhibitions. She practices an aristocratic self-restraint, shows a puritanical estimate of the kind of news that is fit to print, does not indulge in gossip and slander, does not glorify criminals, conceals the identity of persons on trial, deeming no one guilty until he is proven to be so, makes no celebrities the prey of her press hounds, uses headlines in moderation and makes them conform to the substance of the story.

Some ten years ago The Hague was being treated to a sensational murder case. A captain in the Netherland army had been poisoned by a major of the medical staff. The dead man's wife was accused of having been an accessory to the crime. They did not mean to kill, was the woman's defense, but only to daze the victim into semi-unconsciousness and make him sign a document by which he promised to waive all claim to his child in the coming divorce suit. It was disheartening to see how badly the Dutch press covered this case. Covered is the right word. The *Nieuwe Rotterdamsche Courant* stated the bare facts and referred to the accused man as merely Major G. instead of uncovering his full name; it refused to the story the distinction of a front-page spread; it withheld from the public the portraits of the principals; it carried no interviews with Major G. and his paramour; and no reporter tried to extract a statement on the feelings and reactions of the child.

How much better does the American press understand its ethical task. The public has a right to know, and since the journalist's professional modesty forbids him arbitrarily to circumscribe that right, all the news about a sensational murder case is fit to print. To know all is to pardon all, and consequently the minutest reporting is bound to evoke a truly Christian spirit of forgiveness and mercy.

This beneficial effect is especially noticeable in our tabloid dailies. I remember their treatment of the notorious Snyder-Gray case of a dozen years ago: reporters delved so lovingly into the most intimate details that the two principals lost their repulsiveness and became familiar pets of both writers and readers, to be referred to as Ruth and Judd, so well were they known to all. The two had to atone for their crime, but they had at least the sweet comfort of an ephemeral nation-wide publicity. That is what in literature is called poetic justice. But the Dutch daily press lacks poetical sense. It leaves a suspect in nameless obscurity, and even when his confession has removed all doubt as to his guilt, no publicity halo is allowed to suffuse his darkened features with a glimmer of heroism and romance. Such unpoetic justice leaves the criminal no consolation except what little there may be in Emerson's saying that, after all, "every hero becomes a bore at last."

Hollanders find it difficult to grasp the American's estimate of what constitutes news. "What must Americans think of us with our anti-Sunday dancing laws?" asked a Dutch newspaper indignantly of the Burgomaster of Amsterdam, when the latter, an orthodox Calvinist, had proscribed public dancing on the Sabbath. The question revealed how little the editor knew about American ways of thinking. If it is essential to Amsterdam's happiness and self-esteem what Americans shall think of her, the Burgomaster, by prohibiting dancing on Sundays, took the very course by which to attain that end. As a rule Americans never give a thought to Amsterdam. The city was never mentioned in the New York papers when dancing on Sundays was a lawful entertainment. But as soon as it was made a misdemeanor, the New York *World* placed Amsterdam on the reader's map. It filled an entire column with a story of how Amsterdam "howled" while its Burgomaster remained adamant, and illustrated it with a cartoon by Louis Raemaekers of World-War fame. Never before, as long as I can remember, had Holland's metropolis figured thus conspicuously in a New York daily. The Dutch editor who was so much concerned about what Americans think of Amsterdam should take the lesson to heart. It is not by imitating America that Holland can attract America's attention. Let her be her own peculiar obstinate self, and Americans will pause and wonder and write about her.

Every day things must be happening in Holland that will not strike a Dutch journalist as worth reporting, but which, on account of their being so different from what we are accustomed to in America, would lend themselves exceedingly well for a write-up in a New York paper. Miss Janssen of Gouda winning the first prize in a beauty parade on the Scheveningen boulevard has no earthly chance of recognition from the New York press, but the papers would certainly take notice if they could print a story to the effect, "An American who makes it his specialty to organize beauty parades at European seaside resorts was unsuccessful at Scheveningen, the Burgomaster of The Hague having refused his permission on the ground that beauty is its own reward." A Dutch journalist cabling to New York that the headline is coming into vogue in the Netherland press would see his information ignored, but a different reception would be accorded to his message if it contained a news item such as this, "The office windows of the Amsterdam *Telegraaf* were smashed this morning by a person dressed like a gentleman, who declared at the police station that he had acted by way of protest against the discrepancy between a headline in the paper and the story printed underneath." An American's interest in his newspaper is akin to the curiosity with which he visits foreign countries. Otherness is the traveler's aim, and as a reader about foreign lands he is equally keen on finding contrasts. Although he may know that imitation is the sincerest flattery, the American reader of foreign news would rather be entertained than flattered.

A news item having this requirement of novelty was promptly seized upon by the American press in the early days of 1938. A prominent journalist was accused by the Burgomaster of The Hague of betraying an official secret and was locked up in jail for guarding too stubbornly a secret that was not official. The culprit was C. L. Hansen of the staff of *Het Vaderland*, a daily journal at The Hague. He had published in his paper an account of discussions held by the City Council behind · closed doors. Only Councilors and heads of the various administrative departments were present; no stenographers or reporters had been admitted. The inference was clear that Hansen had obtained his scoop from an all too garrulous city father.

The incensed Burgomaster was determined that the guilty one should be detected. He rose, one day, with stern dignity and asked all the Councilors, one by one, "Did you supply this information?" But one after the other shook his head and swore he did not. The Burgomaster was not willing to admit defeat. He could not bring an action against the wicked reporter, for he was not the betrayer of the secret. No one had sworn him to secrecy. The worst that could be charged against him was that he had published information that he must have known to be confidential. But that, in itself, was not an indictable felony. Hansen could not be forced to give testimony to the police. Only a court of justice could make him testify at the trial of the suspected party. So the Burgomaster decided to initiate John Doe proceedings against the unknown City Councilor who had betrayed his sacred trust. An indictment was thereupon brought against N. N., but when Hansen was called to the witness stand, he stubbornly refused to name his informant, pleading that the journalist's professional code of honor would not allow it. The alternative was detention for contempt of court. Hansen had no choice in the matter; he bowed to the unavoidable and went to jail.

He came out of it, thirty-one days later, a national hero. To be sure, there had been something reprehensible in publishing the report of the secret meeting, and in Holland such transgressions of professional decorum are not easily condoned. But with the fervid assistance of Burgomaster De Monchy the reporter's role of culprit who had damaged the self-respect of his calling was changed into that of a martyr to the liberty of the press. By steadfastly concealing his informant's identity he wiped out his guilt in divulging the official secret. It never was a bad stain on his journalistic record. Even the Burgomaster admitted that Hansen's indiscretion had not damaged any vital interests of the city. The secret that the Council had been sworn to preserve was hardly worth guarding. But the Burgomaster argued that when a journalist presumes to judge for himself the measure of secrecy that he would accord to his scoops, there would soon be no limit to the indiscretions of the press.

I venture to believe that His Honor's conclusion was mistaken. What I have seen of Dutch journalism in more than forty years of reading its columns convinces me that the Netherland press has a very high sense of responsibility, which will guard it against excesses. It did not need the deterrent effect of Mr. Hansen in jail to keep it in the straight and narrow path.

Chapter XII

THE DEFEAT OF DRYSTUBBLE

HOLLANDERS are a seafaring nation, as anyone familiar with their history knows. In the seventeenth century they were the freight carriers of Europe, supplying the products of the north to the nations of the south and vice versa. They transported the wines of Bordeaux not only to countries in the Baltic and the Mediterranean, but even to ports along the coasts of France. They shipped grain to the harbors of Spain and Portugal, although at war with both countries; the King of Spain was forced to connive at this clandestine traffic, as without the supplies his people would have starved. Dutch ships passing through the Danish Sound each year outnumbered the combined merchant fleets of all other nations. The Hollanders traded with the Levant and had a consular agent at Constantinople. They sailed to the far north to hunt whales, and the procuring of sperm oil kept a Dutch settlement busy on the island of Spitzbergen during the months that the whale fishing lasted. Hollanders gained a foothold in widely scattered regions of the globe, at the Cape of Good Hope, on the coast of Brazil, in the Caribbean, on the isle of Manhattan, along the coast of Malabar, in Ceylon, in the Malay

Archipelago, in Japan. The map of the world bears witness to their ubiquity in the past by numerous names inscribed by Dutch navigators as mementos of their voyages. Tasmania perpetuates the memory of Abel Tasman, the Dutch explorer who discovered it. Cape Horn was thus called by Willem Schouten in honor of his native place, the town of Hoorn in North Holland. Spitzbergen means Peaked Mountains and was thus christened by its discoverer, Willem Barents. The Hollanders were at home on the five continents and the seven seas, and popular fancy, marveling at the daring of this sea-roving race, created out of the stories of their adventurous life a legend of the Flying Dutchman.

It is a sad reflection upon the nation's creative ability that Dutch literature, in spite of this amazing record, has drawn no inspiration from the sea. Holland's artists have sensed the romance and the beauty of the ship under sail. Vroom, Porcellis, Van de Capelle, De Vlieger, Van de Velde have painted the sea in all its moods. But Dutch poets and novelists have left the sea unexplored. The spell of the great water found no expression in great prose or haunting poetry. Joost van den Vondel, Holland's leading poet, wrote a couple of didactic poems, which he called Hymns, in praise of Amsterdam's Navigation, but they were occasioned by a publisher's demand for a rhymed commentary on an engraved view of the city and its ship-crowded harbor. Hendrik Tollens, two centuries later, rhymed a pedestrian epic of the story of Willem Barents and his ice-locked crew weathering the winter of 1596 on the island of Nova Zembla in the Arctic. Captain Marryat had a feeble imitator in C.

Werumeus Buning. Jacob van Lennep, the chief producer of popular fiction in the middle of the nineteenth century, compiled a dictionary of nautical terms with the assistance of a brother who served as an officer in the Netherland navy, but a novel of the sea does not figure among his collected works. It is true, though, that his masterpiece, *Ferdinand Huyck*, gives the reader a glimpse into the life of the buccaneers in the Caribbean, and this short episode, subordinate to the main plot, is indeed a good specimen of a sea yarn.

Van Lennep did not draw entirely upon his own imagination for his description of the pirates and their manner of life. He took its local color from an authentic account of the life of the buccaneers by Smeeks, a seventeenth-century Dutchman who, as a captive sailor, had served among them and, after his escape and return to Holland, published a faithful story of what he had seen and suffered in his buccaneer days. But Smeeks, again, was not a literary artist, and his book was re-edited, some ten years ago, not as a precious piece of literature, but for its historical value as an authentic and realistic record.

Smeeks was not devoid of literary ambition. He turned his experiences of life on the sea to good account in another book, a novel of wondrous adventure, which may have been known to Daniel Defoe. This story contains an episode of a lone cabin boy shipwrecked on a desert island; the description of his hermit life and the various devices by which he catered to his own comfort in the wilderness offers so many analogies to the tale of Robinson Crusoe that it is not at all improbable that Defoe was indebted to Smeeks for part of the framework of his novel. But the very resemblance between the two stories brings out the more strikingly the Hollander's lack of creative imagination. If Defoe borrowed from Smeeks, he created out of a matter-of-fact account a romance so rich in suggestive power that the book has never failed to thrill each successive generation by its convincing realism. There are few men alive who in their boyhood have not rapturously lived with Robinson Crusoe on his desert island. But I never heard of a Dutch boy who shared in his daydreams the solitude of Smeeks' young hero.

A recent novel by Arthur van Schendel gives relief to this record of neglect of the sea. Upon its appearance in 1930, it was hailed as a masterpiece, and the *Maatschappij der Nederlandsche Letterkunde*, which awards an annual prize to the author of the most distinguished literary work published in the course of the previous year, selected Van Schendel's *Het Fregatschip Johanna Maria* for that honor. It is the biography of a sailing vessel, one of the last of Holland's merchant marine that survived into the age of the steamship. The frigate *Johanna Maria* is Van Schendel's heroine. The hero of his tale is Jacob Brouwer, the sailmaker of the brave ship. He has known her from the day that she was launched, he has served among her crew with a devotion such as no man will give to a soulless thing, he has at last become her owner, and must suffer the pain of parting with the dear one, whom he cannot rescue from the scrapheap, which becomes her burial place. And that pain is the keener for the knowledge that not she alone but all her kind is doomed. The engine has replaced the sail, a man-made driving power has supplanted the force of the wind, and the birdlike beauty of *Johanna Maria* and her kin will be gone forever.

The story is told without sentimentality. As a restrained, objective record of a simple life it approaches greatness in its generous surrender to a single devotion. Still, I cannot join in the general acclaim that the Dutch critics gave it. Van Schendel's technique is that of the unemotional reporter. His narrative lacks dramatic quality. It never breaks into dialogue. The reader is not allowed to hear Jacob Brouwer speak; he is told in the recorder's words what he did, said, and thought. When I closed the book, I felt I had read a skilful résumé of the story, not the novel itself. *Nil desperandum* was the inscription under the bowsprit of the frigate. I wish I could make it my own and, buoyed up by Van Schendel's tale, cease to despair of Holland's inability to create great fiction out of the nation's experience of life on the sea. But it must be admitted, in spite of the Van Schendel award, that there is nothing in Dutch fiction that can compare with *Roderick Random*, or *Moby Dick*, or Joseph Conrad's novels, nor anything that can even distantly approach the haunting beauty of *The Ancient Mariner*.

The reader we used in school in my young days contained a poem greatly admired by the master who forced us to commit it to memory. It was about Piet Heijn, the great admiral who captured the Spanish fleet that carried gold and silver from the mines in South America to Spain. The poet, if he deserved that name, described the hero's reception by his mother on his return from a naval exploit. He rushes across the threshold to embrace her, but she sternly orders him back to the mat to wipe his feet. Thus were we taught hero worship half a century ago. The housewife triumphing over the mother was an edifying example of brave and virtuous self-denial. That was, at least, how we youngsters understood the story. It may be that we did the rhymester an injustice. He was, perhaps, a humorist who intended his tale as a satire on the Dutch women's craze for cleanliness. If that was his aim, the moral was lost on us. Our inference was that the mother, not the son, deserved our worship. I do not remember whether the parable taught us not to put our own mothers to the same hard test when we came home from school. But I do know that we did not recite the poem with the lusty swing that we gave to the singing of the popular song:

> Know ye the defeat
> Of the Spanish fleet,
> Of the silver-and-gold Armada?
> There was a big harvest of ore to reap,
> And oranges of Granada.
> Piet Heijn, Piet Heijn,
> The letters of his name are nine,
> But countless are his deeds,
> But countless are his deeds,
> Piet Heijn has captured the silver fleet!

We loved that ballad. It was written and set to music in the nineteenth century, but it has the directness and simplicity of early folksongs, and a tune that automatically moves the hands and feet to accentuate its dashing lilt. No song of the sea in the national repertoire is more popular among the Dutch. It is a rare example of a sea ballad that has sung itself into the people's hearts. Another is a song that celebrates the capture of Brill by the Sea Beggars. That also dates from the early nineteenth century. The Dutch have no songs of the sea that were made by contemporaries of Piet Heijn. They do exist on paper, but none has survived in oral tradition. D. F. Scheurleer has collected a large number of poems and songs that were written in the days of the Dutch Republic under the immediate impression of the news sent home from the fleet. The thunder of the ships' guns in an encounter with Spaniards or Englishmen never failed to have its repercussions in rhyme. Scheurleer's collection has great historical value, for it shows how the common man reacted to the stirring events of the age; and some of the effusions record incidents that official history has not cared to preserve. But the artistic worth of the collection is slight. Most of the songs were written by amateurs whose patriotism must extenuate their guilt in manhandling the language. Sometimes an enthusiast achieved an effect by the very helplessness of his utterance. The general impression conveyed by this anthology is one of an inarticulate people vainly and pathetically struggling for expression under the stress of emotion.

Professional poets often joined in the national chorus of praise and rejoicing, but their tone is hardly ever in the popular vein. The Reverend Jacob Revius once caught the spirit of the early Sea Beggars' songs, which reveled in satirical invective. But the majority, with

Vondel at their head, summoned the gods and heroes of antiquity from Olympus; under the influence of classical poetry, they staged a baroque pageant that must have been unintelligible to the man in the street. Nearly all these poems sing the praises of victorious admirals, celebrating not the romance of the sea but the triumphs of the Republic in war. The few eulogies of skippers of the merchant marine were not the spontaneous outbursts of poets, but were solicited by the publishers of the seafarer's memoirs. The sea as a field of combat is the theme of this poetry; its terrors, its solitude, its promise of adventure and romance do not haunt the verse of Vondel and the lesser poets of that age.

Nevertheless, good material for both poet and romancer of the sea is available in the logs and accounts of adventurous voyages made by early explorers and navigators. Many of these have been reëdited in the volumes of the *Linschoten Vereeniging*. This is a Dutch counterpart of the Hakluyt Society, and takes its name from Jan Huygen van Linschoten, one of the first Hollanders to visit, in Portuguese employ, the possessions of Portugal in India. He revealed in his *Itinerario* the inner weakness and disintegration of Portugal's colonial empire. That publication became a guidebook to Dutch seafarers and merchants whom it egged on to oust the Portuguese from the Orient. Linschoten was not a literary artist. Neither he nor any of the skippers who wrote after him wrote for effect. Each put down his experiences ·in the course of duty. The picturesque idiom that was their inheritance sometimes enlivens the record with flashes of beauty, but the building of periods was not their job. If they had been content to write as they spoke, they might have written forcefully. But they tried, self-consciously, to write in the style of the printed books and lacking a compass to guide them through the currents and cross-currents of a latinized Dutch syntax, they foundered too often on the shoals of obscurity.

These men were the pioneers who laid the foundation stone of Holland's colonial empire. The Portuguese have an epic of their heroic age in the *Lusiadas* of Camoëns. But the heroes who blazed the trail for the Dutch East India Company in the Malay Archipelago have remained unsung. What is the explanation of their neglect by the poets? Dutch literature is the mirror of a bourgeois society, in whose ears the heroic style has a false ring. The prosperous burghers of the Netherland cities, ever since the late thirteenth century, have set the tone and the fashion of life in the Low Countries. They were the betters of the landed aristocracy in wealth, in knowledge, in political organization.

The beginnings of Dutch literature were, indeed, aristocratic. French romances of chivalry were in vogue among the Dutch nobility and found imitators and adapters among Netherland poets. But with the rise of a well-to-do and self-reliant burgher class in the cities of Flanders and Brabant, the fairy-tale exploits of the knights of Charlemagne and King Arthur became the butt of bourgeois ridicule and scorn. Jacob van Maerlant, who had written romances of chivalry in his youth, condemned them in his riper years for the strain they put upon the burgher's sense of realism. Scripture, repository of truth, and the Lives of the Saints offered more profitable reading than the lies of the poets:

> I hardly know a man, forsooth,
> That liveth now and loveth truth.
> But Lancelot, Percival, Tristram,
> And Galahad, and such as them,
> Feignëd names that never were,
> Of these the people love to hear.
> Leasings of love and lies of war
> The world is reading wide and far.
> The gospel is too hard to scan
> Because it teaches truth to man.

The beast epic of *Reynard the Fox* emanated from the same bourgeois spirit. The poets of this greatest of medieval Dutch poems, preferring, unlike Van Maerlant, entertainment to instruction, did not discard the lies and leasings of romance, but only bared them of the romantic glamour by transposing the exploits of chivalry into the burlesque of animal life. The comic effect of this artifice was more clearly apparent to thirteenth-century readers than it can be to us, who are less familiar with the epic poetry under ridicule. Lines and phrases that were recognized at once as copied from the romances tickled the hearers by their novel application to an odd or a homely incident. No moral was pointed, other than the cynical one that cunning and deceit are of more avail than valor. The poets had a sneaking love for their foxy hero, and felt no qualms of conscience in recounting his repeated escapes from the punishment which, from a knightly point of view, he fully deserved. The Flemish burghers must have chuckled over a story in which the beasts endowed with physical strength were duped by the wit of defenseless little Reynard. It was a parable of middle-class intelligence triumphing over the armed valor of chivalry. But it was at the same time a symptom of middle-class philosophy triumphing over the aristocratic concept of life as a noble and adventurous game.

If there had been in the Netherlands a royal court proud to foster native arts and letters, the history of Dutch literature might have taken a different course. But the Burgundian Dukes, though ambitious for their court to outshine that of their rival, the King of France, never acted as patrons of Dutch letters. They did attract Dutch painters and sculptors. The works of Jan van Eyck and Claus Sluter still bear witness to the high level attained by Netherland art under Burgundian rule. But the language of the court was French. Dutch was the Cinderella, good enough for the converse of tradespeople and craftsmen, but unfit for introduction into the ballroom. She was suddenly proclaimed the most popular beauty when the Dutch rose in arms against Philip II, Duke of Burgundy and King of Spain. The fervor with which the war for freedom of faith and country was fought aroused in the people a new pride in their language. The learned Antwerp physician, Johannes Goropius Becanus, even went so far in patriotic self-applause as to claim for the Germanic, which he called the Cimbric, language the distinction of having been the original speech of our common parents in Paradise. Still, the Prince of Orange, who headed the uprising, though he could speak Dutch, always wrote in French, and at the court of his successors, the Stadtholders, at The Hague, French remained the vehicle of polite conversation. Naturally, the fashion at court set the fashion among the burgher patriciate. The daughters of the ruling families in town and country were sent to the French school, while the sons, after a classical training in Latin, took courses in a French university or went traveling with a Frenchman as tutor and mentor. Thus the practice was for children to learn to write a foreign language before they had learned to write their own, and men might rise to high office who could not express themselves clearly on paper in their. mother tongue.

One of Holland's greatest statesmen, Count Gijsbert Karel van Hogendorp, was unable to write faultless Dutch when he entered public life. He was born in 1762, the son of patrician parents. When he was ten years old, his father sailed for Java, there to restore his shattered fortune, and the boy was sent to Berlin for military training in the cadets' corps. At sixteen, he took part in the Prussian campaign against Austria, and three years later, having completed his studies at Berlin, he returned to Holland and joined the Dutch guard as cornet. In 1783 and 1784 he traveled in America. The record of this journey has been preserved in a collection of letters addressed to his mother. In spite of his Dutch birth and German upbringing these letters were written in French. Once in a while he tried to compose a Dutch letter to his sister, who, if she knew her language better than he, must have chuckled over his sins against Dutch grammar. After his return from the New World, he took up the study of law at Leyden. No doubt he studied also his neglected mother tongue, for, having taken his LL.D., he was appointed Pensionary of his native city of Rotterdam, a position held by Hugo Grotius one hundred and seventy years earlier. During the

French interregnum from 1795 to 1813 he held no public office, but when in 1813 the people revolted against Napoleon, it was Van Hogendorp who took the lead in freeing his country from the conqueror's grasp. Yet, this same patriot, who could not brook to see his country ruled by Frenchmen, felt more at ease in writing French than Dutch. Similarly, his King who had lived in exile while the French domination lasted, and who saw in France the hereditary enemy of the Netherlands, nevertheless corresponded in French with his son, the Prince of Orange.

Nor did the aristocracy of the mind treat the native language with any greater deference. The humanists of the Reformation era refused to follow the schismatic course of the reformers who built up separate national churches in defiance of the one Catholic church of the Middle Ages. The scholars were not anxious to rebuild their Latin temple of learning into a modern tower of Babel. The greatest man of letters in sixteenth-century Europe was Desiderius Erasmus of Rotterdam. But Dutch literature cannot claim him as its own. All that he wrote was written in Latin. He and his fellow humanists rejected the use of a vehicle that would have reached only a small provincial audience. In the patriotic fervor aroused by the Spanish war, the mathematician Simon Stevin set a good example in writing of his science in the vernacular; Hugo Grotius praised him for his loyalty to the mother tongue and made a plea for its wider use among scholars. But the example and the plea were of no avail. Even Grotius himself did not live up to his own preaching. He did write in his mother tongue a handbook on Dutch-Roman law, but the bulk of his prose and poetry was composed in Latin. Dutch scholars continued to publish the results of their research in Latin until the early nineteenth century.

With aristocrats and scholars alike disdaining to cultivate their native speech, its care was left to the middle class, whose chief concern was commerce and trade. The burgher outlook limits the scope of literary interest and expression. Characteristic traits of this mentality are an insistence on realism and the corollary, an aversion to fantastic imaginings; a tendency to travesty the heroic in the burlesque of a workaday garb; and a tendency toward didacticism and moralization.

Jacob Cats was the only poet of the seventeenth century who was widely read in his own lifetime. His verse with its pedestrian philosophy appealed to the masses, who expressed their admiration by calling him affectionately Father Cats. The present-day Dutchmen have lost all respect for his parental dignity. The useful knowledge that he popularized has ceased to be useful, and the verse by which he gave it popularity has ceased to be admired as poetry. Former generations quoted him as readily and reverently as they quoted the Scriptures; in fact, the folio edition of his collected works was a companion volume to the Bible in nearly every Dutch household.

If people still quote Cats they do so unconsciously, not knowing that the proverb is one of his coining. For he was a master of gnomic lore. The merit of proverbs is not in their substance, which is seldom more than mere platitude, but in their form. They strike home by the picturesque wording of a common truth. Cats knew how to make the commonplace sound uncommon by his plastic expression of the truism. Poetry to him was only a means to an end, and that end was edification and uplift of the masses. In order to reach them he wrote in a manner all his own, which, however much it has been parodied and ridiculed, had the merit of accomplishing the end for which he devised it.

He alone among the poets of his time systematically avoided enjambment; the rhyme had to be followed by a rest so as to be distinctly audible to an untrained ear. For the same reason Cats wrote an Alexandrine unique in contemporary Dutch poetry in that the caesura always comes after the sixth syllable, in the middle of the line. This lends to his verse a monotonous lilt which makes it easy to commit to memory. Partial repetition of the same phrase in line after line, and restatement, over and over again, of the same idea in different words and images are his devices to hammer the lesson into unreceptive brains.

He was a better artist than present-day opinion gives him credit for. When modern critics condemn him, it is not his verse but his homely philosophy that excites their scorn. The burden of his monotonous chant is the blessedness of family life. Glory be to the paterfamilias who by dint of industry and thrift builds his home on a foundation of affluence. Father Cats' thoughts seldom wander beyond the precincts of house and garden. Courtship, marriage, childbirth, education, work, prayer, sickbed and death are his favorite topics. The adventurous life on the seven seas is outside his ken and imagination. His concern is with the seven ages of man. The heroism that he celebrated in verse was that of chastity overcoming concupiscence as exemplified in the story of Joseph and the wife of Potiphar. That was the only battle he himself had fought, not always, he was sorry to confess, with victory on the side of virtue. His eye never rolled in a fine frenzy; it could discern no more than the little space of earth in which he moved and, honest realist that he was, he did not strain ambitiously beyond his power. Still, this unemotional, puritanical didacticist, holding the high office of Pensionary of Holland, was a frequent guest at court. He was a favorite of the Prince of Orange, and was employed, late in life, as a special envoy to the Court of St. James's. But court life at The Hague, being an imitation of court life at Versailles, left the Dutch poet untouched.

There was one other poet at The Hague who also moved among the highest circles and went on diplomatic missions to foreign courts. Constantijn Huygens was the private secretary of the Prince of Orange and in constant attendance on his noble master. Still his poetry does not reflect ideals that were beyond the limited ken of Father Cats. Its form, indeed, is different. In diction he is the very opposite of Cats, who never left anything unsaid or unexplained. Huygens strove for distinction through brevity, at the risk of obscuring his meaning. This enigmatic utterance stimulates the reader's interest, whereas Cats' garrulity sends him to sleep. The epigram was a form of expression that suited Huygens' peculiar talent for succinctness. Thousands of short poems in his collected works testify to his wit and ingenuity in hitting upon the terse and telling phrase.

The bulk of his poetry is autobiographic. He has left us a faithful record, in his own inimitable diction, of his daily life at The Hague and at his country seat Hofwyck. This cosmopolitan *grand seigneur* played in his leisure moments with homely fancies that he shared with all prosperous burghers of the Dutch Republic. On one of his diplomatic missions to London he met John Donne, the dean of St. Paul's. He admired the startling felicities of the Englishman's diction, and felt tempted to test his own ingenuity by a translation of nineteen of Donne's poems. But in Huygens' original poetry there is no spark of that frank sensuality and impassioned intenseness that burn in the verse of Donne's youth. What glow of passion there is in the Hollander's poems is a reflection of the controlled woodfire on his hearth. "I did best when I had least truth for my subject," said Donne. Neither Huygens nor Cats could do well without the full support of truth.

There were, at that same time, two poets in Amsterdam whom nature had so richly endowed with imaginative power that they "did well" beyond the truth to which their eyes bore witness. Pieter Cornelisz. Hooft, a burgomaster's son, had visited France and Italy before he came of age. Joost van den Vondel, son of a silk merchant and successor to his father's business, had seen little of the world outside the territory of the Dutch Republic. Of the two, his was the more cosmopolitan spirit. His imagination alone followed the sailor to the Arctic and the Indies, accompanied the Republic's ambassadors to foreign courts, its generals and admirals into battle, its scholars and historians into the literatures of ancient Palestine, Greece, and Rome, and from these flights of fancy into space and time brought home treasures wherewith to decorate his house of poetry. But even he could not refrain from moralizing, in burgher fashion, on the daredevil recklessness of the heroes who sailed to the Arctic in search of a northeast passage to the Indies. Thus he concludes his fable of the serpent that blunted its teeth on an anvil:

This fable warns the reckless whose ambitions tower
To heights where they presume beyond man's utmost
  power,
Such as that foolish crew who, in a vain conceit,
Force Nature's northern passage way, courting defeat,
And with an oaken raft—intrepid crew and master!—
Drift through the mountainous ice-pack, hell-bent for dis-
  aster,
And though a ship may pay the toll and, ice-bound, stand
Fixed as a tower, still onward fares the search-crazed band.

He wrote this not when tired old age had left him without any zest for life, cooped up in his study with books and papers, but at the start of his poetic career. Impassioned surrender to the call of romance and adventure shocked middle-class morality as a revolt against God. No man of noble impulses can live without hero worship. The Baptist Vondel, brought up in the pious sphere of a simple and devout community, found his heroes, not on the quays of Amsterdam's ship-crowded harbor, but in the books of the Old Testament and, after his conversion to the Roman Catholic faith, in the blessed martyrs of the Church. When he looked for a fitting subject for an epic poem, he thought of the Emperor Constantine and John the Baptist; to dramatize heroism, he placed upon the stage the martyrdom of the eleven thousand virgins at Cologne, of Peter and Paul in Rome, of Mary Queen of Scots, all glorified witnesses to the true faith.

Vondel's verse has the majestic sweep of a galleon under full sail. But galleons are a rare spectacle on the sluggish stream of Holland's literature. Its common craft is the *trekschuit*, the horse-drawn canal barge plying between the towns of the Dutch Republic before the invention of the railway. Political pamphlets, in Vondel's lifetime, often took the form, and bore the title, of *Een Trekschuit-praatje*, "A Barge Talk," between travelers of various sorts and conditions who whiled away the tedium of the journey by discussing some burning topic of the day. The *trekschuit* is an integral part of the seventeenth-century Dutch landscape, and the barge talk is of the very essence of the life of the people under the Dutch Republic. The monotonous, unemotional verse of Jacob Cats gives in its *trekschuit* placidity a true reflection of middle-class temper and outlook.

Vondel's age was the highwater mark of Dutch literature. After his death the ebb set in, and for a century and a half the literary output is shallow and sluggish and unemotional, like a neat, placid canal across the polder. However, two figures of that uneventful era were of uncommon stature. Both Willem Bilderdijk and Eduard Douwes Dekker were fired by a spark of genius. Their greatness made them seem strange and exotic to their contemporaries. It set them apart from their fellowmen. It irked them to belong to a bourgeois society of shopkeepers whose only textbooks were the Bible and their ledger. And both sought escape from it in a weird and preposterous fiction, each claiming descent from royal ancestry.

Bilderdijk was a gloomy dean of letters, a bitter and unpleasant critic of his age, a preacher of morality, who in his private life boldly defied the conventional moral code. He was an archconservative in an age that made democracy its gospel, a mystic among rationalists, and a great poet among a crowd of petty rhymesters. He was born in 1756, the son of an Amsterdam physician. At an early age he suffered an injury to his foot, which confined him to his bed for twelve years. Growing up without the friendship of playmates and with no other companions than books, he became a shy, self-centered misanthrope, rich in the knowledge of book-learning, but devoid of all knowledge of his fellowmen.

His encyclopedic mind took a passionate interest in nearly every field of human endeavor. He taught history for a time at Leyden; he published a book on geology; he considered himself an expert on linguistics and engaged in polemics with a Leyden philologist on the proper spelling of the Dutch language; he studied genealogy and heraldry; and corresponded with German scholars on questions of philosophy and religion. His passionate nature was never satisfied with a partial yield, he demanded the utmost from everything and everybody. Disillusionment was, consequently, his lot. He loved his country passionately, but expecting too much from it, he found himself sadly disappointed. It was the only country in which he could endure life, but even in Holland he found it at last endurable only at Leyden.

His wife left him equally disillusioned. When in 1796 he refused to swear allegiance to the Batavian Republic and preferred banishment to disloyalty to the Prince of Orange, she refused to follow him into exile. He took that refusal for an act of abandonment. In London he became acquainted with a Dutch painter, whose two daughters took private lessons from him. The younger one fell in love with her teacher, and he took her to wife, though legally he was still a married man. The couple went to Brunswick in Germany, awaiting an opportunity to return to Holland. But to his growing vexation the release from his exile was postponed from year to year. The long delay embittered him; he satirized the Duke of Brunswick, who had supported him financially, for not supporting him enough; he reviled German life and German manners, and made himself disagreeable to all who came in contact with him. His second wife was a patient Griselda to this erratic Count of Teisterbant. That was the title by which he called himself, not in order to conceal his identity, but because it pleased him to believe that he had a right to the name as a descendant of that medieval house and, through it, of the Knight of the Swan, who was the legendary son of a Byzantine emperor.

In 1806 the Count of Teisterbant was readmitted to his native country, then a kingdom under Napoleon's

brother Louis Bonaparte. The romantic believer in
feudalism and in royalty by the grace of God could
reconcile himself with this new state of affairs. He became the King's instructor in Dutch and his librarian,
and spent a brief period of happiness in the sunshine
of the royal favor. But in 1810 the Kingdom of Holland
was incorporated with the Napoleonic Empire, Louis
Bonaparte was dethroned, and the Count of Teisterbant
relapsed into his former state of hypochondria. The closing years of his life were brightened for him by the
affection and worship of a group of young men who
had sat at his feet in the lecture rooms at Leyden. His
devoted Griselda passed away before him. He followed
her two years later to a grave in the Church of St. Bavo
at Haarlem.

Douwes Dekker's hatred of the Dutch middle class
drove him to create the memorable character of Batavus
Drystubble in his novel, *Max Havelaar*, which he published under the pseudonym of Multatuli. This Drystubble is an Amsterdam coffee broker who, in spite of
his scorn for books and the men who scribble them, is
thinking of writing one himself, or rather of piecing
one together from a manuscript supplied by a former
schoolmate. He is rather ashamed of his acquaintance
with the latter. For this friend of other days is evidently
a pauper; he wears no coat in cold weather, has only
a shawl round his neck, and does not carry a watch.
Still, Shawlman, as he calls him, may prove useful with
his pile of manuscripts which he sent Drystubble in
the hope that, for old acquaintance sake, the rich coffee

broker would be willing to underwrite the publishing costs of a first issue, were it only a small volume.

Shawlman has been in the East Indies, and among his miscellaneous writings are essays on Java and native labor that contain matter of great interest to coffee brokers. It has become clear to Drystubble from Shawlman's essays that a grave danger is threatening the whole coffee market, a danger that can only be warded off by the united efforts of all the brokers. This consideration induces him to lower himself to the level of Grub Street.

Drystubble, however, is not up to the task, or as he would express it, a self-respecting coffee broker cannot stoop to the drudgery of writing. Fortunately there is in his office a young German with literary ambitions. Ernest Stern has mastered the Dutch language fairly well, has a knack for reciting poetry, and a talent for writing. He is, in addition, the son of Ludwig Stern, one of the foremost coffee merchants in Hamburg and one of Drystubble's best customers. The Germans have a romantic regard for scribblers, and Ludwig Stern will be flattered by the recognition of his son's literary talent.

So Stern is engaged to write a couple of chapters every week. But the young German has stipulated that Drystubble must not change one iota of his story. This, it is true, does not please the broker, but he consoles himself with the plan of inserting a chapter of his own composition every now and then to give the book the proper gravity. To their combined, or rather alternating, efforts the reading public in Holland will owe the book which Stern calls "Max Havelaar" after the hero, but which

Drystubble would entitle "The Coffee Sales of the Netherland Trading Company."

Max Havelaar represents the Netherland Government in a district of the Bantam Residency, in West Java. He is all that a hero ought to be: generous, enthusiastic, brave, ready to succor the downtrodden, defiant of the slothful and the wicked who are in command. He finds the native population of his district impoverished and depleted by the emigration of those who prefer exile to misery at home. Who is responsible? Not the Dutch Government, not directly at least. It is the native prince whom that Government has left in charge of his native subjects. He must keep up his princely state, he must be able to cut a figure among his equals, and the simple tillers of the soil must pay for his grandeur, if not with money, then with their labor, or with the buffalo that they need for the plow. The Dutch authorities can stop the outrage by deposing the petty despot, but they are unwilling to take such a drastic step. The system requires that one connive at these abuses as long as peace and quiet prevail. A Resident does not like to report that things are not as they ought to be in the province entrusted to his care, and an assistant who does make such a report is looked upon as a trouble maker.

Max Havelaar is one of these. When his immediate superior remains inactive, he insists on notifying the Central Government at Batavia of the malpractices he discovered. But his zealous advocacy of the native falls on deaf ears. The Governor General, displeased with the manner in which Havelaar has proceeded and with his attitude toward his superior officer, feels compelled to relieve him of his present duties and to order his transfer to a different post. Havelaar, in answer to that order, asks his Excellency to give him his honorable discharge from the service of the State, and therewith ends the story that Ernest Stern has culled from Shawlman's manuscripts.

"Havelaar wandered about, poor and forsaken. He sought . . ." These are the last words that Stern ever wrote. For at this point his pen is taken from him: "Enough, estimable Stern! I, Multatuli, take up the pen. You are not called upon to write Havelaar's life history. I have called you into being . . . I made you come from Hamburg . . . I taught you to write fairly good Dutch in a very short time, it is enough, Stern, you may go!" And when Batavus Drystubble wants to add a final touch of solidity to the narrative, Multatuli again interrupts: "Halt! miserable product of sordid covetousness and blasphemous hypocrisy! I created you . . . you grew under my pen to a monster . . . I loathe my own creation: choke in coffee and vanish."

Such is the whimsical composition of the book that, since its first appearance in 1860, has become a classic of Dutch literature. "If you ask a Hollander for a really good Dutch novelist he refers you to the man who wrote *Old People and Things That Pass* (Louis Couperus), or else to somebody you know nothing about. As regards the Dutch somebody I know nothing about, I am speechless. But as regards *Old People and Things That Pass*, I still think *Max Havelaar* a far more real book." Thus wrote D. H. Lawrence in his introduction to an English translation of the story by W. Siebenhaar. I agree, though admitting with him that, as far as composition goes, it is the greatest mess possible. But Multatuli knew what he was about when he deliberately made it a mess. His alter ego Havelaar had written eloquent letters to the Governor General, but his eloquence had been of no avail. "So if I, Multatuli, wish to be heard —and above all understood—I must write otherwise than he. And that is why my book has such a motley appearance. I make no apology for its form. That form appeared to me suitable for the attainment of my object. That object is twofold: I wished to give my children a patent of nobility from my own hand. And in the second place: I will be read."

He was read. Multatuli became the most discussed writer of Holland. The self-pitying pen name did not disguise his identity. Everybody knew that this "much-suffering" man was Eduard Douwes Dekker, who on account of disagreement with his superiors in Java had resigned from the service. Douwes Dekker, Multatuli, Max Havelaar, Shawlman, are all one and the same. The story told by Stern is a fragment of Dekker's autobiography, his *apologia pro sua vita*. And Batavus Drystubble? In him he has personified and satirized the nation which, for the sake of commercial profits, let the Javanese slave in the coffee plantations and suffer extortion from their princes. If he had thundered his indignation to the people at home they would have remained indifferent. Satire, bitter and scathing, but hiding its hatred behind a humorous grin, would make them listen and take note. He made of his Drystubble a vivid and loathsome reality, so vivid and loathsome that no one could ignore him. His name became a byword, his type a laughing stock among the very nation which in him was satirized. Drystubble's literary success meant his defeat in life, and Multatuli was his victor.

But why did Multatuli entrust the telling of Havelaar's story to a German? That again is part of the satire. A nation of Drystubbles does not produce the talent that can do justice to so moving a tale. It needed a son from the land of Goethe and Schiller to enter into the romantic spirit of Havelaar's tragedy. The hero himself writes German verse when he wants to express the devotion that binds him to his wife and child, and Shawlman at his first meeting with the coffee broker struck the latter as having a touch of the German about him. Among the pile of Shawlman's manuscripts Drystubble found one on "The homage paid to Schiller and Goethe in the German middle-class." Drystubble, on the other hand, who is the middle-class of Holland, calls all poetry nothing but lies.

Multatuli himself, it is true, was of that class. That is to say, in the Amsterdam register of births Eduard Douwes Dekker is on record as having been born on March 2, 1820, as the son of a Dutch sea captain. But he must have been a changeling, in his own opinion. A native chief in Java discovered on the head of Havelaar's little son the double hair twist which, according to Javanese superstition, is intended to wear a crown. "Sir," he said, "the boy is a King's child." And of himself Multatuli wrote to a friend in 1886: "I am like Danton, or Robespierre, or Marat, rather than a Lamartine. Yea, if I had attained the power for which I have striven, hundreds of heads would have fallen at my command." If he had lived in our time, he would have aspired to a dictatorship and crushed Drystubble under an iron heel.

Multatuli's style struck home by its directness and simple beauty. "I do my best," he once wrote, "to write living Dutch, although I have been to school." The sarcasm was prompted by a deeper feeling than mere pleasure in paradox. A rebel by temperament, he hated school for its choking grip on originality, and by shaking off the grip of the literary standard upon the language, which squeezed all expression into stereotyped forms, he started a revolutionary movement in Dutch literature that was rich in results. He himself, however, did not live to see its happy consummation. Drystubble, indeed, was eventually beaten, but he outlasted Multatuli's lifetime and drove the rebel into exile. He found a final home in his beloved Germany, where he died in 1886.

It was, indeed, a dull, self-satisfied, and smug little Holland that he left to Drystubble and his ilk. In the sixties of the past century the chief function of poetry was to celebrate the sweet blessings of the home and the greatness of Holland's past. The versifiers gloried in the laurels won by heroic forbears, but were content, at the same time, to praise a petty-bourgeois present that was incapable of heroism.

When I was in my teens and attended school in Amsterdam, there was a scarcity of heroes in Holland for boys to worship. The popular sports in that country of lakes, rivers, and canals were skating, swimming, rowing, and sailing, but there was little spectacular in these, and the winners of races and regattas never achieved a popularity that made them idols of the public and the press. Hero worship has never been a foible of the Dutch, and in those days they ran very slight risk of succumbing to any un-Dutch idolatry.

The child is father of the man. It is difficult for the man I have grown into to form a clear conception of that particular child that is his father, but he very definitely remembers that, little Hollander though he was, he felt a craving for heroes whom he could worship, and that, not finding any adventure and romance in the actual life of every day, he found a substitute for them in books. Translations of Jules Verne, Gustave Aimard, Fenimore Cooper, Mayne Reid, created for him the world that he loved best, for there was no imaginative literature for boys in his own language. He never could work up much enthusiasm for the heroes of his country's history; they were spoiled for him by the uninspiring manner in which their deeds were recited in the history lesson at school. If you are given marks for your knowledge of what your heroes did, they are bound to lose their vivid reality and turn into little better than dead museum exhibits. One Dutch boy, at least, feels more indebted to the fiction writers of France and America than to the worthy pedagogues and compilers of school books who taught him the history of his country.

When he had reached his Junior year in High School and was able to read foreign authors in the original language, he realized to his mortification how poor and arid, by comparison, was the contemporary literature of Holland. Dutch poetry, in those days, was for a large part the monopoly of very worthy ministers of the Church who were, however, but indifferent poets. They could never forget the part that they professionally performed as molders of public and domestic morals, and in their conscious attempt to make poetics subserve ethics genuine emotion and spontaneity were lost.

There was, it is true, one poet of outstanding merit, E. J. Potgieter. He was not a minister but a merchant; however, his verse suffered from obscurity of thought and diction and was, in consequence, not read as widely as that of the poetic preachers who expressed themselves with such edifying clarity. From 1837 until 1865 Potgieter was editor of *De Gids*, the leading literary monthly, and in that capacity proved himself a relentless critic of contemporary letters. An able and even more relentless assistant in this critical task was C. Busken Huet, who had been a minister of the Church. The love of art was so strong in Huet that it claimed the whole man, and he unfrocked himself to devote all his time to writing. He joined the editorial staff of *De Gids*, and when dissension arose between this fiery, uncompromising spirit and other members of the board, Potgieter sided with him. The two resigned together, leaving *De Gids* in the hands of respectable mediocrity. Huet became editor of a daily journal in Batavia, and on his return from the tropics settled in Paris, remaining a voluntary exile from his native country. Armed with his trenchant pen he had offered battle to the Drystubble forces of conservatism and smug banality and they had beaten him. He no longer felt at home among his own kind.

Hence it so happened that about 1880, when Potgieter had been dead five years and Huet and Multatuli were living among strangers abroad, mediocrity ruled in Holland's little world of letters. And when the boys whose imagination had been stirred by the stories of Verne and Cooper and Aimard outgrew this sort of fiction and looked for something better suited to their adult taste, Dutch literature had little to offer them. They came from an enchanted land into a dull, conventional garden, where emotion and passion and heroism would have been ridiculously out of place.

It was then that we, Juniors and Seniors in High School, discovered heroes whom we could worship: Willem Kloos, Lodewijk van Deyssel, Frederik van Eeden, Albert Verwey. They were a group of young writers who, in 1885, founded a new literary monthly which, by way of challenge to *De Gids*, they called *De Nieuwe Gids* ("The New Guide"). We let ourselves be guided with unquestioning faith by these new leaders. We knew Kloos's sonnets by heart and felt that his impassioned lyricism voiced the longings and emotions of our own inarticulate selves. He could be tender and cynical, ecstatic and profane, devout and defiant, and the music and imagery of his verse seemed always in unison with the mood.

As judges of contemporary literature Kloos and Van Deyssel were bold and aggressive. Their criticism sounded to us like a clarion call to rebellion against all that was smug and humdrum and platitudinous. They dared to use words for the voicing of passion and pride and profanity such as the previous generation had been taught to repress as indecorous and wicked. If they had been merely daring, their revolt would have been a flash in the pan. But they were inspired prophets challenging the age in magnificent prose and verse that burnt themselves into our hearts. They fortunately addressed a generation not merely willing but eager to be saved from mediocrity and smugness. Holland was like a stuffy house with all its windows closed against the blustering winds from east and south that might blow in the dangerous germs of French radicalism and German philosophy. Kloos and his fellow editors forced the windows open and enabled their compatriots to breathe in a European atmosphere.

The fresh air had an intoxicating effect. A new language was needed to give expression to the new sense of elation. The clichés of the figurative speech inherited from preceding generations had become flat and meaningless. There is a distinct cleavage between the literary language of present-day Holland and the Dutch that was written before the nineties of the past century. This profound change was brought about by the writers of *De Nieuwe Gids*. Their revolutionary organ was thrown up like a barricade across the quiet, well-ordered market place of Dutch literature, where poets of various degrees of pedestrianism offered harmless anodynes in rhyme to the lovesick and the lonely. It threw the peaceful scene into a turmoil. It championed the realism of the naturalistic novel, but it also preached art for art's sake, and called the young to the worship of beauty. The triumph of the rebels was quick and decisive. The spirit of Drystubble was driven out of Dutch literature.

The substance of most of the contributions to *De Nieuwe Gids* has lost the powerful appeal which it possessed for this writer's generation. The self-love expressed in them and its corollary, contempt for the multitude, clashed with the social feelings that stirred the generation which grew to manhood in the first decade of this century. The Labor Party came to the fore and won adherents among men of letters: Herman Gorter, a contemporary of the leaders of *De Nieuwe Gids* and hailed by them as a great poet, embraced the cause of the world's proletariat; Frederik van Eeden went in search of God in Tolstoyan love for his fellow man; and Verwey turned from self-worship to the study of man and man's self-revelation in literature. Verwey founded in 1905 a new monthly, *De Beweging* ("The Movement"), which became the rallying point of a group of younger poets who recognized in Verwey their mentor and master. Without being pontifical, he held his following together by the trust he inspired in his aesthetic judgment and by their respect for his uncompromising honesty. *De Beweging* was to demonstrate Verwey's conviction that true poetry has a higher vocation than to express individual moods and feelings in musical and picturesque words. He saw in poetry a social force by which the successive generations and the members of each generation were welded together and made conscious of their unity.

De Beweging was discontinued in 1919. But five years later Verwey was given a new opportunity to exert influence on the nation's youth by his appointment to the vacant chair of Netherland Literature in the University of Leyden. A poet in the professor's chair was something novel in Holland. The experiment turned out to be a great success, to the surprise of the professional educators who valued teaching experience higher than poetic talent. When he was forced to retire on reaching his seventieth year, he had the satisfaction of seeing himself succeeded by the poet P. N. van Eyck, the most eminent of the *Beweging* group. The movement that he started lost its organ nearly twenty years ago, but the spirit that informed it will continue to guide the next generation.

Chapter XIII

INFERIORITY COMPLEXES

WHILE HUNTING for a rare publication in the New York Public Library card catalogue—a thrilling pastime that may lead you on to pleasant discoveries—I found that the library possesses a precious collection of playbills of the Dutch Theater at The Hague covering the period from 1819 to 1867. They are bound together in eleven stout volumes and constitute a valuable record of dramatic production in Holland during the first half of the nineteenth century.

The collection was purchased in 1910 from Martinus Nijhoff, The Hague, although nowhere in Holland, not even in The Hague municipal archives, can its counterpart be found. It is, in fact, a unique file of playbills, which, to judge from notes, corrections of misprints, and changes in the cast and selection of plays scribbled on many of the programs, was kept for reference by the successive directors of the company. That no one at The Hague cared sufficiently for this historic record to prevent its being sold to America is significant of the lack of interest, a generation ago, in the stage and the theater. It is no excuse to say that in the first half of the nineteenth century the Dutch stage had fallen upon evil days, that

Dutch playwrights of whom the nation could be proud did not exist, and that the foreign plays that were performed did not represent the best that was produced abroad. All that is true, but the low caliber of the drama advertised in these playbills does not diminish their value as historical documents. They supply a gauge of the culture and dramatic taste of the playgoing public at The Hague and in the rest of Holland a century ago.

To look through these files of forgotten performances is like going to the theater with one's great-grandparents. It is a more genuine entertainment than the one Christopher Morley treated us to some ten years ago at a Hoboken playhouse; those who went to Hoboken pretended to be their grandparents only in order to pull grimaces at the reflection which they saw in the mirror of the stage. The perusal of the Dutch handbills recalls to the mind's eye not only the scene behind the footlights but the audience in front of it and the picturesque little town that The Hague then was. Its limited size may be inferred from the Directors' manner of addressing their patrons, which seems to imply a personal acquaintance with the individual playgoers and a genuine anxiety to please them. Each bill is phrased in the form of a letter, which was probably handed in at the door a few days in advance of the performance. "Mijnheer," say Messrs Hoedt & Bingley at the top of the bill, "On Monday next we shall have the pleasure of presenting . . ." and they conclude the announcement with the formula, "In the hope that this representation may be honored with your presence, we have the pleasure of calling ourselves respectfully yours, Hoedt & Bingley."

[190]

On special occasions they introduced themselves as public benefactors, ever anxious to please, even to the extent of yielding the playhouse to rivals from out of town. In the second week of March, 1820, the announcement read that "the Directors, ever zealous and inclined to provide the honored public, by means of variety, with those pleasures which they may find at their command, have accordingly signed a contract with the Köbler family, who have aroused general admiration by their excellent talents during a three months' engagement at the Amsterdam theatre." These Köblers were vaudeville artists combining song and dance with pantomime and acrobatics. Their appearance seems to have scored an unusual success, for ten days later the bill made known to Hoedt & Bingley's patrons that "at the flattering request of the general public" the Köblers would give "a fifth and positively final performance, to wit, The Deceits of Harlequin, Great Comical Ballet and Pantomime."

Five performances was indeed a record number. For as a rule no show could be put on twice in the same week, and only very popular plays were offered to the public twice a year. Plays never had a run, they just stood one performance and then were taken off the boards for six months at least. When Hoedt & Bingley announced the forthcoming production of "Jean Calas; or, The Innocent Condemned, Famous Tragedy by M. Victor," they added, as a telling proof of its excellence, that it had run in Paris more than eighty times to the applause of continuous throngs. The Dutch actors at The Hague, playing for an audience drawn from a small community, must have envied their fortunate colleagues in

Paris who could repeat a successful show night after night.

Hoedt & Bingley's company had to work hard to vary their repertoire from day to day. And they gave the playgoer more than he nowadays gets for his money. Each performance consisted of two plays, a serious one followed by something light, a one-act comedy, farce, or vaudeville. That was a very old tradition, which went back to the practice of the late Middle Ages. Only on very special occasions was the lighter entertainment omitted. On February 22, 1820, Hoedt & Bingley featured "The Dead Uncle; or, The Frustrated Deceit, from the German of F. D. Gotter." "This play," says the program, "is one of the most classical comedies of all Germany, and on account of its greatness nothing extra will be shown after it." The same distinction was given to "Cabal and Love; or, The Victims of Ambition and Jealousy, Famous Tragedy by Germany's foremost author, the great Schiller."

Just as rare as the one-play performance was the one-title play. The twin title was a set feature of the drama of that period. I wonder what purpose it was meant to serve. Was the substitute name tagged on as a reserve force wherewith to capture the curiosity of the public in case the first one failed? And was the playgoer's interest won by the enlightening or the mystifying character of the substitute? It is clear that there was no sense in its addition, unless it improved upon the first title; it had to partake of the nature of the adjective, which colors the gray meaning of the noun by putting on touches of the personal and actual. "Edward of Scotland, great and very famous drama from the French of Duval" was one of the attractions on Hoedt & Bingley's repertoire. Its subtitle, "The Night of a Fugitive," is a good example of the species; it limits the story in time and reveals the predicament in which its hero finds himself. But there are many twin titles that are mere juxtapositions of gray nouns, the second adding neither light nor color to the first. "The Merchant from Riga; or, The Lady in Waiting" gives us a choice between a hero and a heroine but nothing definite for the chooser to go by. "The Shipwreck; or, The Heirs" tosses our imagination, like the ship, from sea to land but leaves it a wreck on the shoal of uncertainty. "The Skeleton; or, The Knights of the Lion" suggests a scene-shifting from a cupboard to a castle, but little else to stir our fancy. Such titles are meaningless pairs, of which either half tells us just as much or as little as the whole.

The overwhelming majority of these plays were translations from the French and the German. Dutch children growing up at The Hague in the twenties of the past century must have got the impression that the land of the Hohenzollerns was the nursery of the true drama and that the greatest of its nurserymen was August von Kotzebue. No fewer than forty-three of his plays were put on by Hoedt & Bingley between 1819 and 1821, and several of these were performed twice in the same year. His name appears on these handbills almost every week, and often two Kotzebue plays made up one evening's program. English plays, on the other hand, were seldom seen by Hoedt & Bingley's audiences, and the few that were produced had passed through French or

German versions on their way to The Hague theater. Among the novelties that the management offered their patrons in 1820 was "The Teasers; or, Much Ado About Nothing, after H. Beck's adaptation of a play by Shakespeare"! *Hamlet* was acted in a translation of the French version by Ducis. "Still Waters Run Deep" was featured as "A famous Comedy from the German based on Beaumont and Fletcher's Rule a Wife and Have a Wife."

This neglect of English drama is the more surprising as Willem Bingley, Hoedt's partner, was of English extraction and must have been acquainted with the successes of the London stage. His father, Ward Bingley, the son of English parents who were residents of Rotterdam, made his debut on the Amsterdam stage in 1779. Soon afterwards war broke out between Great Britain and the Dutch Republic, and anti-British sentiment was aroused to such a pitch that the young actor with the English name had to face hostile audiences in the first months of his novitiate. But gradually his great talent overcame the popular prejudice. One of his most applauded parts was that of a comical character in Garrick's *Miss in her Teens*, which Bingley himself had translated into Dutch. In 1796 he left Amsterdam and founded the *Nederduitsch Tooneel* (the "Dutch Stage") in his native city of Rotterdam. After his death in 1818 his son Willem took over the management of the *Nederduitsch Tooneel* in partnership with the actor Jan Hendrik Hoedt, who had married Ward Bingley's daughter. The two brothers-in-law moved their headquarters to The Hague, although they continued to give performances in Rotterdam. Hoedt & Bingley remained "respectfully yours" until 1843 when the death of Bingley dissolved the partnership; Hoedt made his exit three years later. In their honest attempt to please and to make profit, they had, without any ulterior purpose, brought French and German culture to their patrons at The Hague and Rotterdam.

There is good reason to doubt whether the profit of the partners and their company was commensurate with the pleasure of the patrons. We know from the contemporary testimony of reliable critics that the overworked and underpaid actors were, in their art, better craftsmen than the playwrights to whose romantic imaginings they gave an ephemeral life upon the boards, better craftsmen also than the average playgoer was able to appreciate. Spectacular shows, gaudy pageantry, and mechanical marvels were more in demand than the portrayal of human passions and emotions.

One of the chief attractions on Hoedt & Bingley's repertoire was "Love in the Lazaretto," a coarse farce by a seventeenth-century Dutch rhymester. It was not the ribaldry of the main performance that drew the crowds but the short sketches which were put on between the acts, and which could be varied from year to year. In 1821 the intermezzo between the first and second acts consisted of "The Royal Cabinet of Wax Figures, all beautifully modeled from life and presenting striking likenesses of several well-known characters." Between the third and fourth acts appeared "The Automatic Domino Player, Historical and Comical Dramatic Trifle of the Nineteenth Century, equipped with the necessary mechanisms." And before the curtain rose upon the fifth act, the audience was treated to a performance by "The Mechanical Statue," which the handbills declared to be both artistic and comical, adding of course, that on account of the greatness of this representation, no further extras were to be given after it. "Love in the Lazaretto" was on a par with "Cabal and Love, by Germany's foremost author, the great Schiller."

The record preserved by these playbills is a depressing one, indeed. Still, the Hollander of today finds some satisfaction in perusing it, because it serves to point up the stagecraft and dramatic art of modern Holland. One can no longer say that the Dutch theater lives exclusively by third and fourth rate drama imported from abroad. It does rely in part on foreign plays to make up its repertoire, but the managers need not stoop to low farce and spectacular shows to make a profit. On the contrary, they bring before the footlights the very best that can be found. Ibsen, Hauptmann, Shaw, O'Neill, Elmer Rice, Pirandello are as popular at The Hague and Amsterdam as they are in New York. Plays by Shakespeare are often revived and are no longer staged in mangled versions translated from the German or the French. The classical dramas of Vondel, the seventeenth-century Dutch playwright whose age marked the heyday of Holland's dramatic art, are again enjoying popular acclaim, and modern Dutch writers are contributing plays that refute the belief, prevalent a hundred years and half a century ago, that Dutch literature was incapable of producing actable drama.

It is true, there were no authors then whose plays

could spellbind an audience. But the pessimists have been proved wrong who drew from the temporary lack of them the inference that the dearth of good drama was due to a temperamental defect in the Dutch race. During this very period in which the art of the drama sank to its lowest ebb, great actors were among its interpreters on the Dutch stage. A nation that can produce dramatic performers of uncommon talent can not be wholly devoid of dramatic sense.

The decline of the art of the stage had its cause, not in a native defect, but in outward circumstances. Calvinism, the ruling religion in the days of the Dutch Republic, saw in the stage a den of wickedness. Even the Biblical plays of Vondel were frowned upon by the ministers of the Dutch Reformed Church, for they saw in them, not unjustly, survivals in classic disguise of the miracle plays staged by the medieval church, and condemned them, accordingly, as popish abominations. The actor's profession shared in the ecclesiastical ban. In the late eighteenth century it was still possible for players to be disqualified as witnesses in a court of law on the ground of their belonging to a disreputable calling, and a hundred years later they had not yet fully succeeded in living down the evil repute which the hostility of the Protestant church cast upon it.

If, as in Paris and London, the court and the aristocracy had offered the theater their powerful patronage, the Dutch drama might have been saved from degradation. But the court of the Prince of Orange favored the French drama and let the Dutch players shift for themselves. The Hague was never without some French company to entertain high society, and the prestige with which the favor of fashionable circles invested the French drama created a demand for translated French plays among the audiences of lesser degree who patronized the Dutch players. Madame's dressmaker likes what madame approves, and the footman, on his evening off, patterns his amusements after those of his master. Thus the Dutch stage deteriorated into a mere copy, and a bad one at that, of the French, and the educated classes who understood French well enough to follow the action on the stage would rather be seen in the French than in the Dutch theater.

Under such conditions playwrights found little inducement to compete with foreign rivals who were favorites because they were foreigners, nor were the players encouraged to give their best to audiences that did not include the best of society. The company of Hoedt & Bingley was granted an annual subsidy by King William II, but the rival French company at The Hague received twice as much and enjoyed the special favor of the court. In the sixties of the past century the *Théâtre Français de la Haye* succeeded in having the city pay for the music and the settings of two new opera productions a year, but the Dutch company was not permitted to benefit by these settings until they had been used twenty times by the French company, that is, after three or four years. In short, the drama in Holland was a Cinderella among her sister arts, and the actors were the least esteemed among the professional artists.

And yet, there were great artists among them. The greatest of them all, in the last decades of the past century, was Louis Bouwmeester. He was a star of the first magnitude during two generations. My own recollections of him go back to my early childhood, for I saw him first off the stage. Behind our house on the Keizersgracht at Amsterdam was a long garden whose far end was overlooked by the back of a house that was separated from our garden wall only by a narrow yard. We children used to play croquet there, and our game was often watched by an old man—old, that is, in our eyes—who sat in his shirt sleeves at a window of the second floor, smoking a pipe. We watched him in our turn, and with a keener interest than he could feel for our game. To play was work for him and when he took his seat there at the window, it was to rest from playing.

The sight of him fascinated our childish imagination, for we knew that, in the evening, that homely old man in his shirt sleeves might be wearing a crown and an ermine mantle, and be a king or an emperor to the audience in the theater. It made us feel as if we were confidantes of a secret which mystified the public. To have seen him in his domestic homeliness did not spoil our illusion when, afterwards, we saw him on the stage. On the contrary, the man who was able to change from a simple, harmless neighbor into a Richard III, or a Napoleon, or a Shylock, seemed to us the more marvelous for the contrast.

If his native tongue had been English or French and he could have been understood by as many millions as there were thousands whom he held spellbound in Dutch, he would not have sat over a backyard in the shade of trees that were not his. But the life of even the greatest of Dutch actors is not like that of a London or New York star. Two generations of Hollanders have acclaimed Louis Bouwmeester as a great artist, but their applause brought him no affluence. Only in his old age did he win international recognition. Paris, Brussels, Cologne, London, Oxford saw him act and realized his genius. "Even his cane talks," said a celebrated French critic. After a London debut in 1912, which attracted but little attention, he made a second, and this time triumphant, appearance in 1920, when he succeeded Moschovitz as Shylock in Fagan's revival of the *Merchant of Venice* at the Duke of York's Theatre. "That was a red-letter night in the annals of the London stage," said the dramatic critic of the London *Times*. "Bouwmeester came, saw, and conquered. The tragedian, speaking his native language, roused his English auditors to the highest pitch of excitement and enthusiasm. For a veteran of seventy-eight, the merely physical side of the enactment was astonishing. Bouwmeester presented the character uncompromisingly as a monster of revenge—guttural, croaking, blazing, quivering for his pound of flesh. The embodiment of malignity and cruelty, he spluttered, hissed, and raged. In the trial scene he crouched before Antonio, knife in hand, and, after the sentence, he staggered out dishevelled, laughing horribly. Undoubtedly here was a Shylock of renown."

No actor, nowadays, would play the part of Shylock as Bouwmeester conceived it. It was a melodramatic performance suited to the taste of the eighties and nineties of the past century. His success abroad was won when the style he embodied had gone out of fashion.

That his outmoded creation could still impress a postwar London audience is the stronger proof of his greatness. Every age erects hedges of preference and prejudice around the things it admires, but Bouwmeester, though both in space and time an outsider to the British playgoers of 1920, could transcend the barriers and demonstrate by his acting in a foreign speech the power of his art.

His style went out with him. He long survived the passing of its vogue. But he had the satisfaction, in his old age, of seeing the art of the stage in Holland restored to the high level it had occupied in the seventeenth century, and of seeing original Dutch drama restored to the stage, and, in the work of one author, acclaimed in foreign capitals. The restoration of dramatic art was the work of Willem Royaards, actor and stage manager; the successful playwright was Herman Heijermans.

Heijermans' debut occurred in the early nineties of the past century, when the nation was still obsessed by the sense of its dramatic impotence. The public had no confidence in its own playwrights, believing it impossible that any one of them could produce anything of sterling quality. Such scepticism foredoomed all original dramatic writing. Heijermans blamed upon it the cool reception of his first play. A few weeks after that initial failure, a sensational success was scored by the *première* of a play translated from the Russian. The day before, the papers had carried a news item about Ivan Jelakowitch, the unknown author of *Ahasverus*. This item supplied by an interested reader who claimed to have derived his information from an English literary magazine, disclosed that Jelakowitch was born on December 3, 1864, was the author of a satirical novel for which he had been thrown into prison and afterwards banished, and had died in abject poverty in the London slums.

The *premiere* made an enormous hit. *Ahasverus* had been written with tears, wrote a leading critic, and another went this one better by saying that the play had not been written, it had been lived. M. Antoine obtained the production rights in France for his *Théâtre Libre.* But in Paris the play was advertised as a translation from the Dutch by Herman Heijermans. Called to account for robbing the real author of his due credit, Heijermans took pleasure in confessing that he was the Russian Ivan Jelakowitch.

The thirty-year period following this mystification was one of feverish productivity. Heijermans rose to undisputed eminence among the playwrights of Holland. His popularity among his countrymen refuted the charge that Hollanders do not care for the stage. Outside of orthodox Calvinist circles he was warmly admired. When he died, the love the people bore him was apparent at his funeral; the entire route along which the procession passed through the streets of Amsterdam was lined by a dense crowd showing by reverent silence that they had come not for the spectacle but for a last tribute to their hero.

The secret of his popularity was in the intensely Dutch character of his plays. A fondness for the minute portrayal of reality akin to the art of the seventeenth-century genre painters and, coupled with it, a strong sense such as those painters had for the humorous and

farcical made the plays of this Jewish writer colorful
pictures of life in a style that was understood and admired as a truly native art. Among other features of his
work which may have contributed to the general applause it received, were the writer's tendency to cham-
pion the cause of the poor and the victims of our social
order and his manner of painting the contrast between
the underdog and his exploiter in consciously exaggerated colors; by themselves, these could scarcely have
accounted for his extraordinary vogue.

Heijermans' fame among his countrymen is a distinctly artistic triumph such as no social reformer could
have achieved. A social reformer he was and meant to
be, but he owed his success in that field, as Dickens in
the Victorian era, to the persuasive power of his art.
His play *The Good Hope* started in the early years of
this century an agitation for better Government supervision of seagoing craft which resulted in the Ships Act
of 1909; this Act provided much needed guarantees
against ships putting out to sea in unseaworthy condition. Plimsoll, in 1876, accomplished the same thing in
England by his advocacy in Parliament of a Merchant
Shipping bill, but the Dutch politicians had to wait for
the dramatist's voice to waken them to their duty. When
Heijermans died leaving his widow and two little children in straitened circumstances, the crews of Holland's
merchant marine contributed to a fund for their relief,
in recognition of the great service his powerful word
had rendered them and their families. That he was able
so to serve them was owing to his creative fancy, which,

under the strain of emotion, could mold a thing of beauty out of the ugly facts of life.

It takes a consummate playwright to make good drama out of matter that the reformer supplies, and even Heijermans' art was sometimes defeated by his missionary zeal. The hero in *Ghetto*, the rebellious son, bores the audience but does not convince it. If he had felt the pain of parting with orthodox traditions which his reason taught him to despise, the conflict within him between domestic piety and the call of social duty might have made him a tragic figure. But the conflict that we see is one between a son entirely estranged from his antecedents and a father in whom these antecedents are embodied. The picture of that Jewish home is drawn with an artist's loving attention to picturesque detail, and it is that milieu, not the young hero's phrases, that we remember as the essential beauty of the play. In *The Good Hope*, on the other hand, the reformer's purpose does not mar the artist's picture. The unmasking of the merciless shipowner who cares more for the premiums from the insurance companies than for the lives of the crews whom he sends to sea in rotten vessels has nothing to do with the play's persistent success. The playgoer of today sees in the shipowner not the embodiment of a wicked system, but a wicked man as there are wicked men among his victims. The author's triumph in creating a living character out of the symbol he intended his creature to be lifts this play from the mass of timely propaganda literature into the realm of timeless art.

It would be difficult to say to what extent foreign influences molded Heijermans' dramatic work. In his later years, during a protracted residence in Germany, he conceived a deep admiration for Gerhart Hauptmann, which may partly account for his turning from realistic to symbolical drama. But in the bulk of his work he does not appear to have been greatly dependent on literary models. Not literature but life was his source book. His mind was quick to perceive the dramatic possibilities in the most trifling incidents of everyday life and to project them, in picturesque transformation, upon the little world beyond the footlights. That facility proved sometimes a pitfall for his artistic conscience. Too often, also, he let his wit outrun his taste. But when time has winnowed the chaff, there will remain enough of lasting value to warrant classification of his work with the best of Dutch dramatic literature.

While Heijermans restored Dutch drama to the stage, Willem Royaards raised the actor's profession from a means of amusement to an art. His first start in life was in search of adventure in a wider field than the stage. He wore a midshipman's uniform before he dressed up for his first part in a play. The discipline that went with the uniform, however, robbed the adventurous life of its romance. He soon found that the stage behind the footlights promised him more adventure than the deck of a man-of-war. Had he remained on board, he might have become a popular commander, but he would never have achieved the fame that became his on the boards.

As an actor, he retained the sailor's love for a roving life. He tried to surmount the barriers of his native speech and to seek applause abroad. He obtained an engagement at Berlin, where he appeared in the role of Svengali, a successful performance which he subsequently repeated at St. Petersburg. From there he returned to Germany, where he played at Berlin, at Dresden, at Leipzig. From Germany he moved to Great Britain, but there he met with less applause, it would seem, as he was soon back again in Germany, playing under the direction of Max Reinhardt. However, realizing that he would never learn to speak German as perfectly as he did his native tongue, he returned to Holland. While resigning himself to the narrowing of his field of action, he conceived the ambition to rise to undisputed leadership within that narrow area. He would be the Max Reinhardt of Holland.

With irrepressible persistence he succeeded in persuading a number of patrons to furnish the capital needed for his dramatic venture. He called his new company *Het Tooneel* ("The Stage"), and gave his first performance at Amsterdam in September, 1908. Royaards loudly proclaimed his love for the Cinderella among the arts, and raised her from her low estate. He did not court her as an indulgent lover; on the contrary, he proved a severe taskmaster, enforcing among his company a discipline as strict as he would have maintained on shipboard. His profound respect for the poet's work would not allow an actor even the slightest departure from the context, nor would he suffer one of his players to outshine the rest of the cast and unbalance the drama's poise and proportion. Each had to be satisfied with being an organic part of the whole. His stage settings were in accord with this striving after unity of style. They remained subordinate to the act, the beauty achieved by the simplest lines and colors being a plastic accompaniment of the story.

His great services to the nation and the national stage were recognized by the University of Utrecht, which conferred on him the honorary degree of Doctor of Literature. I cannot help feeling that there is something presumptuous in the belief of a body of scholars that a great artist can be honored by being made one of their own. It would be more fitting for the organized actors to elect an eminent teacher of literature an honorary member of their guild, as an artist's creation is a thing of higher order than the learning of a university professor. But Royaards did not see it that way; he was pleased by his scholastic distinction.

In the early summer of 1923 Willem Royaards paid a visit to New York and made the round of its theaters. I had many a chat with him during those days and I treasure the letters that he sent me from the Plaza, where he was staying. In one of these he wrote, "On my return from Coldspring Harbor I received the news of the death of Louis Couperus. I have been miserably depressed ever since . . . Our generation born in the sixties is thinning considerably. Whose turn will come next?" He promised me before he sailed that he would come back the following year and give a recital for the Institute of Arts and Sciences at Columbia University. But he postponed that second visit from year to year, until it was too late. His turn came all too soon. He made his exit in January, 1929, leaving to his people the memory of a heroic part magnificently played and a stagecraft restored to the dignity of a major art.

[207]

The story of the decline and revival of Dutch music offers a close parallel to that of the stage. "The love of music is inborn in the Netherlanders," said Lodovico Guicciardini, the Italian merchant who was a resident of Antwerp, in his famous *Descrittione di tutti i Paesi Bassi.* "Here are the true masters of music, who have restored and perfected that art. For it is so native to them that men and women sing naturally to measure, with great charm and melody. And having joined art to nature, they make such demonstration and harmony with voices and all sorts of instruments as every one can see and hear and may be found in all the courts of Christian princes." That was written in 1566. The sixteenth century has been called the golden age in the history of music and much of its music is the work of Netherland composers. A list of their names is given by Guicciardini. It is long but not exhaustive, for he concludes it by saying, "and many other talented maestros, who are very famous and scattered all over the world in honorable positions and high stations."

The chief patrons of music in the Netherlands were the Church and the dukes of Burgundy. The revolt of the Dutch against both had, consequently, a fatal effect upon Netherlandish music. Since it was the foster child of Rome, the early Reformers, bent on destroying every vestige of popery, banned all music from their churches, and the establishment of the Dutch Republic severed the northern provinces, for good and all, from all contact with the ducal court at Brussels. The synod of the Dutch Reformed Church forbade the use of the organ and ordered its removal from all houses of worship. But the

Calvinist broth was, fortunately, not eaten as hot as the divines chose to serve it. In the Dutch Republic the medieval churches had become the property of the municipalities, and their merchant rulers, less austere and more worldly wise than the preachers, not only forbade the demolition of the organs but encouraged their use for public recreation and uplift, or, as the Leyden magistrates said in their instruction to the town organist, to keep the people, by means of his art, out of taverns and tap-rooms. And in 1641 Constantijn Huygens, poet, courtier, diplomat, and secretary to the Prince of Orange, published a plea for the use of the organ in the church service. His sensitive ear could not endure the cacophony of the congregation's singing of the psalms without instrumental accompaniment. "It was more like howling and screeching than singing," he wrote, "as if there were merit in outshouting one another and the loudest should carry off the prize."

His voice carried weight, for not only was he the confidant of the Prince of Orange, but also a faithful member of the Church whose orthodoxy could not be impugned. Organ music was gradually reinstated everywhere as an essential part of the service, but exclusively for the accompaniment of the psalm singing. Beyond that not even Huygens, who was himself a composer of no mean talent, would allow its wider use for secular music. He was as bitterly opposed to "the frivolous evening organ recitals" which were given in many cities by order of the burgomasters as were the ministers of the Church. "For one psalm that the organist played at those evening concerts, he gave ten madrigals and lighter tunes such as one could not mention in church without giving offense." We should not dream of holding banquets in church, he argued, and what is the difference between feasting our tongues or our ears?

The orthodox, therefore, stayed away from these ear-alluring frivolities. They attracted chiefly the patriciate, the class of highly educated merchants, who spoke foreign languages and admired the manners and the music of Paris and Rome. The lower classes, always inclined to follow the ministers rather than the burgomasters, found in abstention an easy way of demonstrating their piety. Secular music became the exclusive recreation of the upper ten. Jan Pietersz. Sweelinck, the last in the long procession of Dutch composers—he died in 1621—published collections of his songs with dedications written in French to wealthy Amsterdam patrons. The poems that he set to music were Latin, French, or Italian lyrics. Even the four books of his psalms were printed with the text in French.

Music lovers in Holland were ladies and gentlemen who had a snobbish contempt for the songless masses. They fostered the cult of music at home, and formed ensembles that made music for the delectation of friends and social equals. You see such trios and quartets portrayed in many a genre picture of the Dutch school. But while the leisure class played their instruments in drawing rooms, the masses were musically starving. Sweelinck's compositions never reached them. His instrumental music was being copied among his admirers in the upper strata but remained inaccessible to a wider audience. These manuscripts were scattered all over

Europe. When interest in his work was revived toward the end of the nineteenth century, enough was recovered from under the dust of archives to fill ten volumes. But their preservation was due to foreign collectors. In Sweelinck's fatherland there was none to be found.

The nation as a whole, kept intentionally unschooled and systematically discouraged from playing and singing, was like a barren ground from which no talent could spring. The topsoil that was still being tended was too thin a layer to yield a crop with each new generation. After Sweelinck's death Dutch music fell into a decline that lasted until the twentieth century. The art which the early Reformers forswore took its revenge by denying itself to their posterity.

The revival began in the nineties of the past century. Willem Mengelberg, as leader of the Amsterdam Concertgebouw orchestra, was the driving force in the process of regeneration. When he took charge of the Amsterdam orchestra, he found an audience that had been disciplined by his predecessor Willem Kes. The subscribers to the concerts had been taught reverence such as they would render in church to the word of God. Late-comers were no longer admitted while the orchestra was playing and had learnt to submit without protest to their exclusion until the next interval. Private conversations were no longer carried on during the music, for Mr. Kes had shamed the disturbers into silence by suddenly halting the orchestra, turning round to stare in the direction of the whispering voices, and centering the indignant attention of the entire audience upon the embarrassed culprits. Hence the chief task that was left for

Mr. Mengelberg was to educate his audiences to a more discriminating appreciation of music and to stimulate the demand for it all over Holland.

In this he has been successful beyond the most optimistic predictions of a generation ago. Holland, with a population only a little larger than that of New York City, has almost as many municipal orchestras as the entire United States. The Hague, Utrecht, and Rotterdam possess orchestras that are supported by private donations, and thanks to official initiative municipal orchestras have been formed at Haarlem, Arnhem, Maastricht, and Groningen. Dutch music lovers—and they far outnumber the stage fans—are now intimately familiar not only with the great classics of German, French, and Russian music, but also with the works of Mahler, Schönberg, Debussy, Ravel, Dukas, Pierné, Milhaud, Stravinsky.

They know these better than they do their own composers. The disbelief in native talent that thwarted the creative work of Dutch playwrights is also discouraging Dutch writers of music. Nine generations of sterility have fixed in the people's minds a belief that the nation lacks the genius for musical composition. They have now learned to admire their orchestras and to realize that the reproduction of foreign music has attained a high standard in the Netherlands. They acclaim their native singers and concert soloists and fete Willem Mengelberg every time he comes home from a triumphal tour abroad. But the traditional disbelief in the creative power of their own composers had made them deaf to the excellence of modern Dutch music. The Amsterdam Concertgebouw introduced native works to its audience, but the cool reception discouraged the repetition of such attempts. The Utrecht orchestra, under the conductorship of Wouter Hutschenruyter, was more persistent, and did much, during the first two decades of this century, to convert the connoisseurs from their scepticism. At present the Rotterdam orchestra under Eduard Flipse is the chief exponent of the latest Dutch compositions. Since these concerts may be heard over the radio, modern native music is now entering the homes of the many music lovers who stay away from the concert hall and is winning admirers in ever widening circles.

In the recent past a Hollander could not expect to gain recognition at home until his work had won applause in Paris or in Germany. If the foreigner admired it, it must surely be good. But this yielding of the critical dictum to the foreign audience is no longer so common as it used to be. The nation is becoming musically self-conscious. Zweers, Diepenbrock, and Wagenaar, who were in the forefront of the musical revival around 1900, have attained the rank of classics, and the generation of composers born in the seventies and eighties of the past century, Dopper, Ingenhoven, Landré, are gaining in stature in the esteem of their compatriots. Among a crowd of still younger men Willem Pijper, H. Andriessen, and Badings appear to be taking the lead. "Their work shows a tendency to seek inspiration from the great polyphonists of the early Dutch school, to recapture its contrapuntal tradition," says Sem Dresden, Director of the Royal Conservatoire at The Hague. "That is not to say that they have remained aloof from the harmonic and rhythmic evolution of the present day. On the contrary, their harmonic language is audacious, polymetry is incorporated with their music. But these natives of a land perpetually enveloped in a grey mist do not write atonal music. They avoid such excesses. Their work is distinguished by great originality, foreign influences counting for little in their writings."

In music, as in drama, the Hollanders have subdued their inferiority complex. Their present achievements in both fields bear comparison with the best they produced three centuries and more ago.

Chapter XIV

ST. LUKE'S CRAFTSMEN

ST. LUKE is the patron saint of painters' guilds. There is nothing in his gospel that can account for his election to that honor. An early Christian legend, of obscure origin, will have it that he painted a portrait of the Virgin. The Madonna posing for the Evangelist was consequently a favorite theme of medieval artists. Such pictures were destined to adorn the altar which the painters' guild erected to its guardian in one of the local churches.

The guilds in the Netherlands survived the Reformation. But they no longer dedicated altars to their patron. The subject of St. Luke painting our Lady went out of vogue with the people but remained popular with the artists. They found a way of circumventing the Calvinist objection to the theme. It was transformed into a domestic genre piece, the artist substituting himself for the Evangelist and a lady customer for the Virgin. Johannes Vermeer, Michiel van Musscher, Frans van Mieris, and many a lesser master thus portrayed themselves at work in their studios.

Such pictures are valuable documents for the art historian. They show us how little the painter's craft has

changed since the days of Johannes Vermeer. In this
mechanized world the artist is the only craftsman who
still works miracles with his hands, unaided by machinery. In one small detail he has given in to the modern
trend: the old masters ground their paints themselves,
the moderns are generally content to buy them ready
made in tubes. Otherwise there is no break in the tradition. That makes an artist's workshop such a fascinating
place to visit. Coming out of the subway rush and the
tangled traffic of honking motor cars and trucks, one
finds, on entering the studio, peace and serenity, in which
inspired hands perform their still, mysterious labor.

Some years ago, when the technocracy craze had
supplanted the ouija board, Forrest Davis contributed
a clever article to the *Evening World*, in which he expressed his concern for the fate of. artists in the new era
that was promised us by Howard Scott. Would an
industrial state dispense with artists? he asked, or would
some method be found by which to modify the principles of production? Could painters, for example, be
supplied with a technique of mass production, standing
in rows alongside a conveyor, each adding a bit, his
specialty, to the moving landscape?

The suggestion was not so novel as Forrest Davis
imagined. Carel van Mander, who in the early seventeenth century wrote the *Lives of the Dutch Painters*
of a still earlier day, tells that a sixteenth-century artist
called Pieter Vlerick was employed as a young painter
in the studio of a Mechelen master, who produced
painted imitations of tapestries in distemper. His canvases were the products of joint craftsmanship, one

assistant painting heads and hands, another draperies, a third the landscape, while Pieter Vlerick specialized in architectural detail. Here was a case of mass production of art; only the conveying easel was missing.

Rubens also ran a workshop that turned out pictures wholesale, though his manner of production differed from the method of the Mechelen tapestry painters. Dr. Otto Sperling, a Danish physician who visited his Antwerp studio, left a description of it in his autobiography. "We entered a spacious room, which had no windows in the walls but a large skylight in the centre of the ceiling. Many young painters were seated there in front of their easels, each at work on a canvas on which the master had sketched a composition and indicated the color scheme with dashes of paint. The young assistants completed the pictures according to these directions, whereupon Rubens himself added the finishing touch with a few strokes of the brush." These marked them as genuine products of the Rubens workshop. By thus turning out potboilers at small expense of time and effort to himself, he saved his energy for the execution of gigantic masterpieces which he could honestly claim for his own.

Popular portrait painters of that same period employed assistants to paint in backgrounds, draperies, and details of costume, their own contribution to the picture being limited to the heads and hands. The famous master Michiel Janszoon van Mierevelt was thus assisted by five skilful artists, among whom were his two sons and a grandson. They specialized in portraits of the Princes of Orange, for which there was a ready sale among wealthy Dutch patriots.

Such collaboration was a survival of the days when the art of painting was counted among the handicrafts and valued for the precious things it could produce, no matter how and by whom these were executed. One paid for the beauty of the thing, not for the master's signature as a guarantee of its beauty. Hence the buying public saw nothing reprehensible in the master's delegating part of his task to able helpers. The elder Van Mierevelt used to mark the pictures that he had done unassisted with the words *door mij zelven geschilderd* ("painted by myself"), implying that paintings bearing his signature were the products of his communal workshop.

By the end of the seventeenth century, however, Dutch notions as to the propriety of joint craftsmanship in art production seem to have changed. This may be concluded from a remark by Houbraken in his sketch of the life and career of Godfrey Kneller, the fashionable court painter of King Charles and his three successors. "Kneller's portraits," he wrote, "differ widely in value, owing to the fact that the painters he employed at different times were not equally skilful, some being more capable in imitating his manner than others. For they consider it proper in England that the masters paint only the faces and hands and leave the costumes and other details to assistants. But in Holland such a procedure would not pass muster."

Was it fortuitous that this change in opinion coincided with the decline of Dutch art? When pictures became the making of artists, artists could no longer afford to collaborate in the making of pictures. Joint devotion of the craft gave way to a scramble for individual distinction, and big prices were paid not for beautiful paintings but for signatures of celebrities.

The bulk of early Dutch art is anonymous. Few signatures or monograms aid the historian in ascertaining authorship. The primitive painters of the Netherlands were craftsmen pure and simple, to whom their art was a means of earning a living, not a road to posthumous fame. Margaret of Savoy, aunt of Charles V and ruler over the Netherlands during his absence from the Low Countries, possessed a valuable art collection in her palace at Malines. In 1516 she wrote with her own hand an inventory of her treasures. The only artists of the fifteenth century who are mentioned by name in this list are Le Maistre Hans (by which she meant Memlinc), Jheronimus Bosch, and Dirck, that is, Dirck Bouts. A second list compiled seven years later omits even these few names. Instead, it mentions two living artists, Mabuse and Maistre Conrad, that is, Conrad Meyt, Margaret's court sculptor. The early sixteenth-century collectors looked at pictures and overlooked signatures. They knew less about the primitive painters than the modern art historians who, aided by the archivists, have discovered facts about the lives of these artists which their contemporaries did not care to know.

Primitive painters is a misleading term. It describes not the naïveté of their art, but the insufficiency of our knowledge, for it only means that we know little of their predecessors and that to us their art is the beginning of Dutch painting. But in reality it was the full blossom of a long growth, whose earlier phases are veiled in obscurity. We know more, though, at present than was known at the time when the name primitives came into vogue, and a modern history of Dutch painting will take the reader back to a starting point two centuries and more beyond the age of Jan van Eyck.

Illuminators of manuscripts were the precursors of the primitives, whose works, painted on panel, remained subservient to poetry and fiction. They were illustrators not from choice but from necessity, for they were dependent on patrons whose demand was for illustration of literature. These patrons included the Church, from which came orders for murals and altar pieces; the secular powers, who ordered historical or mythological paintings for the decoration of court room and council chamber; and wealthy noblemen and burghers, who commissioned triptychs portraying the martyrdom of their patron saints and showing the donors kneeling with their offspring. As illustrators of Biblical scenes, of secular history, and legends of the saints, the primitives belonged to a craft that might justly be called the younger sister of poetry. But the younger sister was apt to resent the older sister's guardianship. She found a way of pleasing herself while seemingly obeying her senior's lead. The so-called primitives of the Dutch school, when they executed orders for a holy family, a scene from the passion, or the martyrdom of a saint, placed the action of the figures in a realistic Dutch setting, and crowded the scene with many accessory details, in the painting

[220]

of which they could give vent to their love of the picturesqueness of everyday life.

A Portuguese painter, Francesco de Holanda, wrote
in the early sixteenth century a collection of aesthetic
speculations, which he put into the form of dialogues
with Michelangelo. In these the Italian master found
fault with the manner of the Dutch primitives who
"tried to paint many things together in their full beauty
of which one alone is important enough to engage all
one's talent in its portrayal." Michelangelo, enamored
of the heroic, and therefore conscious of his kinship with
the poets, could not appreciate the reasons that made the
Dutch painters overcrowd their scenes. It was for them
an escape from what they felt, unconsciously, perhaps,
to be the dictatorship of literary art. They sought refuge
from the impositions of foreign fiction in the loved and
admired reality of their own milieu.

In the sixteenth century it became the fashion for
young Dutch painters to go to Italy for their schooling,
and many of those who went came back converted to
the Italian conception of the heroic as the proper subject for the painter's art. Rubens is the chief representative of that Italianized school. But the stay-at-homes did
better. They disarmed Michelangelo's criticism of the
overcrowded scene by breaking it up into its component
parts. The frame of the open window giving a glimpse
of the market place in an interior of a Flemish primitive
was lifted out of the picture and became the picture
frame round a view of city architecture. The landscape,
originally background to a scene of human activity,
gradually took preëminence over that scene, reducing

it to a mere decorative device or accessory to itself, until finally even the accessory faded into nothing and left the landscape bare of all but its own loveliness. The portrait of the wealthy burgher, who posed for the early painter amid the trappings of his trade or profession, stands out on Rembrandt's canvases against a mysterious darkness, which compels the beholder's entire interest toward the face, and the trappings—the scholar's pile of books, the treasures of the goldsmith, the paraphernalia of the alchemist, the vase of lilies in a scene of the Annunciation—were given an importance of their own in the exquisite still-life scenes of Rembrandt's contemporaries. In this way the Dutch created new genres by revealing the paintableness of the simplest and homeliest, even of the ugly, things of life. In other words, the painter became, from a mere illustrator and follower of the poet, a pioneer in new realms of unsuspected beauty, where the poet, reluctantly at first, was tempted to follow him.

Brueghel, Avercamp, Van der Neer, and many other lesser painters, made landscapes of the four seasons of the year, a genre developed from the medieval books of hours, in which miniatures depicted various human activities from month to month. But to them the landscape had become the chief concern and man at work or at play merely a means of enlivening the scene. A century later James Thomson brought out his *Seasons*, which has been praised for inaugurating something new in literature because the role of man in the landscapes described is incidental, being introduced only so far as it forms a telling feature of the scenery. "It is Thomson's peculiarity," says the *Cambridge History of English Literature*, "that the description of natural phenomena, in an age which overlooked their artistic value, was his chief concern." But it had not been overlooked in the preceding age by the landscape painters of the Dutch school. Again, at a time when literature was still incapable of sensing the beauty of nature except as a setting for a pastoral idyll, Jacob van Ruysdael and Allart van Everdingen painted mountain scenery of forbidding grandeur. Europe had to wait until the age of Rousseau for literature to become aware of the beauty that these Dutch painters discovered in scenery of awe-inspiring solitude.

The discovery of beauty in an unidyllic landscape was only one of similar achievements of the Dutch school of painting. There was hardly any aspect of life that their inquisitive eyes did not detect to be paintable. This is, indeed, the great achievement of Dutch art that it has demonstrated the fallacy of the common belief that the beauty of a picture is due to something inherent in the subject portrayed.

It took a long time for poetry to accept the lesson. The eighteenth century remained impervious to it. Not until Wordsworth wrote of his *Lyrical Ballads* that "the feeling therein developed gave importance to the action and situation, and not the action and situation to the feeling," did poetry formulate what the Dutch painters had shown to be true. Lessing never saw the light. He tells his readers, on the authority of Pliny, that wealthy collectors in ancient Greece paid huge sums for pictures by the artist Pyreicos, who painted barber shops, dirty

workshops, donkeys, and vegetables with all the industry of a Dutch painter, as if these possessed some charm
and were rarely to be seen; and he adds with approval
that this misguided man of talent was given the nickname of Rhyparographos or Painter of Filth. But this
painter of filth was no doubt one of those explorers who
taught people to see beauty where they had never seen
it before. Says Browning's Fra Lippo Lippi,

> We're made so that we love
> First when we see them painted, things we have passed
> Perhaps a thousand times nor cared to see.

Beauty is omnipresent and surrenders itself to the genius
of the artist who discovers it. An historical picture on
a large scale by an Italian master may fascinate us more
than the portrait of a homely burgher or a still-life scene
of fish or fruit or a pile of books, but its greater fascina-
tion results from its appeal to our intellect, which reads
a story in the painting, and not from a sense of its greater
beauty.

Unconsciously the painters of seventeenth-century
Holland understood this elementary truth. They did not
theorize about their art, but they did what they intui-
tively felt was the right thing for them to do: to paint
their own life, no matter how simple and homely, as
they saw it. To them nothing was unworthy of their
loving observation. They discovered the beautiful even
in the ugly. Jan Steen did not love drunken riots because he loved debauch, but because he loved life in
all its manifestations. If Rembrandt was the interpreter
of the highest and best that lives in the race from which

he sprang, Jan Steen's *oeuvre* is the expression of the people's healthy joy of living. They represent two sides of one nature, just as idealism is embodied in Don Quixote and materialism in Sancho Pancha.

The seventeenth century was followed by a period of decline. The painters of the eighteenth and early nineteenth centuries kept up the tradition in the choice of their subjects, but their workmanship lacks that instinct for truth which was the secret of the older masters. But about 1850 Dutch art revived in the works of the Hague School. Josef Israels, Johannes Bosboom, the brothers Maris, Anton Mauve were realists like the old masters, but reality affected them in a different way. Their predecessors were enamored of the outward show of life and reflected it in their work with all its picturesqueness of detail. But the paintings of the Hague School render the mood or the sentiment that pervades the scene. Emanuel de Witte's church interiors are beautiful studies of architecture, Bosboom is the painter of reverie and reverence under the vaulted roofs of the aisles. In the old genre picture the figures merely pose, the poor as Israels painted them are workers and sufferers. He was the painter of human toil and sorrow. The landscapists of the Hague School did not paint trees and cattle and windmills, they painted the sunlight, the silvery morning haze, the shadow of the clouds, and their effects upon mills, cattle, and trees. The street scenes of the Berckheydes are historical documents precious to the student of Holland's past though he may care little for art. But, beautiful though they are, life is lacking in those pictures; they strike one as stage sets revealed to view at the raising of the curtain before the action of the play has yet begun. Breitner, on the other hand, painted Amsterdam alive, a moody city susceptible to fits of depression and gloom. Rembrandt alone among the artists of the seventeenth century was more than a recorder, being, like these later painters, an interpreter of life. And it was in him that they recognized their master.

The Dutch painter's detection of beauty in the commonplace is not like the discovery of unknown land, which thereafter has its immovable location on the map. The artist who finds it recreates it for once on his canvas, and each successor must rediscover it for himself and transform it in his own way into a work of art. Creative talent, however, is rare, and the members of the painting craft are many. The bane of each movement is the host of its soulless followers, who do mechanically what the leaders do creatively. Everyday reality is being represented wholesale by painters who do not invent new beauty but simply reproduce subject matter that their betters discovered to be beautiful and re-created into art. The naturalistic novelist follows suit. "Little obviousnesses," says Aldous Huxley, "fill (at a moderate computation) quite half of the great majority of contemporary novels, stories, and films. The great public derives an extraordinary pleasure from the mere recognition of familiar objects and circumstances." To the novelist, though, man and the life of man remain the center of interest, whereas to the painter inanimate things are of no less importance; the light that falls upon his subject is of chief concern, not the passions of the human heart.

I remember reading an essay by Aldous Huxley in which he made the remark that in modern fiction art is apparently tabooed. He cites as an instance Hemingway's *Farewell to Arms*, in which there is one reference to painting, but it is made almost shamefacedly, as if the author was conscious of mentioning a forbidden subject. Huxley sees in this a symptom of vulgar snobbism that affects to be afraid of all high-brow discussion. I believe the explanation lies elsewhere. The painter and poet have lost touch with each other. Naturalistic fiction lives by insight, impressionistic painting lives by sight only. In an age that has been taught by Freud to spy and grope into the recesses of the subconscious, an art that shows nothing but the obvious can hardly appeal to the poet.

Expressionistic painting is the natural reaction to the impressionist's cult of the obvious. In *Old Pictures in Florence*, Browning speaks of the early Italian painters as in revolt against Greek art and fired by one ambition:

> to become selfacquainters,
> And paint man man, whatever the issue,
> Make new hopes shine through the flesh they fray,
> New fears aggrandize the rags and tatters:
> To bring the invisible full into play!
> Let the visible go to the dogs—what matters?

To paint the invisible is also the aim of the expressionists. A landscape by Isaac Israels is the reproduction of a moment's visual impression, a landscape by Van Gogh is the reflection of a state of mind. The representation of nature means little to the expressionist. He strives to apprehend the essential reality below the surface, and to express in aesthetic form the emotions astir within himself. Thus, art, in its most recent development, has come closer to her older sister poetry by forsaking the sole guidance of the eye for the promptings of the subconscious self.

The abstractions produced by these modern self-acquainters are so hyperindividualistic that the circle of responsive souls who honestly grasp what they mean has dwindled to a few intimates. Is this art not out of step with the trend of the present, which is away from individualism and toward socialism? The cult of the ego was characteristic of the period that divides our time from the Middle Ages. Our surrealists are not pioneers of a new art. They are the last survivors of an era that is passing, and their work, which suffers from hypertrophy of the ego, is a reduction to absurdity of the ego cult inaugurated by the Renaissance. They show themselves followers along a beaten track, instead of blazers of new trails, by producing pictures enclosed in frames. These are evidently intended as wall decoration. But this is an old-fashioned notion dictated by that same tradition which the surrealists claim to abhor. Look at our modern architecture: walls of glass admitting a maximum of light and reducing the space in which paintings may be hung, are a striking feature of its latest development. Furthermore, the beautiful wall surfaces and coverings produced by modern techniques tend to discourage the superposition of canvases and painted panels. The heyday of the picture painter is over. The artist will have to adjust his production to the requirements of a new age. He is losing a patron in the individual collector. His patron of the future will be organized industry. The true modernist is that artist who, far from trying to startle the public by the cryptic abstractions of his subconscious self, is willing to merge his personality in collaboration with the engineer and the architect under the unified control of a master builder.

Chapter XV

RESPECT FOR THE PAST

IN MY YOUNG DAYS the Rijksmuseum, now in the center of the metropolis, stood at the edge of a green sea of waving grass. I was only a little boy when the National Gallery of the Netherlands was opened with great ceremony by J. Heemskerk, the Minister of Home Affairs, but I clearly remember the excitement and the festive aspect of the city, bedecked with the national colors for the occasion.

I knew nothing of Mr. Heemskerk and, had I been told his title, would have denied that his affairs had anything to do with the home. But I did know the importance of the edifice that was opened to the nation on that day. I had heard grown-ups discuss the style of the architect's creation, which left no one indifferent. As Berlage's Amsterdam Exchange was to do a generation later, it aroused ardent admirers and indignant critics. "Looks like a medieval monastery," sneered the faultfinders. "A bold break with dull tradition," said the enthusiasts. The pioneer who had conceived this neo-medieval building was P. J. H. Cuypers, a pupil of Viollet-le-Duc. His style, inspired by the Gothic and the Netherland architecture of the sixteenth century,

[230]

reconciled medieval conceptions with the practical demands of modern life.

It cannot be denied that the paintings of seventeenth-century Holland look somewhat out of place on the walls of this art cathedral. Johannes Vermeer and Pieter de Hooghe have painted the sober dignity of the Calvinist Hollander's home, which is alien to this pre-Reformation atmosphere. But the art of the Netherlands is not restricted to one period. The iconoclasts, unfortunately, destroyed a great deal of the treasures produced by the artists of the fifteenth and early sixteenth centuries, but enough has been saved to fill part of the wall space in the Rijksmuseum, and for the works of painters such as Jan van Eyck, Roger van der Weyden, Dirck Bouts, and Petrus Christus the National Gallery that Cuypers built is an ideal setting. A museum that must house the treasures of a nation's creative efforts through the ages cannot possibly be in harmony with the spirit of each successive age.

- The plan for a Gallery that would contain all the art treasures of the Netherland nation was, strange to say, first conceived by a ruler of foreign birth. Louis Napoleon, who was made King of Holland by his brother the Emperor in the year 1806, chose for his royal residence the City Hall of Amsterdam, and by decree of April 21, 1808, he ordered the establishment in his new palace of a "Great Royal Museum destined to become a storehouse of paintings, drawings, sculpture, cameos, antiquities, and various other objects of art." Its beginnings were modest. Five rooms in the former City Hall were set aside for the collection, which included from the start Rembrandt's *Nightwatch* and his *Syndics*, both the property of the city of Amsterdam. During the four years of Louis Napoleon's reign valuable additions were made to the new museum by the purchase of private collections. In 1809 the Van Heteren Cabinet of one hundred and thirty-seven paintings was acquired for the sum of $25,000. It included the famous *St. Nicholas Eve* by Jan Steen, which alone may now be worth fifty times that amount.

After the King's abdication in 1810, the city of Amsterdam was made responsible for the upkeep of the Hollandsch Museum, as it was officially called, and the municipal government was authorized to increase by ten percent the local taxes for this purpose. In 1815 the collection was removed to a patrician mansion called the "Trippenhuis" on the Kloveniersburgwal. The house took its name from the original owners, the brothers Louis and Hendrik Trip, two seventeenth-century capitalists who had made a fortune as gun founders and dealers in ammunition. There the pictures remained until the opening of the Rijksmuseum in 1885.

I still remember being taken by my father to the Trippenhuis and getting my first impression of Rembrandt's *Nightwatch*. The building was at the same time the headquarters of the Royal Academy of Sciences, whose members met once a fortnight among the masterpieces of the Dutch school. The smoke of their churchwarden pipes must in the course of years have covered the canvases and panels with a misty film that eclipsed both color and design. The house was not fireproof and was surrounded by warehouses in which inflammable goods were stored. The walls became more and more crowded as fresh additions came in through purchase and bequest. Warnings and complaints at last aroused the citizens of Amsterdam to a realization of the danger to which the treasures of nation and city were exposed. In 1862 a committee was formed for the drafting of plans for a new museum. But ten years later nothing had as yet been accomplished. In 1872, however, the Second Chamber passed an amendment to the budget to the effect that the foundation of a National Gallery was the task of the central Government, and should not be left to private initiative or to the enterprise of Amsterdam. Thereupon this city pledged itself to contribute the land and a subsidy of $25,000, and to loan to the new art home the paintings in its possession. Cuypers started work in 1876, and nine years later the Rijksmuseum was inaugurated.

Amsterdam has taken better care of the art collection within its walls than of the old City Hall in which that collection had its modest beginning. After Louis Napoleon's abdication, the building was never reoccupied by the city government, which nevertheless considered itself the rightful owner. A dozen years ago the question of ownership became a matter of controversy between the central Government at The Hague and the City Fathers. This royal residence belongs to the State, said the former. The building belongs to the city, retorted the City Council; it has only been loaned to the State. One of the members of the Council proposed in 1926 that Amsterdam should cancel the loan and recover possession of its property. A committee of learned historians and jurists was appointed to find out which of the two was the actual owner, and their unanimous verdict fully confirmed the city's claim.

How was it possible for a building of such importance to lose track of its rightful owner? There never was any doubt as to whose it had been originally. Amsterdam built it for a City Hall, Amsterdam's money had paid for the costly structure, Amsterdam artists, in the service of the burgomasters, had adorned it with paintings and sculpture, the Amsterdam government had resided under its roof for a period of one hundred and fifty years. But when King Louis Napoleon made Amsterdam the capital of his realm, the city had to pay for this distinction by the cession of its City Hall, which the new King claimed for himself as a palace.

The municipal government removed its headquarters to the Prinsenhof, an old building which, in the days of the Republic, had been used for the reception of honorable guests of the city. It stood on a narrow canal, the Fluweelen Burgwal or "Velvet Moat," so called from the rich burghers clad in velvet who used to live there in earlier days. But Amsterdam had since expanded toward the south and built a triple girdle of more stately canals, which became the residential section of the city. The Fluweelen Burgwal, in the nineteenth century, had become one of the backwaters of the metropolis. No wonder, therefore, that the people resented the removal of their government to a neighborhood that had known better days. They cared but little for the King's choice of Amsterdam as his capital; they would rather he had lived elsewhere than that they should lose the old City Hall, symbol of Amsterdam's greatness.

The city's playgoers, one evening, had an opportunity of expressing their injured feelings, when the municipal theater produced a dramatization of the popular story of the miller of Sans-Souci. Frederick II, King of Prussia, annoyed by the incessant din and whir of a windmill near his rural retreat at Potsdam, summoned the miller before him and offered a big sum for the mill. But the fellow would not sell. His grandfather and father had lived and died there and he intended to die there too. He refused to part with the family property. The King was not accustomed to seeing his wishes thus naïvely treated as wishes. Did the fellow not realize that the King's wishes were commands? If he did not obey, that nuisance of a mill would be demolished. "Your Majesty forgets that there is such a thing as a Court of Justice," was the miller's reply. King Frederick saw the aptness of the retort and decided that the wisest course for him to take was to shut his ears to the whir of the sails. And the mill still stands where it stood, a monument to the miller's blunt honesty.

It was no accident that this play was chosen for production on the evening of February 13, 1808, the year in which the building on the Dam changed occupants. The audience perceived the analogy between the mill and the City Hall, and loudly applauded the miller when in his uncouth speech he voiced the outraged feelings of the citizenry. But the miller on the stage was less successful than his Potsdam prototype. King Louis had his way, after all, and the City Hall, having been turned into a residence for His Majesty, remained in use as a Royal Palace when, after the fall of the Bonapartes, the Prince of Orange was made King of the Netherlands.

To say, as I did just now, that the building has remained in use is to speak euphemistically. The use that Queen Wilhelmina makes of her city palace is limited to one week a year, when, in April, Her Majesty pays her annual visit to Amsterdam, an honor to which the city is entitled in virtue of its still being the nominal capital of the Kingdom. The rest of the year, during fifty-one weeks, the palace stands empty and lifeless, its eyes shut to the life of the city around it, a mummified relic of the past devoid of usefulness and purpose. It is an offensive sight to the citizens, this dead colossus throwing its shadow across the chief public square in the original center of the city. They would like to see it restored to its former dignity and made serviceable again to the municipal government as an official home, where the burgomaster would have his office, where the Council could meet, and where the city could offer a ceremonious welcome to royal visitors and other worshipful guests of Amsterdam. The seventeenth-century building could not house all the offices of the various departments of administration into which the city management has ramified. Those could remain in the old Prinsenhof or wherever they are now established. But the royal palace would eminently serve the same kind of purpose to which New York has turned its decorative City Hall. That is what the Councilor had in mind who moved, in 1926, that the city cancel the loan of the palace to the State.

But had the building been loaned? That question had first to be settled. The committee of experts found that, after the collapse of Napoleon's Empire, King William I, yielding to the wishes of the citizens of Amsterdam, had returned Louis Napoleon's palace to the city without binding this act of restitution to any condition whatsoever. He only expressed a wish that some apartments might be reserved for his use whenever he should pay a visit to the city. King William intended to come oftener to Amsterdam than his great-granddaughter cares to do. In the past Amsterdam had repeatedly been the leader of the anti-Orange faction in the Republic, and the Prince of Orange, now raised to the dignity of King of the Netherlands, was anxious to enter upon his reign assured of the support and loyalty of the metropolis. The city government, appreciating the King's expressed intention of honoring Amsterdam with his royal presence at regular intervals, offered the provisional use of the entire building to His Majesty, following a vote to that effect of the City Council of January 28, 1814. This provisional arrangement became in course of time so firmly established that the manner in which it came about was entirely forgotten and the authorities at The Hague came to regard the palace on the Dam as State property.

The central Government accepted the findings of the experts as conclusive. But it did not admit that reoccupation by the city must follow as a matter of course. It addressed a note to the government of Amsterdam, offering to the city the State's collaboration for the erection of a new City Hall, on condition that the palace on the Dam be ceded to the State. The burgomaster and aldermen were inclined to accede to this proopsal. They submitted to the City Council the draft of a contract to be concluded with the State, under which the city would turn over, free of charge, its former City Hall, in exchange for the State's financial aid in the building of a new City Hail, to which the central Government would contribute up to a maximum of fifteen million guilders.

The citizenship felt grieved and disappointed by this action of the burgomaster and aldermen. They never suspected that this barter would result from the committee's findings, which they had hailed as a signal victory for Amsterdam. To them it was not a matter of fifteen millions that was at stake, the city's honor was involved. If Amsterdam should need a new City Hall, it would be able to build one without State support. But that was not what Amsterdam needed. It wanted its old City Hall back, because in it the people saw the palladium of their city's dignity and greatness. The municipal government, until the days of national disgrace under Napoleon's rule, had always resided on the Dam, the public square that was the hub round which civic life revolved. When the present palace was built in the middle of the seventeenth century, it was erected on the very same spot on which the old Stadhuis had stood. That spot has been hallowed by tradition; no other place in the city could vie with it in wealth of historical associations. The people of Amsterdam would like to see their government return to that spot. They wanted the dead palace revitalized into the busy Stadhuis for which it was intended. The place which the burgomaster and aldermen had chosen for the new City Hall was in a part of the city that was developed in the nineteenth century. No memories that could awaken civic pride attached to the spot. As a native of Amsterdam I shall be sorry to see Amsterdam's government move thither in order to enable its rightful residence to continue a mummified existence on the Dam.

That the Royal Palace on the Dam has ceased to be a home is proved by its inclusion in the official guide to the Netherland museums, a publication of the Ministry of Education, Arts, and Sciences. This useful little book contains in brief outline information on the whereabouts of the country's museums,[1] the hours of admission, the dates of their founding, the nature of the exhibits, publications concerning them, and the average number of visitors per year. A table at the end gives an instructive survey of the steady increase in the number of museums. Only nineteen collections date back to a period prior to the nineteenth century. In the years from 1800 to 1875 thirty-two were added to that original number, the last quarter of that century witnessed an increase of thirty, in the first two decades of this century fifty-one museums were established, and in the past eighteen years no fewer than one hundred and seventeen new ones opened their doors to the public.

They are to be found in the most unexpected places, in small villages that even most Hollanders have never heard of, in churches, almshouses, hospitals, schools, town halls, and private homes. Private collections, however, must be open to the public, otherwise the Nether-

---

[1] *De Nederlandsche Musea: Uitgegeven vanwege het Departement van Onderwijs, Kunsten en Wetenschappen* (The Hague, 1938).

land Ministry does not recognize them as museums. The Ministry defines a museum as "a collection which, either in its entirety or in part, is on permanent exhibition for the public benefit and accessible to visitors at stated intervals or upon request, either for a fee of admission or gratuitously." The *New English Dictionary* omits accessibility to the public from its more elaborate definition. But I agree with the editor of the Netherland Ministry's museum manual that this constitutes the essential character of what is called a museum.

Prior to the nineteenth century, collectors of books, pictures, curios, and *objets d'art* were wealthy capitalists, not the State or the municipalities. Holland in the eighteenth century was rich in private collections. Proud owners were always glad to show them to connoisseurs who came with reliable credentials, but callers were not admitted indiscriminately. The current name for such a private treasure house was not museum but cabinet. The small nucleus was first locked up in a cabinet, and though the collection might outgrow its space, gradually overflowing into several cabinets and finally filling the house from attic to cellar, it retained the name of its original depository. The word is still in use in isolated cases. The Dutch name for print room is *prentenkabinet*, for numismatic collection *kabinet van munten en penningen* ("cabinet of coins and medals"), and the picture gallery on view in the Mauritshuis at The Hague bears the official name of *Koninklijk Kabinet van Schilderijen* ("Royal Cabinet of Paintings").

The nineteen museums whose origin antedates the year 1800 were not known by that name and were not museums in the sense of the Ministry's definition. Among them are collections belonging to art schools and universities, royal cabinets and palaces, treasure rooms of medieval churches, almshouses, and ancient town halls with well preserved interiors. They became museums by being made accessible to the public. And that did not happen before the nineteenth century.

Americans may wonder what there is about an almshouse that could make it a showplace for tourists and sightseers. The early homes and furniture of these charitable institutions were preserved for generations, until the things of daily use, unvalued in the past, became precious samples of primitive handicrafts highly prized in an industrialized age. And then the public gained admission to these homes to view treasures that were never collected for show but solely for the utilitarian purposes of everyday life. There are four of this type among the early nineteen, and they are the most attractive kind of museum. For each is the survival of a domestic unit presenting a picture of home life of an earlier age preserved intact. The collector's storehouse is like the dictionary of a dead language. It contains all the things, as the lexicon contains all the words, that were in use in a bygone period. But neither can show us how the things and the words were arranged for the purposes of social life. These ancient almshouses and townhalls that became museums by no collector's effort but as it were automatically, by virtue of their well-preserved old age, are like plays by Plautus and Terence, which show the use and arrangement of old things in daily life. There are, to be sure, Latin scholars who can imitate Terence and compose a Latin play from the words in the lexicon. And even so there are learned museum directors who can piece together an early living room from scattered exhibits in their collections. But these composite reconstructions of the past lack the charm that invests the genuine survival. They instruct, but cannot convince.

For the guidance of the specialist who is interested in only one subject the editor of the museum manual has drawn up an alphabetical list of all the various categories represented in the Dutch museums. Each collection is given its number, and the name of each category is followed by the numbers of those collections that are partly or entirely devoted to that special field.

A highly specialized kind of museum is that which is dedicated to the memory of one man. Such is the Spinoza House at Rijnsburg, near Leyden, the home of the philosopher in the early sixties of the seventeenth century. It was opened in 1899. Copies of the books Spinoza is known to have read have been collected by the founders, and this reconstructed library is the chief attraction of this modest place of pilgrimage. Another is the Rembrandt House in the Jewish quarter at Amsterdam. These two are not survivals but restorations. After the great men moved out, their houses were occupied for more than two centuries by generations of tenants who did not care for, or were ignorant of, the mighty presence that had once pervaded the rooms they occupied. Rembrandt's house, after he left it, was divided in two, and each half was raised by one story. De Bazel, a leader among modern Dutch architects, undertook its restoration in 1908, and rebuilt the two parts into the one house that was the master's from 1639 to 1660. Etchings, drawings, and paintings by Rembrandt and contemporary artists who influenced his style are hung upon the walls, and furniture of the period creates a semblance of a home. But the life is gone from it.

On one visitor, at least, the Rembrandt House made the same impression that spoilt his pleasure in a pilgrimage to Williamsburg, Virginia. The faultless restoration of eighteenth century architecture aroused his respect for the designers and builders, but in wandering through this reconstructed village he felt as though he were inspecting a stage set and waiting for the play to begin. But the play was over; the actors had made their exit long, long ago; an artistic make-believe now takes the place of the scenes in which they did not act, but lived, their parts.

I much prefer the picture galleries that do not pretend to be anything but showrooms. They do not, it is true, bring out a picture to its best advantage. The large majority were not painted for wholesale exhibition. Rembrandt's portrait of his mother would be far more impressive if we could still see it hanging in the living room of his parents' simple home rather than on the wall of a gallery where, among the crowd of other scenes, the essence of its intimate beauty is lost. Still, Johannes Vermeer's famous *Milkmaid* in the Rijksmuseum now gives joy to untold numbers, whereas it used to enchant only the few who were privileged to see it in the intimacy of the Six home. What man would deplore that the sun shines upon all and everyone, though he may love it most for the beauty it adds to his own garden? I am not one of those who repeat the cynic's sneer that museums are mausoleums of art. The crowds that visit the museums of Holland do not regard them as burial places. If the Mauritshuis at The Hague were a home of the dead, it would not attract fifty thousand visitors a year. Besides, Dutch individualism and local pride protect the art lovers against the deadening effect of centralization of the country's art treasures. The Rijksmuseum, richly stocked though it be, is only the largest among a host of lesser collections scattered all over the country. No gifted peasant boy need die an inglorious Rembrandt. In the treasures on view in the local museum of the nearest market town he will find inspiration and guidance for his budding talent.

Chapter XVI

RELIGION AND POLITICS

IT IS a common complaint of Dutch writers on politics that the Hollanders lack political sense. I must confess that I have a very vague notion of what constitutes political sense. My ignorance on that score is doubtless due to my Dutch birth. If political sense is not bred in you, it is difficult to form an accurate conception of its real nature.

It is, perhaps, more to my discredit that, after twenty years of continuous residence in America, where political life is so much more active and alert, my mental conception of this sixth sense has not become any clearer. Gladstone has defined the true political spirit as the faculty of nation-making, but that, of course, refers to a statesmanlike attitude toward matters of government. Political sense as these Dutch critics understand it is, apparently, the politician's astute perception of the best ways and means to score a success at the polls. The politicians are not bent on nation-building but on nation-splitting. Do not entrust the other party with the government, they tell the voters, for if you do, the country will go to the dogs. But if success in splitting the nation be a test of political skill, the Dutch cannot be so sadly devoid of it after all. They have managed to split themselves up into ten parties, each of which claims to be the most reliable trustee of the national interests. Only the Communist party is modest enough not to make that claim, for it champions the cause of the Dutch workers not as Hollanders but as members of the international proletariat. As far as the Communist politicians are concerned, the country may perish if the world be made safe for the Third International. That is one thing the other parties want to make the country safe from; in this respect they show a united front.

It is difficult to give Americans a clear idea of Dutch party aims and party methods, for they differ in every respect from what we are accustomed to in America. There are Democrats there as here, but these Dutch Democrats do not keep up a brave pretense of perfect accord on all matters of principle. There are among them Democrats pure and simple, there is a Christian variety of Democrats, there is a brand called Liberal Democrats, and last, but not least, there are, of course, the Social Democrats. The four together should doubtless be able to make the country safe for democracy, but the trouble is that they find it so difficult to collaborate. Instead of making the most of their common denominator, they stress their Christianity or their Liberal ideals, or their Socialism.

Hollanders are very particular in dotting their i's. A Dutch politician who bolts his party does not run over into a rival's camp, he sets up a platform of his own to advertise his particular brand of heterodoxy. At the elections of 1925 there were, in addition to the seventeen parties officially recognized at that time, no fewer than twenty political groups which, in the name of some particular interest or principle, put up their own candidates for membership in the Second Chamber. There are politicians in Holland who find much more pleasure in running their own private party than in running an automobile.

This national tendency toward disruption has derived additional strength from the system of proportional representation, which was introduced some twenty years ago. The principle on which it was based was laudable to a degree. Before its adoption the country was divided into as many election districts as there were members of the Second Chamber, one hundred in all. The votes of scattered minorities were always wasted under that system. At present each vote counts, for the elector no longer casts his ballot for a particular local candidate, but for the party of his choice, and the sum of all the votes cast in the entire country in favor of each party list of candidates decides the number of seats to which each party is entitled. In other words, the old division of the country into election districts has been abandoned for a system that recognizes one election district only, encompassing the entire country.

The principle, unfortunately, proved less admirable in practice. Pothouse politicians, political cranks, social reformers, noble idealists, and every shade and variety of political thought saw a chance of returning a spokesman to Parliament. A political creed was not even indispensable to cement such factions together. People who shared certain grievances or hobbies, members of one and the same profession, even the scoffers at politics found in their likes and dislikes and occupations a common basis for new party groups. In the elections of 1918, the first to be held after the adoption of proportional representation, the Dutch police came out with their own candidate; the music-hall artists did the same; in the elections of 1924 the Freethinkers mustered 3,649 votes, and the scoffers, organized in what they called the Rabble Party, even beat the Freethinkers by more than a thousand, not enough, though, to win them representation. Mushroom factions went begging for votes which at the polls could not muster more than a couple of hundred supporters. It was the reduction to absurdity of an experiment noble in motive but vicious in its application. One of its foibles has since been corrected. It is still possible for signers of a list of candidates to obtain recognition of their faction at the polls, but they must deposit a sum of F. 250, which is forfeited if the number of votes mustered on election day remains below a stated minimum. As a result the mushroom crop has been less prolific of late years.

Another peculiar feature of Dutch politics is the claim of certain parties that their binding force is a religious principle. Of the four major parties only the Social Democratic Labor Party does not build its platform upon a confessional creed. The orthodox Protestants of the Dutch Reformed Church have their political organization in the Christian Historical Union, the members of the dissenting Calvinist churches form the Anti-revolutionary Party, and the Roman Catholics are also politically organized. Agnostics and churchless citizens who

are averse to Socialism cannot unite on a common platform, and, therefore, scatter their votes on a multiplicity
of little groups and factions. The Protestants, far from
dreading the direst results from the Catholics coming
into power, see in the Catholics their natural allies
against those parties that leave God and religion outside
the sphere of politics. They together are the Christian
forces that will save the country from the rationalism and
unbelief of Liberals and Socialists.

From September, 1918, until August, 1925, Holland
had a Roman Catholic Prime Minister who was brought
into power with the aid of the orthodox Calvinists. This
Christian coalition was dissolved in 1925 in consequence
of a dispute over a matter of apparently but slight importance. Appropriations for the continuance in office
of a Netherland envoy to the Vatican were rejected by
a majority which comprised many members of the two
Calvinist parties. The Catholics would have won, even
in spite of Calvinist defections, if the members of the
Liberal Democratic League, then holding seven seats in
the Second Chamber, had voted with them. In principle,
the League was not opposed to diplomatic representation
at the Holy See, but when the leader of the Catholic
Party in the Chamber declared that rejection of the
appropriations would spell the breakdown of the Christian coalition, the seven Liberal Democrats, who held the
coalition to be detrimental to the country's well-being,
voted as one man with the opposition. Their aim in
rejecting the appropriations was not to break off diplomatic relations with the Vatican, but to break the politi-

cal union in Holland between the Churches of Rome and Calvin.

The Calvinist defection caused a breach in the Christian union that was slow in healing. During the ensuing twelve years no party and no combination of parties had sufficient backing in the Second Chamber to dare assume the reins of government. The diversity of interests and ideas represented in Parliament made parliamentary government impossible. The Ministry in office could not be a party Cabinet based upon a solid majority among the people's representatives. Its members had to be chosen for their expert knowledge of the affairs controlled by their departments regardless of party affiliations.

The hobnobbing of religion with politics causes incidents that are unthinkable in this country. What would happen if Secretary Ickes or some other member of Mr. Roosevelt's official family should announce one day in a Cabinet meeting, "Mr. President, I want you to know that I have become a Roman Catholic." The President would doubtless radiate one of his most charming smiles and wish the happy convert all the blessings that he might expect from his spiritual rebirth, all his colleagues would probably concur with the sentiment, whereupon the meeting would resume the business in hand, and that would be all.

They take things differently in Holland. Early in May of the year 1935, rumors were rife at The Hague that H. P. Marchànt, the Minister of Education, had been received into the Church of Rome. This was startling news, for Marchant was the leader of the Liberal Democratic League, one of the minor parties of the Left, in

which from the outset agnosticism had prevailed. The
League was represented in the Cabinet by one other
member, P. J. Oud, the Minister of Finance. Oud was
alarmed by the rumor, and completely bowled over when
the convert confirmed it. He felt that he could not remain in the Cabinet with his renegade colleague. Either
Marchant should resign or he himself would step out.
The Liberal Democratic League does not bar Roman
Catholics from its membership. It is open to all who subscribe to its political tenets, and considers a man's religious convictions his private concern. Why then Oud's
consternation?

He would have remained impassive had Marchant embraced Islam or Buddhism, or had joined the Holy
Rollers. But his reception into the Church of Rome was
a different matter. Since in Holland the Roman Catholics
are politically organized, the question at once arose: Is it
possible for a Roman Catholic to be a member of another
than the Catholic State Party? There was the rub. The
Liberal Democrats would accept him as a member, but
would not the Catholic Party claim him as its own? And
in the case of Marchant the question of conscience was
especially ticklish, since as Minister of Education he was
the chief administrator not only of public schools but
also of all confessional schools subsidized by the State.

For half a century the question of equal rights for private confessional and neutral public schools had vitiated
the political life of the country. A solution was found
during the World War at the expense of the taxpayer.
All private institutions that conform to the standards set
for public schools are now entitled to a Government

subsidy. The post-war depression led to drastic retrenchments of appropriations, and subsidies had to be reduced in proportion to the diminished budget. A Minister of Education appointed as a Liberal Democrat and administering his Department as a potential member of the Roman Catholic State Party was placed in a very ambiguous position. Marchant might still adhere to the political doctrines of the Liberal Democratic League, but his Roman Catholicism would make it hard for him to convince its members of his unshaken loyalty to those doctrines. The convert admitted this, withdrew from the party that he had headed for so long, and realizing that its representation in the Cabinet was impaired by his action, handed in his resignation to Her Majesty the Queen.

Marchant was the man who, as leader of the Liberal Democratic League, was instrumental, in 1925, in removing the Netherland Envoy from the Vatican. Ten years later he went himself to Rome as a convert. The step that he took was a symptom of the profound change that has affected the spiritual atmosphere within his own party. The first leaders of the Liberal Democrats were—to quote Marchant's own words—able and learned agnostics whose thinking was confined within the limits of the domain of positive science. Religion was not mentioned among them; that was not considered a topic of discussion in a political organization. But under the leadership of Marchant that attitude was gradually abandoned. The annual Party Congress is nowadays preceded by a devotional service, which from year to year attracts a larger number of participants, and in the party's declaration of

principles the value of religion as a factor in political life
is now explicitly recognized. The agnostic indifference
of nineteenth-century Liberalism is on the wane. The
trend now is towards definiteness, towards absolute
denial as in Russia and Germany, or towards a firm
anchorage in the one Church that has survived the storms
of the ages.

When proportional representation was introduced, its
begetters enacted, at the same time, the principle of the
duty to vote. The new system, they argued, could not
yield a true reflection of the political sentiments among
the people unless the entire electorate exercised their right
to the suffrage. Hence the exercise of that right was
made a duty, and the slackers and shirkers became liable
to prosecution. The measure caused considerable resent-
ment at the time of its enactment, and to judge from the
number of voters who stay away from the polls it is not
any more popular now than it was twenty years ago.
A right is a right only if it leaves one the free choice
between exercising it or not. By being enjoined to use
it the citizen ceases to enjoy it. You cannot take pride in
doing what you are forced to do.

In a country politically so divided and where a large
percentage of the electorate expresses its opinion at the
polls, the Chamber of Representatives must in its composition reflect a great variety of thought and interests.
A large number of deputies are lawyers, teachers, and
clergymen; a great many come from the working classes,
representing either rural or industrial labor; and there
are, of course, the professional politicians. Big business,
on the other hand, has very few spokesmen in Parlia-

ment. At a meeting, in 1928, of the Netherland Employers' Federation, the President, in his opening address, deplored that the leaders of industry did not possess that influence on legislation and government which he considered theirs by right and desirable in the interest of the nation. The few thousands of men, he said, who were in control of the national production had about as much to say in the government of the country as had the employees of one factory of average size or a few thousands of unemployed receiving doles. The suffrage system was partly to blame for this, but the chief fault lay with the leaders of business and industry themselves. They kept aloof from political activities, from a mistaken feeling that it was beneath their dignity to become mixed up in them. The leading industrial concerns should, on the contrary, realize that an increasingly large part of their success depended on the degree in which they were able to influence the work of the Government and the Chambers in the fields of economic and social legislation.

This picture of Dutch politics is in every detail the very reverse of conditions in America. Parties galore, religion injected into politics as a matter of course, proportional representation, the electorate under compulsion to vote, the business world without influence on the trend of political affairs! Here is a system that has obviously many flaws, which, however, often reflect distinct virtues of the Dutch. But it is also true that political bosses under this system do not have easy sledding, and party machines are not apt to run smoothly. That may be the reason why the Hollanders prefer their system to

the American one. But then, you remember, they have
not much political sense.

There is one party that has set itself the task of ridding
Holland of its checkered party system. The National
Socialists advocate "revision of the suffrage with a view
to eliminating the electoral conflict, which is assuming increasingly immoral aspects and is becoming increasingly
meaningless." One of these Dutch Fascists promised his
hearers, in the fall of 1933, that his party would turn
the Dutch into a nation of which Queen Wilhelmina
would have reason to be proud. That certainly is a noble
aim. The implication that Her Majesty does not feel
any pride in her people as they are in their present unre-
generate condition is indeed disheartening news. We
must assume, of course, that the speaker, before making
his announcement, had satisfied himself that royal pride
and Fascist pride are plants of a common soil and thrive
on the same fertilizer. Since the Queen is so popular,
the happy prospect of making her proud of her Hollanders for the first time in a long reign of more than
forty years must persuade the whole nation to don black
shirts—they wear them black, not brown, in Holland,
for they must make *some* show of independence from
the German model—and parade by the Palace in the
Noordeinde with arms upraised in the Fascist salute.

Dutchmen, unfortunately, suffer from an almost angelic timidity to tread where fools rush in. I do not mean
to say that they consider these Fascists to be fools, but
they like to be sure that they are not, before joining
the movement, and cool deliberation is not the kind of
climate in which the Fascist fervor flourishes. The Hol-

landers will ask irritating questions and turn the answers over and over before they can make up their minds. I can imagine them asking, "Would the nation, after having been disciplined into an object of royal pride, have any reason left to be still proud of its Queen? Is it not true that the news from Italy that is allowed to be spread abroad never concerns King Victor Emanuel III? Would not Queen Wilhelmina, under National Socialist rule, disappear backstage, while the full glare of the footlights would fall on the figure of Mussert, Holland's would-be dictator? Mr. Mussert is not the only pretender. There are several rival Fascist groups. In this respect they conform to the nation's tendency toward factionalism, though they are bent on inhibiting most other national tendencies. But Mussert, it must be admitted, stands out among his competitors, and if he continues to make progress he may ultimately purge Dutch Fascism of the schism bacillus and justly proclaim his own brand the genuine article.

It is an article, though, to which the Dutch, obstinate individualists as they are, have always refused to give currency. Dictatorial methods have never been popular among them. That was one of the characteristic traits for which they were praised by Lodovico Guicciardini, who was a resident of Antwerp in the days when Italians were capable of admiring and emulating love of freedom. Guicciardini testified to his love for the Dutch people among whom he had settled by writing, in the sixties of the sixteenth century, a voluminous *Descrittione di tutti i Paesi Bassi* ("Description of All the Low Countries"), which is still the best description we possess of the Netherlands in the Reformation period. One may well wonder why he should have taken such a pride in his adopted country. King Philip II, the sovereign Lord of the Low Countries, was anything but proud of his Dutch subjects. He was forced to send the Duke of Alva to make them behave and give him reason for pride in them. But that was after Guicciardini wrote. In his time they were not yet properly disciplined. He tells us, without a show of disapproval, that the delegates to the States General were apt to raise objections to the proposals laid before them by the Sovereign or his Governor. And, says he, "if the latter is not satisfied with their reply, he tries to bring them round to his point of view by means of much reasoning and argumentation, for according to their guaranteed rights he may not settle anything except by discussion, it being not customary here, as it is in many other places, for the ruler to say *Sic voleo, sic jubeo,* Do as I tell you." This sixteenth-century procedure is, strange to say, still the practice in Holland in our more enlightened age, and Mussert will find it difficult to educate his countrymen to a cheerful acceptance of his superior do-as-I-tell-you policy.

Guicciardini also states, with evident satisfaction, that in the Netherlands it was possible for individuals to bring suit against the officers of the Crown and even against the Sovereign himself, and he cites, by way of illustration, the case of a Lord of Anhalt in the Duchy of Guelders who won an important suit against Philip II. No officer could be found, however, who dared to execute the verdict, whereupon the King himself gave orders for its being done in strict adherence to the law.

"O giustissimo Principe!" exclaims Guicciardini, who admired both the law and the sovereign who obeyed it. His Dutch translator, the Antwerp scholar Kiliaen, rendered this passage accurately, not omitting the Italian's praise of the King as a very just prince. And yet, Kiliaen had witnessed all the horrors of the Spanish Inquisition and the Duke of Alva's reign of terror. How could he bring himself to repeat the eulogy of the monarch who had become a persecutor of his people? Perhaps he dared not omit it because he lived in Antwerp under Spanish rule? But see then what Petrus Montanus did, who in 1612 published a new edition of Kiliaen's translation. He again left the entire passage intact, including the apostrophe to the very just monarch. Montanus' version was published at Amsterdam, where Spanish censors had no power. This Dutch historian, who well knew what his country had suffered under Spanish tyranny, saw no good reason for excising a eulogy to which few countrymen of his would have subscribed. But the King did act justly in this case of the Lord of Anhalt, and Montanus, priding himself on being an impartial historian, did not feel justified in denying him Guicciardini's praise.

Dutch historians of the present day are still given to the same spineless preoccupation with fairness. Mussert will have to do something about it. Impartiality and tolerance weaken the nation's moral stamina. Historiography is not a science but an art, and a good artist disregards the intermediate shades and stresses the contrasts of light and darkness. The latest findings of some biologists show that Nature does not act otherwise. People

are Aryans or they are not Aryans. Half-Aryans do
not exist. Montanus should have realized that a vestige
of justice in a tyrant does not make him a just king.
Neither does a vestige of Aryan blood in a Jew make
that Jew an Aryan. True, a vestige of Jewish blood in an
Aryan makes that Aryan a Jew, but that is one of those
erratic caprices of Nature that still await the explanation of Science. It is probably due to the inherent weakness of the Aryan strain, which cannot survive in the
struggle for existence with its more powerful Semitic
rival.

However that may be, this exceptional effect of a
dash of Jewish blood shows nevertheless that Nature
favors opposites and eliminates intermediates. There is
nothing half-hearted about her, and in a well-ordered
State the liquidation of all superfluous distinctions would
have the wholesome effect of reducing an unwieldy
social machinery to the simplicity of primitive times. In
the Fascist State people belong to The Party or they do
not, and those who don't are Communists. It is as de-
lightfully simple as a fairy tale. In the primitive fiction
of our early ancestors we are told of the wickedest and
the holiest queens that ever lived, of devilish ogres and
godlike heroes, of angelic maidens and fiendish villains.
There are no degrees of good and bad between the best
and the worst. The clamor for a simplified social order
springs from the same subconscious urge to which we
owe the return to primitiveness in art. "Your little boy
could have painted that," Matisse was told by a friend
who inspected one of his pictures. "That is exactly what
I am aiming at, I want to paint as children see," was the

artist's reply. Let us turn back to the childhood of the race. Let us learn to see as children see, and trust to the intuition of the untutored mind. Let us be ruled by that unspoiled sense of right and wrong that is in children and, perhaps, in adults whose mental growth came to a stop at the age of ten.

Are the Dutch people ready for this return to the primitive? I very much doubt it. The Hollander's habit of analytical reasoning makes him unfit for a social order that tolerates no fine distinctions. He is a critical animal with a keen eye for detail. His joys are seldom exultant, his sorrows are seldom black with despair. For in the good that he experiences he will notice the flaw that prevents it from being very good, and the bad that he must endure is never so bad but he discovers in it some saving grace. He moves in a world of moderation, where progress is neither tardy nor headlong, where the great are neither idolized nor damned, where the wicked are neither punished with death nor pampered with an easy life in hotel-like prisons, where crime waves and religious revivals do not sweep the masses, where few drink to excess and few preach prohibition, in short, a dull world unrelieved by crass contrasts, adventure, and romance. And the amazing thing is that the people are proud—not excessively proud, for they distrust excess, but still proud—of that dull scene. They imagine it to be the best social scheme so far evolved, not the very best possible, for they know their own faults, but better than what they see among their neighbors.

Chapter XVII

A DEMOCRATIC MONARCHY

IN THE CENTER of Het Plein at The Hague stands a statue of William the Silent. Trolley cars circle round him from morning till night, a never ceasing cavalcade of bicycles forms an outer circle, which is enclosed, in its turn, by the procession of pedestrians along the pavement. And this merry-go-round is hemmed in by a square of massive buildings, whose dull, forbidding façades seem to frown upon the noisy revolutions of the three concentric rings. The pivotal figure of the Prince of Orange stands immovable amid this *perpetuum mobile*, as its living prototype stood immovable amid the vicissitudes and turmoils of his age.

"Which way does he face?" I was asked one summer in a company of friends at The Hague. I was not sure of the right answer, but as I had not lived in the city for seventeen years, I had less reason to be ashamed of my ignorance than had the others, all residents, and all equally uncertain about the exact position of the statue. No one looks at the sights in his own town. It is only the transient tourist who, guidebook in hand, inspects the monument, and reads the inscription on its pedestal.

A sense of shame made me go next morning on a pil-

grimage to Prince Willem on Het Plein. I found that he
looks northward, in the direction of the Foreign Office.
He turns his back toward a strange looking building
squeezed in between the massive piles of the Departments of Justice and Colonies. It looks like a cross between a Greek temple and a neo-Gothic Methodist
chapel. But if your guidebook mentions it at all, you will
find that it is neither temple nor chapel, but the home
of the Supreme Court of the Netherlands.

Holland, indeed, possesses a Supreme Court, in common with all civilized and self-respecting countries. Its
home looks dwarfed between the Ministries on its right
and left; it is pushed back from the street as if it were
too modest to stand in line and claim equality with its
next-door neighbors. It is apparently a Court that strives
for dignity by self-effacement. As a matter of fact, I
have no recollection of its ever having been the storm
center of a political conflict. It is so seldom talked about
that I dare say the average Hollander scarcely knows
the names of the Judges. They are never called names,
either, nor denounced as petrified supporters of "the
tottering capitalistic structure." Their leanings toward
either the left or the right are never a subject of discussion, and neither the legislative nor the executive
branch of the Government would care or dare to criticize
their decisions. The Supreme Court of the Netherlands
is beyond cavil and reproach, not because it has the
power to make the cavilers atone for their presumption,
but thanks to strict limitations set upon its competency,
which save it from becoming involved in the political
combat.

These limitations detract, indeed, from the supremacy of the Court. But the name by which it is officially known does not proclaim it to be supreme. Though it is the highest Court of the land, the Constitution withholds from it the superlative title. It has to be satisfied with the positive degree: *Hooge Raad,* that is "High Council." The choice of that name was not a deliberate implication of curtailed power, for the name is older than the curtailment; it was dictated, no doubt, by a native dislike of superlatives. All the same, the avoidance of a term equivalent to "supreme" happens to be in accord with the actual restrictions of its power. According to Article 166 of the Constitution the function of the *Hooge Raad* is to insure the orderly conduct and disposal of lawsuits and the compliance of the judiciary with the existing laws of the land. When it finds the latter to have been infringed by the actions, decisions, and verdicts of the lower courts, it has the right to reverse the findings. In other words, it is a Court of Cassation. Its function is to guard against infraction of the laws by the courts; it is never called upon to decide whether these laws themselves are infractions of the Constitution.

In 1911 the High Council was asked to pass upon the legality of a set of regulations affecting the white-slave trade. It was charged that the regulations in question were illegally incorporated with the law of 1911, because the Council of State had not been consulted, although Article 75 of the Constitution makes such consultation mandatory. The *Hooge Raad,* however, rejected this alleged irregularity as a ground on which it could base its right to invalidate the incriminated regulations.

The complainants were referred to Article 121 of the Constitution, which declares laws that have been passed by the legislature and approved by the monarch to be binding by virtue of their proclamation.

The *Hooge Raad*, therefore, may submit a law to three tests only: it may ask, Has it been passed by the legislature? Has it been approved by the monarch? Has it been duly proclaimed? A law that fulfills these three requirements cannot be invalidated by a decision of the High Council. Article 121, which thus curtails the authority of the *Hooge Raad*, was inserted into the Constitution as long ago as 1848. Thorbecke, who at that time was Holland's most eminent statesman and constitutional lawyer, did not approve of the provision. As a result of its adoption, he said, the Constitution had ceased to be the Constitution, and the legislature, which derived its existence and its power from the fundamental law, had taken ascendancy over it.

"The Supreme Court," said Lord Bryce, "is the living voice of the Constitution." In Holland the *Hooge Raad* is the living voice of justice as it is defined by the laws of the land. This definition may happen to conflict with the letter or the spirit of the Constitution, but the Constitution does not authorize the *Hooge Raad* to vindicate the superiority of the fundamental law. This seems illogical to the point of absurdity. Still, the Dutch people are perfectly satisfied with this state of affairs, and although now and then a reformer raises his voice in favor of the American system, pleas for investing the High Council with the power to test and invalidate laws have never received strong backing. R. Kranenburg, of the

University of Leyden, admits in his standard work on Netherland Constitutional Law that the legislature has often made light of the provisions of the Constitution, but he does not believe that great harm has been done by these infractions of the fundamental law. On the contrary, "our constitutional law has remained more elastic as a result." Moreover, there are provisions in the Constitution which are due to a political compromise, such as Article 195, which settled a long drawn-out battle between the liberal upholders of the public school and the clerical advocates of state-subsidized denominational education. It is preferable, says Dr. Kranenburg, that the interpretation of such provisions be left, in principle, to the legislature, which, he says, "is a better interpreter, not because the Constitution is public law, but because it contains many solutions of political conflicts." The judiciary ought to be kept out of politics at any price.

The executive branch of the Government has little say in the matter of appointments to the *Hooge Raad*. The monarch, it is true, appoints the judges, but must make the choice from a list of three candidates which is drawn up, in case of a vacancy, by the Second Chamber of the States General. It has become an established convention for the monarch to appoint the candidate who heads the list. It is, accordingly, in the majority of the Lower House that the appointive power is actually vested. The people's representatives decide the composition of the *Hooge Raad*, and make laws which, if passed by both houses, approved by the Crown, and duly proclaimed, cannot be invalidated by the judiciary, even though it may be proved that they infringe the Constitution.

Under the American system the executive branch of the Government has the power to veto laws passed by the legislature. In Holland, on the other hand, the right of veto can hardly be said to exist. It may be applied only to laws initiated by members of the Second Chamber. But the right of initiative is seldom used. The framing of legislative proposals requires a great deal of preparatory labor and research, for which the members are not free to enlist the assistance of the departmental staffs. The large majority of bills emanate from the monarch, who submits them to the legislature through the Crown's responsible ministers. If the Chamber should pass amendments that are unacceptable to the Government, the latter withdraws its proposals, as no longer representing the intention of the Crown. But if changes are made that the Government is willing to accept, it goes without saying that the originator of the act will not undo his own work by pronouncing his veto upon it.

In theory the right of veto cannot be exercised, either, in respect to proposals initiated by the representatives of the people. The Crown's collaboration is required for the enactment of bills, as proposals passed by the legislature do not become law until approved and proclaimed by the monarch. It would, therefore, be more correct to say that the monarch may refuse to approve a bill, as a result of which it fails of enactment. The Crown has doubtless the right to withhold approval. But it is customary for the monarch not to withhold it. An exceptional breach of that custom occurred in 1917, when a proposal to increase teachers' salaries was passed by the legislature but failed of approval by the Crown. This happened in wartime, when public attention was absorbed by the news from the front. It was, says Kranenburg, an experiment which might not safely be repeated in normal times, especially with regard to proposals of greater public concern than a raise of teachers' salaries. The Hollanders call themselves a democratic people. They are not satisfied with the mere name democracy, they stubbornly want the very thing.

This same democracy does not, however, insist on having its way all the time. It does not believe itself competent to settle matters of jurisprudence. The jury system does not, and never did, exist in Holland. In Montesquieu's opinion the jury system was the best system that could be devised because "in that way the power to pass judgment, held in such awe among men, becomes, so to say, invisible and naught." The daily press in America takes good care that the full glare of the limelight shall fall upon this allegedly invisible power. The good men and true are lined up before the camera and reporters write stories about the foreman and his fellow jurors divesting them of the awe their power might inspire.

In Holland judges shun publicity and advertisement. Their features are of slight interest to the public, and the power they wield is that of the impersonal court, not of His Honor whose portrait appeared in the morning paper. Attorneys for the defense do not attempt to make speeches in court that move the emotional to tears. They know that they face judges who are not swayed by irrational impulses, and public gallery hysteria cannot save the poor woman under indictment for a crime of passion from the punishment that the law demands.

That punishment is seldom oversevere. There is no death penalty, and the judges, when they err, are apt to err on the side of leniency. But they are never lenient under pressure of some influential politician.

The bench in Holland is absolutely free from sinister interference with its jurisdiction, for no judge owes his high office to the choice of the electorate. Every judge, from the highest to the lowest, is appointed for life by the Crown, and not even the Crown which appoints him can dismiss him. No judge can be ousted from office except by a verdict of the *Hooge Raad*, the Supreme Council, and only at his own request can he be retired by the Crown. Thus the judge has no reason to curry favor with any authority, including the monarch, as no one can tamper with his tenure of office. Does appointment for life exclude the possibility of fixing a retirement age? That was long a moot question, and in order to give its solution constitutional authority, a provision was inserted into the Fundamental Law as revised in 1922, to the effect that the law may decide that judges shall be retired on reaching a certain age.

Another office independent of the votes of the electorate is that of Burgomaster. In the days of the Republic there were twelve Burgomasters in Amsterdam, four of whom were entrusted with the administration of affairs. These four were called the Reigning Burgomasters, and each of the twelve took his turn in serving on the executive committee. In other Dutch cities the government was differently organized, but all were alike in having more than one mayor elected by the City Council. The present system does not recognize the commune's right to the election of its own ruler; the city council is still elected by the voters, but the Burgomaster—there is never more than one—is an appointee of the Crown.

When the city of Rotterdam lost its Burgomaster, ten years ago, the Queen appointed as his successor a man who had gained his spurs as comptroller of the city of The Hague. The Rotterdam council, jealous of their city's prerogatives, passed a resolution, with only one dissenting voice, deploring the failure of the central Government to consult the wishes of the council before making the appointment. This was a futile protest, as the Minister of Home Affairs was entirely within his legal rights in refusing to ask for the council's recommendations. The law does not contain a single provision on which the Rotterdam council could base its complaint. Article 148 of the Constitution, it is true, recognizes the right of municipal governments to advocate the interests of their commune with the Crown, the States General, and the Provincial States, and under that provision the Rotterdam council could have made its wishes known to the Minister. But it did not avail itself of that opportunity, and the Minister was under no obligation to solicit guidance from the council.

One cannot blame him for relying on his own judgment. A variety of parties are represented on the council, and one wonders how so divided a body could have agreed on the choice of the best man. Where political dissension necessitates a compromise, excellence is apt to yield to mediocrity. The appointment by the Crown of an outsider chosen not for his political affiliations but solely for his proven merits as an administrator is the best guarantee for honest government. Even "a little bit of honest graft" is thus eliminated from the management of city affairs.

In a country where the power of the Crown is restricted to such an extent that the monarch cannot veto, nor withhold approval from, any bill passed by Parliament, and where judges, once appointed, cannot be removed by the monarch who appointed them, it is easy for the hereditary ruler to retain the loyalty of the citizens. Suspicion, fear, and hatred are the creatures of despotism. On the other hand, confidence and trust are inspired when authority is circumscribed. And when, apart from this limitation of power granted by the people, the ruler possesses character and dignity and true devotion to the ruler's task, traditional loyalty to the dynasty is strengthened by personal loyalty to the monarch.

Republicanism, as a consequence, is a dead issue in Holland, except among a small band of Dutch Communists. Even the Socialists are no longer opponents of the monarchy. Twenty-five years ago, Troelstra, then the leader of the Social-Democratic Labor Party, was offered by Her Majesty a seat in the Council of Ministers. But he declined the honor as incompatible with his principles and his pledges to the Internationale. The Socialists, at that time, though they respected the Queen for her eminent qualities, were more distrustful of the monarchy than the monarch was of Socialism. But recent developments in Soviet Russia and in the Third Reich have taught the Dutch Socialists that a Republic is not necessarily the natural habitat of freedom, and that the Bill of Rights is safer under a constitutional monarchy than under any other form of government. The very excesses into which arbitrary power is betrayed in totalitarian countries serve to establish the constitutional monarchy more solidly in the people's affection. Spontaneous demonstrations of popular devotion to the Royal House have been more frequent and impressive in the post-war period than they were in the early part of Queen Wilhelmina's reign.

A memorable incident occurred in 1932 at the ceremonious opening of the States General. Parliament is a word that is alien to the Dutch vocabulary. The legislature is officially called States General, a name that has come down from the Middle Ages, but the colloquial term is simply the Chambers. On the third Tuesday of September, which tradition has set aside for the opening of the States General, the time-honored appellation is, however, appropriate to the solemnity of the occasion. The Queen, on that day, departs from the simplicity that marks her life, and appears before her people in the pomp and splendor that a bygone age considered the natural trappings of royalty. She drives in a gilt coach from her palace to the Ridderzaal, or "Hall of Knights," the oldest building in The Hague, whose foundations were laid as far back as the thirteenth century.

The scene always reminds me of a picture that fascinated me as a little child. It showed Cinderella driving to the ball at court in the gorgeous coach created by the good fairy from a cabbage—or was it a pumpkin? The miracle of the transformation was suggestively stressed by contrast with the picture, on the preceding page, which showed the ragged little maid crouching by the extinguished fire. The clash of extremes is the stock-in-trade of fairy tales, for it delights the naïve imagination of children. Grown-ups in the mass are like children in their love of just that kind of contrast. What fascinates the crowd in this third-Tuesday-of-September spectacle is the Queen's appearance in a role that, judging from her habitual simplicity, is entirely foreign to her nature. People flock to The Hague from all parts of the country to watch a pageant possessing all the charm of a fairy tale. And the charm is enhanced by the fact that its heroine is a real queen, their own Queen Wilhelmina.

In the year 1932 The Hague was more crowded than ever on the third Tuesday of September. But there were many among the spectators who had not come to watch a fairy tale enacted. They had come to scoff at the beautiful show, which was nothing to them but a senseless farce. The Communists had chosen that day for a mass demonstration. The State railways ran special trains to transport the Red comrades to The Hague. This will amaze Mayor Hague and patriots of his stripe. Hollanders labor under the delusion that repression is a less effective means of preserving the public peace than an impartial concession of facilities to all alike, be they conservatives or radicals. They believe that by refraining from supplying an opponent with a just grievance, you make it hard for him to put conviction into his protests. The unchecked invasion of the Communists actually made less effect upon the country than would have been achieved by well-founded protests of a few, voiced on behalf of comrades who had been prevented from being there by the State's refusal to grant them railway transportation. Two of them were present at the ceremony in the Hall of Knights in their capacity of members of the Second Chamber. In previous years the Communist deputies demonstrated their contempt for these farcical proceedings by staying away from the joint opening session. This time they attended the ceremony and listened to Her Majesty's speech from the throne. When the reading of the message was completed and the cry of "Long Live the Queen!" resounded through the Ridderzaal, the two Communists were heard to raise their voices to a shout of defiance. What they actually said no one knew for certain. Those nearest to them interpreted the shout as, "Away with the Queen"; others caught words of a different content, while the shouters themselves subsequently claimed they had called a curse, not upon the dynasty, but upon the government in power. However that may be, the fact of their hurling some insulting remark at the throne did not pass unnoticed. The Queen herself, taken aback for a moment, immediately recovered her self-control and bowed with stately dignity in the direction whence the protest issued, whereupon spontaneously the entire States General rose to their feet and, discarding their habitual immobility and solemn decorum, sang the national anthem *Wilhelmus van Nassouwe*. A wave of enthusiasm swept over the assembly, and in its onrush the Communist protest was overwhelmed and drowned. Never before had the opening

[273]

session of the States General presented such a spectacle
of spontaneous emotion. The tense excitement, in some
mysterious way, affected the waiting crowds outside in
the streets, and when the royal procession returned from
the Ridderzaal to the Palace in the Noordeinde, a thun-
dering ovation met Her Majesty along the route.

Such scenes never occurred half a century ago. The
monarchy, in those days, was taken for granted. It was
not prized because it was not attacked. The revolutions
in Russia, Italy, Germany, and Spain afforded an object
lesson that was not lost upon the Dutch people. It
shocked their trust in the permanence of their political
inheritance, and brought home to them that their democracy under the House of Orange is the precious palladium of their ancient freedom. They had known this
before, but were apt to forget it, as a man in perfect
health forgets to be grateful for that best of blessings.
He will give thought to it when an epidemic makes even
a perfect physique a precarious boon. And so the Hollanders, living on the edge of a diseased, plague-ridden
continent, have been shocked into grateful awareness of
their political sanity. This sense of gratitude and the
realization that their country might not prove immune
to the contagion account for repeated outbursts of
patriotic fervor in the past few years such as were unknown in less perilous days.

The Hollanders are believed to be a phlegmatic kind
of people, but that word does not describe them cor-
rectly. It is true that their emotions are not easily aroused.
Demagogues, to their dismay, find them cold and unre-
sponsive to catch-phrases and slogans. The critical minds

[274]

of the Dutch will carefully examine each panacea that is offered for the cure of political ills, and in the long exposure to the cool air of reason the champagne of political oratory loses its kick. The Hollanders are also a self-conscious people. They criticize themselves as freely as they do others, and an awareness of their shortcomings, no less than the critical temper of their neighbors, makes them hesitant in giving vent to their feelings.

But these inhibitions are not always in force. In the national rejoicings over the betrothal of Princess Juliana all restraints were loosened and the people let themselves go in happy abandon. More than three hundred organizations paraded past the Royal Palace at The Hague to greet the young couple with a demonstration of the nation's joy at the betrothal. Schools and stores and offices were closed for the afternoon, and the streets swarmed with a holiday crowd of townspeople and countryfolk from the rural environs of The Hague. Restaurants and cafés lacked space and staff to cater to the multitude. The wise and thrifty had brought their own provender and camped out in the streets, on private stoops or public benches. Acrobats, magicians, and monkeys supplied entertainment to this open-air audience, street singers hawked the latest ballads in praise of Juliana and her Bernhard, and venders of postcards with the picture of the young couple did a roaring business. All day long, hours before the parade began and hours afterwards, a packed crowd stood waiting in front of the palace, hoping to catch a glimpse of the royal family. The spontaneity of this popular outburst must have impressed Prince Bernhard. Such demonstrations cannot be stage-managed in a nontotalitarian state. The Netherland Government cannot order the Queen's subjects to march and cheer and wave flags with military precision. They are free men and women, who will do as they like. These tens of thousands who, from one mighty common impulse, wished to pay tribute to their Queen's daughter and her fiancé staged unintentionally a more imposing spectacle than could have been produced by an army trained by drill sergeants.

When Juliana married Prince Bernhard on January 7, 1937, she did so, as must all Dutch maidens, before the Burgomaster at the City Hall, in strict conformity with the law of the Netherlands. That law does not recognize any marriage solemnized by the church alone; and the parson, priest, or rabbi presuming to consecrate a marriage before the civil ceremony has been performed commits an unlawful act and runs the risk of being sent to prison. Hence in Holland marrying parsons can do no business, Little Churches around the Corner cannot corner the wedding market, and Gretna Green blacksmiths cannot strike marriage fees out of their anvils. You never hear in Holland of runaway matches, or of weddings of persons who met for the first time a few hours earlier, or of one-day brides or grooms disclaiming any intention of marriage and charging that they were tricked into signing the contract while under the influence of liquor or drugs. In short, marriage in Queen Wilhelmina's kingdom is divested of the glamor, adventure, and romance that attend it so gloriously in this country.

The law courts, which are deprived of salacious actions for annulment, the attorneys specializing in divorce, the "true story" magazines, which cannot print fiction that could not happen in reality, are the chief sufferers from the dull, respectable regularity created by stringent marriage laws. These make it impossible for the reckless to rush headlong into bliss by the provision that the would-be groom and bride, three weeks before the date fixed for the ceremony, must register at the town hall their intention to be married. The interval gives ample time for recovery from the effect of drugs or liquor or other artificial stimulation.

When I was young, there was an official custom which lent added force to this precautionary delay. At noon on the Sundays falling in the three-week interval, the town clerk mounted the steps of the *Raadhuis* and read aloud to passersby the names of couples registered in the preceding period. Any person, thus publicly notified, who objected to a match, could then submit his objections to the magistrate for consideration and action. This public recitation was abolished in 1913. A copy of recent registrations is now affixed to a bulletin board on the outer wall of the town hall, where any passerby can consult them at leisure. Even persons under thirty years of age need the consent of their parents, but they may appeal, which minors may not, to the district judge and obtain reversal of a parental refusal. The plaintiff need not satisfy the judge that the parents' reasons are insufficient grounds for preventing the marriage; the judge has no choice in the matter, he acts merely as registrar of the intention to marry. The right thereto is automatically granted when the application is made. Resort to the courts is also required when the applicants claim to be orphans. They must be able to produce the death certificates of both parents, and when the authorities are satisfied that father and mother are no longer among the living, a court license must be obtained in lieu of the unfurnishable consent of the parents. The prospective bridegroom must also produce documentary evidence that he has duly served his time in the army or that he was legally exempted from military service.

In short, getting married in Holland is no easy matter. You cannot do it on a sudden impulse, or on a dare. Special licenses are unobtainable; the three weeks that must elapse between the registration and the wedding stand as an inexorable barrier between the impulse and its consummation.

Princess Juliana had to conform to the law as any other citizen. There was no special license issued to Her Royal Highness. She appeared with her fiancé at the City Hall in The Hague, where both signed the register in token of their intention to be married. Prince Bernhard signed it as a Netherland citizen. A Dutch girl marrying a foreigner loses thereby her Dutch citizenship, so a couple of weeks before the Prince signed the marriage register, he was naturalized by a special act of Parliament. Three weeks later, the Burgomaster of The Hague united Juliana and Bernhard in wedlock.

At the first cry of a new-born baby in the palace of Soestdijk in the morning of January 31, 1938, the telephone wires started buzzing, the guns in the various garrisons boomed fifty-one salvos, the red, white, and blue flags appeared at the windows, and people ran out into

the streets to give vent to an emotion which, like a ground
swell lifting the ocean's surface, caused a sudden surge
of the nation's soul into a frenzy of joy. When the can-
non ceased booming after the fifty-first salvo, no shadow
of disappointment fell across the land. One hundred and
one would have proclaimed the birth of a Prince of
Orange. Whether girl or boy, it was the continuance of
the monarchy that mattered.

The wall of the nursery in the palace of Soestdijk is
decorated with a large map of the world. The little eyes
that are beginning to look around in wonder will be
attracted soon by the splotches of bright color, weird
and meaningless but beautiful. They are still weird and
meaningless to us, who see nations wantonly attacked by
other nations, and one-half of a nation waging war upon
the other half, and innocent noncombatants, men,
women, and children, massacred in cold blood by a hail-
storm of bombs. And yet, it is beautiful too, this world
with its undying dream of a better future, with its millions trying to build upon the ruins they have made new
homes and temples of new faiths. By the time the map
on the wall in the royal nursery acquires meaning to the
little princess, it may be a symbol of a different reality
from the one we know. The colors may have changed,
from black to red, or from red to black, boundaries
may have been retraced, flags hauled down and other
standards raised instead. Even the spot that her little
index finger will most readily point to may look different. A green dot may cover part of the blue that indicates the Zuiderzee. "That is our conquest," she will say
with pride. But God forbid that anything else in that

small corner of the world should change in color. "Where is Soestdijk, Your Royal Highness?" "Do you see that green spot with an orange edge around it? That is Netherland. And this tiny orange dot, that is Soestdijk." "The Dutch are good painters, Princess Beatrix. They will keep the spot green on your map of the world, as green and fresh as the grass of their polders. They will keep its protective edge of orange unsullied like the loyalty to the House of Orange in their hearts."

REFERENCES FOR FURTHER READING

HISTORY

Barnouw, A. J. Holland under Queen Wilhelmina. New York: Scribner, 1923.

Edmundson, G. History of Holland. Cambridge: University Press, 1922.

Geyl, P. The Revolt of the Netherlands, 1555-1609. London: Williams & Norgate, 1932.

COLONIES

Furnivall, J. S. Netherlands India, a Study of Plural Economy. New York: Macmillan Co., 1939.

Klerck, E. S. de. History of the Netherlands East Indies. Rotterdam: W. L. & J. Brusse, N. V., 1938.

Torchiana, H. A. W. van C. Tropical Holland. Chicago: University of Chicago Press, 1921.

Vandenbosch, Amry. The Dutch East Indies. Grand Rapids, Mich.: Eerdmans Publishing Company, 1933.

ART

Collins Baker, C. H. Dutch Painting of the Seventeenth Century. London: The Studio Limited, 1926.

Kaines Smith, S. C. The Dutch School of Painting. London: The Medici Society, 1929.

Wilenski, R. H. An Introduction to Dutch Art. London: Faber & Gwyer, Ltd., 1929.

LITERATURE

Barnouw, A. J. Vondel. New York: Scribner, 1925.

Grierson, H. The First Half of the Seventeenth Century. Edinburgh: 1906 (Vol. VII of Saintsbury's Periods of European Literature).

Russell, J. A. Dutch Poetry and English. Amsterdam: H. J. Paris, 1939.

TRAVEL

Bricklayer, Peter. Holland's House: A Nation building a Home. Haarlem: Enschedé en Zonen, 1939.

Capek, Karel. Letters from Holland. Translated from the Czech by Paul Selver. New York: Putnam, 1933.

Clark, Sydney A. Holland on $50 (A concise, amusing, and well-informed guidebook). New York: McBride, 1936.

De Leeuw, H. Crossroads of the Zuider Zee. Philadelphia: Lippincott, 1939.

Jungman, Nico and Beatrix. Holland. Illustrations by Nico Jungman, text by Beatrix Jungman. London: A. & C. Black, 1904.

Lucas, E. V. A Wanderer in Holland. New York: Macmillan, 18th ed., 1924.

Meldrum, D. S. Holland and the Hollanders. New York: Dodd, Mead & Co., 1898.

Rice, W. G. Carillons of Belgium and Holland; Tower Music in the Low Countries. New York: John Lane Co., 1915.

Scheffler, Karl. Holland. Translated from the German by Caroline Fredrick. New York: A. Knopf, 1932.

Tuyn, W. Old Dutch Towns and Villages of the Zuider-zee. Illustrations by W. O. J. Nieuwenkamp and J. G. Veldheer. London: T. F. Unwin, 1901.

Van Loon, H. W. An Indiscreet Itinerary. New York: Harcourt, Brace & Co., 1933.

LANGUAGE

Kruisinga, E. A Grammar of Modern Dutch. London: Allen & Unwin, 1924.

Zonneveld, K. van. Simplified Dutch Grammar for Americans. Groningen: Noordhoff, 1929.

INDEX

Aalsmeer, College of Horticulture, 71; garden industry, 68-72; half a century ago, 68
Aalsmeer Horticultural League, 71
Abyssinia, 4
Actors, 191, 194, 195, 197, 198, 205
Adagia (Erasmus), 29
Advertising, 26
Aggressor, sanctions against, 6
Agnosticism, 248, 251, 252, 253
Agricultural colleges, 72, 107
Ahasverus (Jelakowitch), 201
Aircraft, *see* Aviation
Aleander, Hieronymus, 77, 78
Alexander the Great, 117
Almshouses as museums, 241
Alva, Duke of, 257, 258
America, *see* United States
America Set Free (Keyserling), 14
Amersfoordt, J. P., 37
Amsterdam, American newspapers and, 151; architecture, 61 ff., 230; art collections, 231 ff.; Burgomasters, 268; City Hall as art Gallery and royal palace, 231, 234; City Hall ownership controversy, 233 ff.; Concertgebouw orchestra, 211, 212; conditions in early nineteenth century, 54-57; conditions in early seventeenth century, 56; "Free University," 106; how built, 52; landscaping and planting, 52; leader of anti-Orange faction, 237; made the capital,

234; municipal headquarters, 234 ff.; municipal officers, 57; paintings of, 226; patron saint, 124; Prinsenhof, 234, 236; rebuilding of modern, 57 ff.; sanitation, 54, 56 f.; slum clearance, 57, 61; Stadhuis on the Dam, 238; university of, 94, 99, 107, 125; water supply, 56, 57
Andriessen, H., 213
Anhalt, Lord of, 257, 258
Anrooy, Peter van, 105
Anti-revolutionary Party, 248
Architecture, beauty, 20, 63; Berlage's leadership, 61; modern, and its effect upon painters, 228; Rijksmuseum, 230
Armaments, budget for, 3
Army, 7
Art and artists, 215-29; adjustment to modern world, 216, 228; beauty in the commonplace, 222, 223, 226; Burgundian patronage, 165; decline and revival, 225; ego cult, 228; expressionistic, 225 ff.; homes as demonstration of, 63; illuminators of manuscripts, 220; impressionistic, 227; Italianized school, 221; joint craftsmanship in workshops, 216-19; landscapists, 221, 222, 225, 227; Louis Napoleon's collection, 231; museums *vs.* restored places, 243; overcrowding of scene, 221; primitives, 219, 221; private collections, 219, 239,